E. M. Forster

A Literary Life

Mary Lago
Emerita Professor
University of Missouri-Columbia

MACMILLAN

First published 1995 by
MACMILLAN PRESS LTD
Houndmills, Basingstoke, Hampshire RG21 2XS
and London
Companies and representatives
throughout the world

ISBN 0–333–57723–X hardcover
ISBN 0–333–60956–5 paperback

A catalogue record for this book is available
from the British Library.

10 9   8   7   6   5   4   3   2   1
04 03 02 01 00 99 98 97 96 95

Printed and bound in Great Britain by
Antony Rowe Ltd
Chippenham, Wiltshire

To P. N. Furbank

Contents

Preface

A sequence of literary genres suggests one key to the shape of E. M. Forster's working life. A specific form made him known to the public in a certain period, after which he laid it aside. His short fiction is the variation in this pattern. It was his first published work of consequence, and one of his last concerns was for a group of short stories that pleased but also grieved him, for he knew that, like the novel *Maurice*, they could not be published in any future that he could foresee. I have considered these works as in a way an epilogue, for their posthumous appearance made them an epilogue to his publishing history.

The novel is the form most readily associated with Forster's name. During five of the Edwardian years, from 1905 to 1910, he wrote four novels about dwellers in the rural suburbs of the Home Counties, of whom he himself was one. They were a social class in transition between environments, and they belonged to a society in transition between centuries: from the Victorian age to an era still undefined. For Forster, the citizens of the new suburban communities possessed many of the middle-class virtues that had given England her distinctive character. Their great fault lay in their being too often complacent and too seldom uncertain about their place in the new scheme of things. They were absorbed in the minutiae of position and prestige and property-owning. They wished to be thought cultured but seemed not to understand Culture. After *Howards End*, the fourth and last of these novels, he laid aside any major fictional treatment of this theme. Critics and thesis-writers have wondered why this was so, since *Howards End* brought him his first real popular success, and there seemed much still to be said on the subject. However, *Howards End* marked the end of an era in history as well as a phase in Forster's literary career, for King Edward died in the year the novel was published. The sense of an ending was doubly pervasive, for although the King had seemed to be England's reprieve from Victorian restrictions, at the same time Edward VII was 'the last genuine link with the Victorian age' and, in the words of a contemporary journalist, 'who is now so bold as to dare forecast the nature of the epoch that is now opening?'[1]

Fourteen years elapsed between the end of Forster's suburban

series and the next major work to bring him forcibly to the public's
attention. Much happened in that interval, however. He visited India and wrote a few chapters of a novel with an Indian setting but
was dissatisfied and laid them aside. He wrote instead a draft of the
novel that would become *Maurice* and laid that aside, not only out of
dissatisfaction but also because of the criminal penalties for homosexuality. Then came war service in Egypt and a second visit to
India. When at last he could complete the Indian novel, it became
something entirely new in a fictional sub-genre, the Anglo-Indian
novel.[2] That had adhered to several standard patterns: Kipling's
scornfully affectionate stories of late-Victorian India; romances of
oriental derring-do and beleagured innocent, genteel but intrepid
English ladies; and fictionalised versions of English heroism during
the 1857 Mutiny. All of these seem crude beside *A Passage to India*
with its subtleties of characterisation and plot and, above all, its
implications of great uncertainty about the future of the British Raj.
In fact, it was Forster's Indian continuation of a central theme from
the suburban novels: complacency, the absence of a saving uncertainty, obsession with the piece of imperial property that was India.
Again a Forster novel marked the end of an era. There could be no
question that Indian nationalist ferment would grow and grow until
it had serious consequences for England and the Empire, which
would fall to the forces of British exclusivism and philistinism. He
was one of a small minority who held that view. Many readers
resisted it. Of those who grudgingly accepted it, few wished to be 'so
bold as to dare forecast the nature of the epoch that is now opening?'

Nor could anyone have forecast the future of BBC broadcasting,
the enterprise through which Forster, after a few years of indecision,
again had a wide public audience. The radio talk was a completely
new genre, a re-invention of the spoken word. He brought to it a
uniquely personal style, a human voice of technology. For thirty
years he talked most often about books that he thought valuable and
outstanding, but his inclusive subject was the Culture that rests on a
foundation of all the arts. Where Culture is absent, the spirit is
impoverished and practical enterprise as well as personal relations
will suffer. This conviction has been inherent in all of his works,
from the beginning of his career. That is why I have begun with the
example of a radio talk of 1946, another time of transition whose
future was difficult to forecast – although many dared. Again he
pointed out that the issue was a choice between mechanistic and
humane values. This talk is more about the problems of providing

postwar housing than about the arts as such. However, in it Forster demonstrates how the humane attitudes shaped by attention to the creative arts can illuminate the most mundane human enterprise.

If he had this important message to deliver, why had his career this pattern of stops and starts? For one thing, when he looked at some literary lions of his acquaintance he feared what literary fame might make him become. His commitment to Culture kept him from doing the fashionable thing and consulting a psychoanalyst about the sources of his fear, for 'these people have no sense of literature and art and I regard with foreboding and resentment their offers to turn an artist upside down.' He had 'stopped creating rather than become uncreative: . . . It's rather that the scraps of imagination and observation in me won't coalesce as they used to.'³ He was intimidated by the popular assumption that a novelist once begun must go on producing at a regular rate in order to keep the franchise; literary history is littered with proofs of the unwisdom of this assumption. But the salient point about the progression of Forster's literary life is not that he twice abandoned the novel form. It is that however often he wrote, in whatever form, he brought to it a sense of history's turning-points so keen that it turned the genre itself in a new direction.

All passages from E. M. Forster's published and unpublished writings are © the Provost and Scholars of King's College, Cambridge (1994), the Executors of the E. M. Forster Estate. I wish to thank them for permission to use this material, and I am grateful for special assistance from Dr Donald Parry; Miss Jacqueline Cox, Western Manuscripts Archivist, King's College Library; and also her predecessor, Dr Michael Halls.

I wish to thank the Master and Fellows of Selwyn College, Cambridge University, for the Visiting Bye-Fellowship in the winter of 1991–92 during which I completed research for this book. The Research Council of the University of Missouri-Columbia assisted with a travel grant. Grants in earlier years from that Research Council and from the National Endowment for the Humanities, while not specifically applicable to this project, made possible the gathering of many materials of both direct and indirect use here.

I wish to thank the many friends and associates, both old and new, who have given me thoughtful assistance, advice and hospitality. My first and greatest debt is to Mr P. N. Furbank, authorised biographer of Forster and co-editor with me of Forster's *Selected Letters*, for his unfailing kindness and wise counsel. I am further indebted to others who have shared with me their personal knowledge of Forster and of those whose paths crossed his, most especially Mr Anthony Barnes, Mrs May Buckingham, Mr and Mrs Eric Crozier, Miss B. J. Kirkpatrick, Miss Jean Rowntree.

Directors and staff members of many libraries and archives have provided materials, answered my questions, and suggested new sources. I wish most particularly to thank the King's College Library and the University Library, Cambridge; the British Library; the Britten-Pears Library, Aldeburgh; the London Library; the Working Men's College, London. I have had assistance over many years of work on Forster's papers from Dr Richard Bingle (India Office Library), Mr David Burnett (Durham University Library), Miss Cathy Henderson (The Harry Ransom Humanities Research Center, University of Texas at Austin), and Mrs Jacqueline Kavanagh (BBC Written Archives, Caversham Park, Reading).

E. M. Forster's diaries are among the Western Manuscripts at King's College, and unpublished letters from that archive quoted here are as follows: to Florence Barger, Sir George Barnes (14 October 1946), Henry Brooke (later Lord Brooke of Cumnor), Robert Buckingham, Goldsworthy Lowes Dickinson, Alice Clara Forster, Christopher Isherwood, Elizabeth Poston.

Recipients, with present owners, of other unpublished Forster letters quoted here are as follows: J. R. Ackerley and Malcolm Darling (Humanities Research Center, Austin), Sir George Barnes (23 May 1940, 5 February 1942: BBC Written Archives), Benjamin Britten (Britten-Pears Library), Paul Cadmus (Recipient); Eric Crozier (Britten-Pears Library), Christopher Isherwood (Don Bachardy), Arthur Koestler (Koestler Estate), William Plomer (Durham University Library), Forrest Reid (Stephen Gilbert), D. K. Roberts (British Library). Siegfried Sassoon (Sassoon Estate), Elizabeth Trevelyan (Wren Library, Trinity College, Cambridge), Lorna Wood (Hofstra University Library), Leonard Woolf (Sussex University Library).

I wish to thank the following for permission to quote from unpublished letters other than Forster's that are now in the Manuscripts Department of the University Library, Cambridge: Mr Nicholas Smith, for Sir Harcourt Spencer Butler; Mary, Duchess of Roxburghe, for Lord Crewe, 1st Marquis; Lord Hardinge of Penshurst, for Lord Hardinge, 2nd Marquis; Mrs Mary Bennett, for H.A.L. Fisher; Miss Anna Gelder, for the Rt. Hon. Edwin Samuel Montagu.

For a letter from Jane Harrison to Gilbert Murray, I thank Newnham College, Cambridge. For access to letters addressed to Sir George Barnes, I wish to thank Mr Anthony Barnes, the present owner, and, for permission to quote from them, the copyright owners: Mr Nigel Nicolson, for Sir Harold Nicolson; Mrs J. B. Priestley, for J. B. Priestley. I am grateful as well to Mr Barnes for access to and permission to quote from his father's letters, notes of travel and memoranda about his work for the BBC and particularly for the Third Programme. Mr and Mrs Eric Crozier and Mrs May Buckingham allowed me to quote from their privately recorded reminiscences about Forster; and Miss Jean Rowntree, from a private memoir of her years with the BBC and from her letters to myself.

Passages from Briggs, *The History of Broadcasting in the United Kingdom*; Fielden, *The Natural Bent*; Grisewood, *One Thing at a Time*; Matheson, *Broadcasting* are used by permission of the copyright owners.

My valued friend Martha Alexander, Director of Libraries, University of Missouri-Columbia, gave me the ideal office in which to finish writing this book, and her expert staff has been ever helpful with every kind of bibliographical and lending assistance. Miss Connie Reece, English Department Secretary, has seen me through manifold mysteries of word-processing.

Finally, but by no means least, Dr Richard Dutton, General Editor of the Series, has been always ready with advice and encouragement for which I am most grateful, and I wish to thank Macmillan's editors, Miss Margaret Cannon and Miss Charmian Hearne, for their kindly and informative guidance.

Columbia, Missouri   Mary Lago
November 1993

1

E. M. Forster:
Self and Neighbours

In the spring of 1946 E. M. Forster was one of ten BBC radio speakers invited to discuss 'The Challenge of Our Time'. Since the time was the beginning of a momentous postwar era and the challenge was enormous, the series was intended to make radio listeners stop and think: in particular, to think ahead to what they hoped might be the future shape of the civilisation they had fought to preserve. Four scientists, two historians (Arthur Koestler being one), a classicist, a theologian, a philosopher and Forster were to consider 'whether and how far the ills of our present world are traceable to causes in human thinking'. Was the war just concluded only a symptom of general unease about the durability of tradition? Was the nation-state consuming the individual? 'Is there a chance of re-creating the social mould?' What about a new synthesis? The present chaos was the dire alternative.[1]

Forster's assigned topic was 'The View of the Creative Artist'. In 1943, in another radio series called 'Security for What?' he had declared himself 'a fanatic on the subject of art'. 'Art' is his comprehensive term for all that makes life more than a routine existence: literature, music, the fine arts, the decorative arts. He believed that it is art that 'distinguishes us from the animals . . . if we stop practising it we shall not rise higher.'[2] In 1946 he expanded this into a messsage about the conditions essential to the enhancement and preservation of Culture. 'Message' is the correct word, for where Culture was concerned he was an evangelist ardent and single-minded. His definition of Culture included tradition and its continuities, the ability to select wisely for the enlightenment and enjoyment of future generations, personal relations founded upon the holiness of the heart's affections, and the ability to draw delight and nourishment from the arts. Much of the education for Culture begins where formal education leaves off, and this learning does not come easily. Invariably it involves difficult choices. In 1946 Forster talked about the choice between the kind of life created by mechanistic planning and a life

1

shaped and informed by the creative arts. The series quickly became a debate about choices between morality and expediency. Koestler, the first speaker, drew an analogy between the fate of the Scott Polar Expedition and the sacrifice of Czechoslovakia. The Expedition's remnant might have struggled to safety, had they not tried to carry the failing Evans with them. But the sacrifice of Czechoslovakia saved none of the other countries that fell before Hitler. 'By that time,' said Koestler, 'the number of individual Evanses is counted by the millions'. Morality versus expediency, or utilitarian compromise, or justifying the end by the means is never a philosophical question, but a daily dilemma to which there is no 'final solution' (Koestler's phrase, but poisoned for ever by its Nazi connections). Each generation must find the solution adapted to its own conditions and must act as if ethical absolutes *do* exist. We must, he said, 'apply the brake, or we shall crash'.[3]

Thereafter, with invocations of Wordsworth and Wells, Milton and Marx, the debate concentrates upon the question of whether scientific planning or humanist sympathy is society's best hope. Forster's talk is quite different from the others'. Theirs have the tone of scientists standing firmly on certainties confirmed in the laboratory, or of academics arguing learnedly with one another. Forster speaks gently to the unseen audience. He reminiscences about his late-Victorian childhood – irrelevant, surely, after the calamities and upheavals of the war just ended? He says that he is uneasy about his subject. He realises that he is older than the others, perhaps a little out of date. He declares himself an individualist who values old-fashioned reticence and privacy, and courtesy in approaches to society's problems. Looking back, he saw himself as a part of 'the fag-end of Victorian liberalism', when 'challenges were moderate in their tone'. And perhaps more important, people who lived comfortably but not lavishly – that is, the middle classes – felt that all the challenges were manageable. Forster had known and cherished memories of individuals who embodied ideals of intellectual curiosity, respect for the humane virtues, belief in freedom of speech. His own education 'in those far-off and fantastic days made me soft and I am very glad it did', for his experience since then had shown him how harshly the world could treat even the most deserving of individuals. No, he is not out of date, for he knows now that that education, although humane, had been imperfect because economic well-being was taken for granted. Persons of great domestic and civic virtue gave little or no thought to the plantations and mines overseas that stocked their well-filled larders and swelled their annual dividends. Victorian dividends were fat, and middle-class notions were dim with respect to the overseas exploitation that made such easy income possible. Forster remembered all too well the childhood admonition: '"Dear, don't talk about money, it's so ugly" . . . a Victorian defence mechanism' if ever there was one. Now all that had changed, and he speaks out of his experiences of India and Egypt: the so-called 'backward races', as well as the poor at home, had rebelled and now demanded that they be heard – a development that Forster applauded.

Nor does he wish to be the creative artist who withdraws to the ivory tower and scorns the practical concerns of scientists and economists. In that case, how could he answer the Challenge of Our Time? The answer is to be found in a combination of the new economy and the old morality. Laissez-faire in economics will not work, for the result has been the greed for power that has culminated in the war just over. Some economic planning is essential, most especially at a time of such widespread loss and dislocation. On the other hand, the doctrine of laissez-faire works admirably in the realm of mind and spirit; there, control spawns totalitarianism. Planners tend to scoff at the idealist's fears of totalitarian tyranny, but, said Forster, although the abstract idea of 'the people' is held up as the ideal, he puts his faith in the individual. 'He seems to me a divine achievement and I distrust any view which belittles him.' Here he slips into the direct address to his radio listeners, urgent but encouraging and personal, that made him so successful as a broadcaster. 'If anyone calls you a wretched little individual – and I have been called that – don't you take it lying down. You are important because everyone else is an individual too . . .'

How to resolve this collision of principles? Here Forster invoked his long-loved childhood house and emotional continuing-place: Rooksnest, the original of Howards End, near Stevenage in Hertfordshire. He loved that countryside with a passion. It has no Lake Country attractions, no romantic scenery, only gently rolling farmland and villages of ancient history and custom. It was his 'abiding city', and he returned there whenever he could, to visit his childhood home and the people who had become its tenants and his friends. He cherished the sense of the continuity of generations, and sometimes he saw the boy with whom he had played as a child, both of them now in their sixties and his old playmate a grandfather. Perhaps because Forster knew that his immediate family would come to an end with him, the sense of a line inherited from the past and continuing into the future had all the more meaning for him. Hertfordshire seemed unchanged and unchanging, and therefore reassuring – until a local resident who asked 'permission to lay a water-pipe was casually informed that it would not be granted since the whole area had been commandeered. Commandeered for what? Hadn't the war ended?'

But this *was* war, and the foe was a London bureaucracy of planners who lacked even the simple courtesy to inform the local people that a Stevenage New Town of sixty thousand people was to be constructed there. 'Garden City' used to be the name and plan for the ideal suburban development. Now 'satellite town' was the nomenclature for a development that would gobble up whole fields and bring in a population whose traditions were those of London, not the countryside. 'Meteorite town would be the better name, for it has fallen on them out of a blue sky.'

Planning asks: why so sentimental? People must have houses. But there was no escaping the fact that if this New Town happened as projected, with a stifling density of new houses, a way of life would be destroyed for ever. Those who moved into the new houses would never know that a way of life had existed that, once eliminated, could never be reconstructed, for it belonged to 'the world of the spirit'. Bombed-out Britons needed houses, but the planning need not be an assault on the spirit. Expediency had ousted morality and courtesy.

Had he strayed from the topic assigned? Not really, for he wished to state what one writer, at least, saw as the need for some means of satisfying both expediency and morality, planning and laissez-faire. Now was the time to speak out, when the end of the war had forced so many new beginnings. And the intellectual has a duty to speak out, for he thinks more consistently in human terms than does the scientist. In Forster's view the scientist 'patronises the past, oversimplifies the present, and envisages a future where his leadership will be accepted'. It is easy to imagine a scientist dismissing Forster's argument out of hand as one-sided and unrealistic. He was accustomed also to being called unrealistic, and that also did not trouble him. He knew that he spoke across a generation gap, not only because the other speakers on this panel were younger, but also because the advocates and practitioners of the new technologies were younger still. Nevertheless, he invited the scientist to 'come down from his ivory laboratory' and talk. The humanist's ascending the tower was no solution, for he keeps his bearings by being in touch with people. Together at ground level, the scientist-planner (expediency) and the humanist (morality) might together answer the Challenge with houses for the homeless and less damage to landscape and spirit.[4]

This was not Forster's first comment on the ivory tower. In l938 he had meditated upon its importance to the poet as a retreat in which to convert thoughts and impressions into art. Staying there too long courts sterility, for the real world is inescapable: 'Consequently, [man] is always contradicting himself in his conduct and getting into muddles . . .' Milton, for example, began in seclusion as a Cambridge intellectual, then found that he had no choice but to take sides in the Civil War. After twenty years he returned to the tower and produced works like *Samson Agonistes* and *Paradise Lost*. Milton was sour and prim, stubborn and opinionated, but he knew when to ascend the tower and when to come down: that is the key. Britain's postwar planners had stayed so long in their tower laboratory that they had lost touch with the spiritual realities.[5]

That flawed Victorian education was at the root of the problem. By trial and error Forster had discarded what had proven unfruitfully utilitarian and had substituted his own philosophy of the developed heart. He was uncomfortable with abstract theorising and often said that his mind simply did not work in that way. He remembered once scolding himself as he fretted up and down a railway platform while awaiting a delayed train. Instead of wasting this time he would consider some Important Abstract Subject: he would think upon Education. But nothing, nothing at all, came to mind, for heart was advising mind.[6] Education in the abstract did not speak to his condition; nor, in his opinion, had it much to say to the condition of England. The really effective education knits itself into every aspect of one's life. It is effective because it is inescapable. The most difficult and perplexed characters in Forster's fiction are those who have stopped learning; some have never even begun. They drift anchorless through life and smash up smaller craft as they go.

Thus his writings contain teachers of various kinds, a variety of educational agencies, and emphasis on possibilities of endless learning. Of the novels, *The Longest Journey* has a boarding school and a master who finds no joy in teaching. In *A Passage to India* the English Principal of a government school, who loves to teach, contends with the rigidities of the British Raj. Italy herself is the teacher in *Where Angels Fear to Tread* and *A Room with a View*; some of the English are receptive pupils, while others remain unaware that a lesson is offered. *Howards End* shows us two attempts at self-education, both unsatisfactory. Margaret Schlegel relies on books and concerts and genteel discussion groups but must begin again to educate her heart; and Leonard Bast, who realises vaguely that books alone are not enough, does not know how to begin again.

Forster believed that human beings could be taught to pick and choose from among the contents of Culture's storehouse. In 1971, a year after his death, Eric Crozier recorded a conversation with Forster's friends Bob and May Buckingham, a police constable and a nurse, both of working-class background.

E.   You both told me separately that Morgan educated you.
B.   He certainly educated me, not in the formal sense, but he directed my taste, suggested things I ought to read . . .
M.   He lent us books, and we talked about them.
B.   When we talked about something that interested us, he would say 'Why don't you read so-and-so?'
E.   Was he tolerant? – patient, if you didn't like his suggestions?
B.   Yes indeed.
E.   Because he could be trenchant in his criticism, couldn't he?
B.   Yes. He taught me to be critical, too.
E.   What about you, May?
M.   I used to read everything that came my way . . . But Morgan taught me how to read novels, to pick and choose.[7]

In his fiction and essays, in his travels, his teaching at the Working Men's College and his talks for the BBC, Forster taught himself to pick and choose the best from that Victorian tradition of which he was a grateful if often irritated inheritor and 'fag-end'. Facile acceptance of ideas irritated him. In 1948 he found himself angry with Bob Buckingham and their friend E. K. Bennett, 'for misunderstanding education – or rather one of its functions', which in Forster's view is to encourage variety, not to standardise opinions.[8]

The middle class, because it enjoyed particular advantages of mobility, was the destined carrier of the torch and with certain modifications of character would discharge that duty well. His essay, 'Notes on the English Character', sets forth both its virtues and its deficiencies. The middle class is 'the heart of England'. Its values and mores had become the national characteristics that made England most recognisable abroad. Those were products of an Age of

Reason, and the English middle class desired above all to be thought *reasonable* and to be admired for its practical uses of reason. It has energy and initiative. It works very hard. It can be generous. It has feelings – else how could England have produced Shakespeare and the other great poets? But it does not know how to admit or show them, for imagination remains unnourished. It lacks a sense of humour. Consider *Punch*, which has 'neither wit, laughter, nor satire, . . . only the snigger of a suburban householder who can understand nothing that does not resemble himself.'⁹ Suburban seclusion and exclusion were a large part of the problem. The middle class had broken out of a prescribed place on the social scale only to shut itself up in suburbs where it clung to hard-won respectability, mindlessly imitated the manners of the aristocracy, and tried to avoid the contaminating ways of the lower orders. These suburbanites acquired properties but lacked sufficient sense of *place*. Education was too much a matter of school prizes and good degrees. The arts were suspect. When that middle class went abroad to rule, it did not change; imperial compounds simply replaced the suburbs. 'Victorian middle-class culture,' says F.M.L. Thompson, 'was dedicated to separate spheres: separate single-family houses, separation of work from home, and separation of women from work.'¹⁰ And, Forster would have added, separation from the great world, its fascinations and its lessons. This was his own class. In his suburban neighbours' foibles he saw some of his own. It is worth remembering that when in his writings he struck notes now often called 'Forsterian' – proportion, continuity, connection, Culture – he addressed himself as well as his neighbours.

2

The Suburban Novels

By 1894, when Morgan Forster was fifteen, Rooksnest, the house near Stevenage, Hertfordshire, had become his Arcadia, cherished in memory but unattainable. In 1894, when he began a detailed description of the house in order to fix it firmly in mind, he could not remember the act of first entering the house, but he was clear about his first memory connected with his being in and of Rooksnest: 'playing with bricks on the drawing room floor'. They had arrived in March 1883 and intended to stay for no more than three years. They left in 1893 because the landlord would not renew their lease, in part because Mrs Forster could not make up her mind about it. In those ten years her son developed his lifelong attachment to the house, its wych-elm and meadow, and the farm beyond.

In Forster's memoir 'Rooksnest', he describes with loving detail the rather eccentric interior plan, then passes on to neighbours. A somewhat difficult family was named Plum, whose children tended to a dismaying disorderliness. The Franklin family at the adjacent farm supplied fresh milk and butter, but the farm hands sometimes stole the Rooksnest apples. Rooksnest's own meadow was let to Mr Franklin with the stipulation that only orderly animals be admitted. There were cats, a dog, a pony, games in fields and hayricks with the Franklins' son. There were also disadvantages, which the Forsters seem to have borne more easily than the friends who wondered how they put up with such inconvenience. Rooksnest had no well, and for six years rainwater from the roof was the water supply, supplemented by pails of overpriced water from the farm. Colonel Wilkinson, the landlord, promised that water would be pumped to the house after the town built its waterworks. The waterworks materialised, 'but lo! Colonel Wilkinson said we had got on all right for 6 years & could go on for longer.' At last he gave in, and the result was 'a cross between a Noah's ark & a sardine-box', which supplied them with water but was grotesquely ugly and interfered with the view of the countryside in all directions. (When Forster ended this memoir in 1947 the water-tank was still there, still in use, a monument to the awful tenacity of ugliness.) On the other hand, there were the wych-elm with the pigs' mystic teeth embedded in the bark and the ancient vine that linked the house to the soil.[1] The early portion of this memoir, in Forster's squarish schoolboy hand, forecasts the principles that the mature author will outline in his BBC talk on 'The Challenge of Our Time'. Forster did indeed belong to what seemed 'the fag-end of Victorian liberalism'. It had reached him through his father's connection by marriage to the Thornton family, and it echoed in Forster's ideas and behaviour right to the end of his life. Forster's great-great-uncle, Henry Thornton, merchant, banker, and Member of Parliament for Southwark, was born in 1760 and died in 1815, the year of Waterloo. He built a splendid house, Battersea Rise, on the edge of Clapham Common, at that time shady and uncrowded, five miles from the centre of London. The house, the bank and Henry Thornton's activist tradition passed in turn to his son Henry, Forster's great-uncle, who was born in 1800 and died in 1881. Battersea Rise became the centre of activities of the like-minded families who built their own homes around the Common and became known as the Clapham Sect, an early suburban community of Macaulays, Trevelyans, Grants, Stephens, Wilberforces, Thorntons. They were so vigorous in founding and maintaining Bible societies, foreign missions, societies for the abolition of slavery and other means of doing good, that outsiders dubbed them the Saints. The Sect were Church-of-England Evangelical in faith, generally Utilitarian in secular philosophy. 'It was not a closed sainthood', Forster wrote in 1956, for others who shared their views and their sense of social and evangelical mission were welcome to join in their efforts. They may have appeared a closed clique to those who did not understand them, for their common interests had drawn them together as the enclave at Clapham. Proximity made it so much easier to get on with the organisation of good works.[2] With relatives and connections through friendship and marriage they comprised what Noel Annan has called England's nineteenth-century 'intellectual aristocracy'.[3] They concerned themselves with every facet of Victorian life (except serious art): politics, legislation, the judicial, church polity, education, commerce. Duty ruled them, but they were not humourless, and they did not make the younger generation's life a misery of all duty and no play. They were financially secure and seldom, if ever, idle. They were thrifty but not stingy in the uses of their worldly goods, for themselves and for others. They were not ascetics. 'Deep in the Thorntons' character, deeper even than they suspected, was the disinclination to inflict pain,' Forster wrote, and that outlook also he inherited from them.[4]

Deeper, probably, than Morgan suspected at the time was his mother's growing impatience with the enveloping Thornton influence. His father, Edward Morgan Llewellyn Forster, was a Thornton nephew. In 1877 he married Alice Clara Whichelo, whom the Thorntons and Marianne in particular, daughter of the first Henry Thornton and sister to the second, took under their wing after her father's death. When Edward Forster died in 1880, less than two years after Morgan's birth, Marianne's attention fixed firmly on the widow and her child. She had aggressively definite ideas of how she wanted Morgan to turn out, so that the move to Rooksnest in 1883 became Mrs Forster's cautious declaration of independence. She took care not to cut the Thornton tie altogether, but the move made her son more than ever the centre of her existence. The distance between Rooksnest and the village encouraged this, and Mrs Forster remained on the whole aloof from local society. Margaret Ashby, in her history of Rooksnest and Stevenage, says that the Forsters 'continued to live very secluded lives', but 'the unhurried pace of life gave Mrs Forster and Morgan time to enjoy the simple pleasures of each season and to find amusement in small, unexpected incidents.'[5] Ties formed there were too strong to be loosened in later years, and they would mark Morgan's adult life, not only with dilemmas regarding responsibility toward his mother, but with the effects of an environment dominated by women who hovered over him, depended on him, expected undefined but great things of him.

Because their influence was so powerful, understanding the Thorntons was one way for Morgan to understand himself. Marianne had lived until 1887, and Morgan could remember her. A principal source was her 'Recollections', and through them he could trace some of his own characteristics to her: his attitude toward money, for instance. Money was not for show. It carried moral responsibility. The Thorntons had plenty and to spare and were serious about the morality side of that equation. Money must earn its keep. A surplus must be shared, but prudently.

Marianne adored her grand-nephew Morgan, but she took precautions when providing for him because she was a little worried about the intensity of his feelings for favourite belongings and surroundings: an expression, perhaps, of his need to put down roots, a need that only grew stronger as he grew older. She worried because he made emotional investments in belongings and in bits of his physical surroundings, an affection as intense as 'the attachment of grown up people for each other . . .'[6] In the absence of the father he would never know, Marianne took on the role of a provider. She left £8000 for his education and maintenance, but he did not get the principal until he was twenty-five. She need not have worried, for he grew up extremely conscious of and often worried about money's power over human beings, and particularly about its effects on friendship. He managed his own income on lines as strict as Marianne's own. He lived modestly, even frugally, even after his publication royalties increased greatly. He gave away his surplus according to the Thorntons' rule: if he made a gift, he wanted to hear no more about it. If a loan were requested, even if only a few pounds, the money must be repaid, and promptly, for borrowing is a solemn responsibility. Letting the borrower off weakens his moral fibre.

Responsibility was the lesson of the Thornton family's financial epic, which concerns the family bank, its near-failure in 1825, and its daring rescue by Henry Thornton the younger, then aged twenty-five. He kept his head, acted quickly, and earned the confidence of officers of the Bank of England when many who were older and more experienced succumbed to panic. A second panic and a reorganisation followed, and Marianne wrote with much satisfaction that 'it still appears to me magic' that Henry had risen so spectacularly in his profession instead of having to work his way up through the family's banking hierarchy.[7] There was no magic, but some luck and a great deal of courage. The crisis became a bit of Forster's own moral and financial history, for by saving the bank Henry Thornton incidentally assured Marianne's bequest that not only paid for Morgan Forster's education but would one day make possible his career as an independent writer. He took pride in Henry's exploit and would remind himself and others that banking was in his blood.[8] Of Henry, Marianne wrote that the family's standards of 'high honour, strict principle, and fearless integrity' that had created the bank had now saved it, a source of immense satisfaction to her upright soul and to Morgan Forster as well.[9]

To the fifteen-year-old Forster at Rooksnest, Colonel Wilkinson's integrity was less than fearless. He made a promise and did not keep it. He had to be made to 'give in'. Young Forster treats him with the irony that the novelist will deal out to fictional characters similarly flawed, for lo! the Colonel had an ungenerous heart. Worse, he does not know that that is so. Individuals of ungenerous heart will be the most difficult adversaries in Forster's novels.

Failed generosity suggests a deficient imagination. That was the flaw in the local planner who placed the new water-tank at Rooksnest. Forster's schoolboy memoir simply forecast his criticism of the national planners in 1946. The water-tank was efficient but grotesquely ugly and a blight on nature, just as the postwar satellite town, which would have obliterated Rooksnest altogether, would consume whole miles of uniquely beautiful landscape. A little more thought and courtesy might have placed the new water-tank and expanded Stevenage more felicitously, for the greater happiness of the tenants and the integrity of house and countryside. Forster's feeling for inanimate objects, which Marianne Thornton had found so striking, became a settled part of his emotional equipment. He was repelled when an acquaintance gave him and his mother a leaf from an ivy branch that had grown through a cottage roof: '"taking away a bit" from everywhere' was a 'hateful custom'.[10]

In 1901, his handwriting now evolving toward the familiar mature script, he added a little more to the Rooksnest memoir, then nothing until 1947, when he was alone and had settled in his last home, King's College, Cambridge. He still thought of the house as 'my Rooksnest', for it renewed the seal on his identity, 'my childhood and safety. . . . Only a little of my passion and irrationalism was used up in *Howards End*.' His domestic totem, the mantelpiece designed by his architect father was one of those inanimate objects that represented his roots. It had been installed at Rooksnest, then had accompanied him and his mother to Tonbridge, to Tunbridge Wells, Weybridge and West Hackhurst and finally went with him to King's, where it may be seen today.[11]

Those locations in Kent and Surrey trace the wanderings of the Forsters, mother and son, after they left Rooksnest in 1893 and Mrs Forster took a house in Tonbridge so that Morgan could attend Tonbridge School. His earlier experiences of formal education had been often unhappy, and one of those preceding Tonbridge had brought him so close to hysteria that his mother had had to withdraw him. Tonbridge offered low fees for boys living within ten miles of Tonbridge church, so that there was financial advantage in Morgan's being a day-boy. But day-boys were by definition outsiders, and his caution and reserve that Morgan hoped would protect him from extroverted heartiness and unkindness became a second handicap. In 1956 he told himself that he had long forgotten Tonbridge School, but he never forgot it, if only because *The Longest Journey*, in which Tonbridge is the prototype for the deplorable Sawston School, remained the book he was 'most glad to have written'.[12] He remembered something else that his Tonbridge education only intimated: the mind's expansion through entry into a literature other than one's own. He reread Virgil's description of Aeneas' shield and thought of Mr Floyd, a Tonbridge form-master, who read aloud to the end 'and squeaked "Marvellous, but you cant see it, wretched boys, cant see it – – –"'. Forster, like the other boys, could not see it at the time, but he had an early intimation that the purpose of education was to create curiosity and make connections between ideas merely suggested and ideas understood. 'His squeak survives as a fruitful sound, . . . and I pay him this faint far away tribute.' Forster's first book, an edition of Virgil's *Aeneid*, was an early part of that tribute, and in *The Longest Journey* he would try to advance the solution to that puzzle.[13] Why should education not carry the wretched boys beyond puzzlement and mere intimations of enlightenment to come?

P. N. Furbank says that when Forster arrived in Cambridge in 1897 he was 'already, in some ways, a very wise young man . . . it was not an awestruck provincial who entered the gateway of King's, and he would not have been over-impressed by the picture-book setting'. Nevertheless his first year was rather bleak, and he recalled himself as 'immature, uninteresting, and unphilosophic'.[14] He discovered at once that his Tonbridge School preparation had been deficient. He lived in lodgings and made friends only slowly. Several of those he saw most often were relentlessly, humourlessly religious and got on his nerves. In his second year he lived in College, and his view began to brighten. It also broadened under the influence of his tutor, Nathaniel Wedd, who was unconventional, outspoken and Fabian; and Goldsworthy Lowes Dickinson, political philosopher and advocate of the Hellenic approach to life. Knowing individuals like these soon disposed of Forster's conventional Christian beliefs, for which he began to substitute a philosophy of humanism. By the time he was elected, in his fourth year, to the Cambridge Conversazione Society – the Apostles – he was ready for their free and wide-ranging enquiries, which gave him his first experience of serious discussion of sex. He must have realised by this time that he was homosexual, but he had only vague ideas of what that entailed and of whether fellow Apostles were actively engaged in affairs in or out of their Colleges. The revelations were an abstract, not a physical liberation. But intellectual liberation, which made clearer what education at Tonbridge had only intimated, brought him friends like Robert Trevelyan and Lytton Strachey, and a little later it would carry him into the orbit of the Bloomsbury group.

A vague family assumption had accompanied him to Cambridge, that he would become one of those university intellectuals who took a hand in administering Britain. While he was there, his connections to the Clapham Thorntons had enabled him to see a good deal of their friends and relations among Darwins, Wedgwoods, Trevelyans and Grants. He found the rather strained gentilities and social assumptions of middle-class academic intellectuals sometimes amusing and sometimes irritating. But along with liberating new ideas he absorbed also the 'Cambridge prejudice that it was scholars and civil servants, not business men, who ran Britain'.[15] Forster's University record, however, was neither brilliant enough to start him up a government administrative ladder nor to secure a College appointment, which was what he really wanted, more for personal than for scholarly and pedagogical reasons: 'I would have given and would give anything to be [a don]. I can't think of any body who is in a better position for making new friends and keeping old ones.'[16]

The alternative was the year that he and his mother spent in Italy, from the autumn of 1901, during which he prepared himself to be a University Extension lecturer on Italian art. That year held a mirror to middle-class English travellers, and he became very conscious that he was one of them. 'John Bull Abroad' was easily and persistently caricatured. Stereotypes mocked unkindly the gentlemen of 'long, lean face, the hook nose, and Holmesean getup' of Inverness cape, pipe and hat. They were even more unkind about those women, all too plainly domestic rejects, with 'pince nez, the prominent front teeth, the skirt which droops amorphously at the back and the feet as flat as her chest'.[17] But there were others, serious-minded and courageous, and Mrs Forster was one of those, as conscientious as her son about systematic tours of galleries, churches and landscapes. A lively sense of the absurd and liberal political views protected her from falling into the pattern of the heedless tourist. The Forsters did, however, belong to the category of persons who made Thomas Cook's business so successful, those with an average assured income of between three and six hundred pounds a year. Gentility and composure were expected of them. Forster's travel diary shows him to be one of the approved type, respectable and conscientious. Preparing himself to lecture on Italian art was his primary purpose, but the diary shows that he recorded experiences and impressions with literary flair and care. As yet, a literary career was not a fixed idea. He had begun to write short stories, although at the time writing seemed possible as no more than an intermittent and supplementary activity.

Long before Forster's time many of the British abroad gave the impression of wishing they had never left home. Cook's enterprise was barely begun when John Henry Newman felt compelled to warn, in *The Idea of a University*, that travel alone was no substitute for education. His portrait of British tourists was not flattering, for 'nothing which meets them carries them forward or backward to any idea beyond itself. Everything stands by itself, and comes in its turn, like the shifting scenes of a show, which leaves the spectator where he was.'[18]

Of course there were exceptions. G. M. Trevelyan's 'poor Muggleton', a fictional composite but a recognisable academic type, was 'a failure at the classics' when in school, but the classical education whose pedagogical sterility he deplored did not destroy his love for the classics themselves. He still opens his Homer with reverence and 'is often found sitting in front of the Elgin Marbles'. His ideal achieves apotheosis when he visits Athens: 'I have made my pilgrimage and touched the gods of my idolatry.'[19]

As traveller in 1901 Forster wished to be that kind of exception, and there was a great deal of Marianne Thornton in him. In 1816, at the age of nineteen, already a canny observer, she went to France and found that she disliked English insularity and the unreasoning dislike and suspicion of the French, and tourists who excoriate them and say 'nothing but old England for me', when a less prejudiced outlook often revealed the despised French as well worth knowing.[20] Why did the reserve and caution that made the English so steady and admirable at home become disadvantages when they went abroad?

At Lucerne the Forsters did become very British, then were contrite, after they were 'attacked by Miss Stackpole' (not her real name). 'British like', they snubbed her – as she reminded them when they relented and allowed themselves to become better acquainted with her. Forster even refrained from arguing with her about the relative sizes of Cologne Cathedral and the Hof Kirch, no doubt an amends for his fit of British standoffishness. 'She says that everyone would be kind if you only gave them a chance, and that she for one means to give it them.'[21] But at Como the Forsters made little effort to be gracious, for they found their hotel taken over by English tourists, 'mostly T[unbridge] Wells old ladies', exhausted and argumentative. However, he and his mother felt that on the whole they had 'escaped the burden of people like ourselves'.[22]

Italy took up where Cambridge had left off. Forster was filled with
the pleasure of recognition – and perhaps also some disappointment
at the lack of surprise – on his second day there, for he felt 'that I
know it well already'. He had done his homework and now 'nothing
comes as a surprise'. Immediately, however, he got one, for curiosity
took hold when he went from full sunlight to very chilly shade at
Cadenazzo and understood suddenly 'why Virgil & Theocritus always state so definitely whether their shepherds are in the shade or
the sun'.[23]

He turned a severely clinical eye upon himself and added some
philosophy for good measure. On Lake Como the wind had been
violent and he and his mother were tired. However, he prided
himself on missing none of the details of the scene in the sky, on
water and on shore. He was not the type of traveller who gushes
over one moment and then forgets all about it in ecstasies over the
next scene. He must wait, he adjured himself rather sententiously,
until his impressions and his ideas about them had had time to
mature, for 'the while we are young a little time purges away our
frailties and leaves us with the pure gold. But I would rather have
the pure gold at once.'[24]

He got the gold, not at once, but in the relatively short period of
five years, from the two 'Italian novels', *Where Angels Fear to Tread* in
1905 and *A Room with a View* in 1908, which examine middle-class
tourists abroad; to *The Longest Journey* in 1907 and *Howards End* in
1910, which consider them in their home settings. In a sense they are
all 'suburban novels', for his Italian travels made him ponder more
extensively than ever before the suburban environment – which was
his own – from which so many of the English travellers came. The
Forsters still lived in Tonbridge when he went up to Cambridge in
1897, but in September 1898 Mrs Forster moved their home to
Tunbridge Wells, six miles to the south. In received social opinion,
that would have been a step up. Tunbridge Wells, laid out in 1606 as
a rustic spa, tended to look down upon less fashionable, more utilitarian Tonbridge. In 1724, Daniel Defoe noted with disapproval that
'those people who have nothing to do any where else, seem to be the
only people who have any thing to do at Tunbridge.'[25] In 1923 the
official guide book still stated winningly that 'the town is never
over-run with trippers', or 'defiled by the vulgar or the inane'. Its
well-to-do inhabitants 'naturally create social atmosphere tinged by
culture and refinement'. Discerning members of the aristocracy come
there to recover from the 'ceaseless social duties of the London

season', and when London is '"empty" in the society sense, Tunbridge Wells is at its liveliest and best'.[26] Forster conceived an abiding dislike for the town. He had always thought its 'tinge of culture and refinement' not even skin deep, no more than a cosmetic. In 1912 he passed judgement, rather viciously, at the end of a three-day visit: 'Filthy self righteous place, full of Dorothy Perkins roses. I stifled.'[27]

His disaffection came not only from the contrast with Cambridge or his unfavourable opinions of the behaviour of suburban tourists on the Continent. He criticised because he invested so much hope in the possibilities of the middle class. He was already formulating the analysis that he would publish in 1920 in his essay, 'Notes on the English Character'. England's essentially middle-class character was expressed in 'solidity, caution, integrity, efficiency'; but also in 'lack of imagination, hypocrisy'. Middle classes everywhere tended to caution and a certain rigidity, but in the case of England he lays much of the blame for those on the public school as an institution, the 'heart of the middle classes' and a machine for standardising those who will obtain a highly disproportionate number of responsible positions in the civil, military and ecclesiastical establishments of realm and Empire. Its exclusivism spread to many in the middle classes who had never been to public schools, and it matured as the snobbery that separated them from the rest of society. What then of the middle-class energy and ingenuity that had helped to make England great? 'Saint George may caper on banners and in the speeches of politicians, but it is John Bull who delivers the goods.'[28]

But delivering the goods kept John Bull so busy that he seemed unaware of the provincialism and suburban isolation that so disturbed Forster. Prosperity now meant, at relative social levels, the ability to turn one's back on the city and move to the new commuter suburbs. The shift was part of a much greater change in Edwardian England. The agricultural depression of the 1870s, and higher taxes and death duties, forced owners of large estates to sell off parts of their urban and rural holdings, on many of which the new suburbs then sprang up. At the same time, middle-class professional persons and university intellectuals found more places in county and national government, Parliament and the Cabinet, the Civil Service and the Courts, the Foreign Service and the Armed Services.[29]

When the Forsters returned from Italy they improvised for a year in a London flat. Then, in 1904, they settled at Weybridge, Surrey. Weybridge lacked the educational tone that an ancient and well-known school gave to Tonbridge, and it did not have Tunbridge

Wells' fashionable cachet. In fact, history allowed Weybridge scant character. The Surrey historian in *The Victoria History of the Counties of England* says that in the fourteenth century it was 'a place of very small importance'. It had once included a royal property, but instead of basking in reflected glory the village, which had only one cart, became peevish about the 'burden of [providing] carriages for the royal removals'. During the Restoration the Duke of Norfolk rebuilt a house there, which John Evelyn thought was 'in a miserable barren sandy place by the street side; never in my life had I seen such expense [£10,000] to such small purpose.'[30]

The Forsters' Weybridge house cost fifty-five pounds a year. It faced a small green with a Hanoverian monument too modest to compete with Tunbridge Wells. The house, which still stands, is detached, but just barely, so that although it had a pleasant garden it could not be said to stand amid 'grounds'. It is an enduring English suburban type, solid and unimaginative. The Forsters called it 'Harnham', and it had 'a beautiful brass bound door stop' unique in the neighbourhood. The 'best families' would soon call, and Morgan would attend the new Literary Society 'if invited'.[31] They did, and he was.

Despite its age as a settlement and the Roman ruins in the environs, Weybridge at that time, at least in Forster's perception of it, invited his ironic nudge at self-conscious gentility: a brass door stop for neighbourhood one-upmanship, strictly selective calls on newcomers, a brand-new Literary Society to certify the presence of Culture. Weybridge at the turn of the century was more and more a London commuters' town, with 'whole colonies of new houses' proliferating along the Thames and the railway 'to the annoyance of the Surrey Union Hunt'.[32] The Forsters' house was not one of the raw new ones, but the atmosphere, like that of Tonbridge and Tunbridge Wells, struck Forster as restricted and restricting. Questions of national and international import remained for the most part outside the reposeful round of domestic arranging, genteel amusement, day-trips to London shops, and, very occasionally, a cautious tour of approved Continental countries.

After he had finished *Where Angels Fear to Tread*, Forster had another opportunity for a long perspective on English suburban life when he went in 1905 to Nassenheide as tutor to three of the children of Elizabeth von Arnim, the 'Elizabeth' of that very popular book, *Elizabeth's German Garden*. There he wondered whether he had lost his own soul by investing his energies in descriptions of the trivialities of English Suburbia. It was too easy to gush over the picturesque poor, but at least the Working Men's College would show him how to meet them without condescension. But facing up to 'the vulgar and genteel' was another kind of problem. 'To know and help them are we to lose our souls – or how much of them?' This, Furbank says, 'was to be a central question for him. The kind of life he had chosen for himself, full of aunts and tea-parties and little jokes and chocolate hares, was a thoroughly dowdy and tame and suburban one, beset on all sides by the "vulgar and genteel".' In fact, he felt that he had had no choice, for 'it had chosen him'.[33]

His suburban novels have a principal context from an activity that took him right out of Suburbia: his teaching at the Working Men's College in London, whose students were seldom picturesque but were solid and determined and terribly in earnest about self-improvement. This was his first sustained contact with members of the urban working class. Shortly before he came down from Cambridge, he had informed his mother that he had been to 'a meeting about the Working Men's college, which [G. M.] Trevelyan set up... [It] sounds a wonderful thing and I want to hear more about it'.[34]

It was, and still is, a wonderful thing. It was quite different from the community centres or leisure-time clubs for working men that many Oxford and Cambridge colleges sponsored under Nonconformist or Church of England auspices. The dangers of class condescension were always present in programmes that inserted privileged young men into short-term, part-time activities with persons whose background they understood only theoretically. Samuel Butler, in *The Way of All Flesh*, a book that Forster took seriously to heart, lays bare a weakness of such enterprises when he lets poor Ernest Pontifex, earnest but hopelessly naive, come to grief in his central London parish because he is so ignorant of the facts of his parishioners' lives.

The new Working Men's College was intended from the beginning as a *college*. Its founders knew that they must deal with the academic assumption, from which Forster himself was not exempt at the time, that the good life was not really possible outside Oxford and Cambridge. But they would do their best to combine university ideals and social life on the university pattern with teaching to fit the abilities and aspirations of working men (and, as much as possible, women). It would not insult them with a juvenile curriculum warmed over. The atmosphere would be collegial: a community, a club, a centre for friendship and leisure activities as well as for study and some practical training. So far as was humanly possible, there would be no artificial social or professional barriers.

This vision grew from the Christian Socialism of the Reverend

Frederick Denison Maurice and his friends who sympathised with
Chartism and commiserated its failure. Education, they believed,
might accomplish what Chartism had failed to obtain through public protest. The College, an entirely new departure in adult education, would be closer to Newman's idea of a university, liberal and
liberating. Maurice intended it, in the words of one historian, as 'an
association of men *as men* – an association not formed for some
commercial purpose and not limited by coincidence of opinion, and
to represent, therefore, that union which he was always striving to
bring about' – that is, reconciliation within and between classes.[35]

The immediate realisation of Maurice's vision followed upon
expulsion from his Professorship at King's College, London, after his
lecture, 'On Eternal Life and Eternal Death', in which he rejected the
doctrine of eternal death and punishment: it cancelled out the doctrine of God's mercy. During the ensuing row he insisted on his right
to 'bear what testimony I can for the right of English divines to
preach the gospel of God's love to mankind . . . '[36] He could have
resigned quietly but chose not to do so. More than 900 working men
from ninety-five different trades signed a statement of sympathy
and support, and out of that came a specific request that he become
the Principal of a Working Men's College. In January 1854 the College, a durable act of 'moral imagination', opened in makeshift
Bloomsbury quarters; in 1857 it moved to 45 Great Ormond Street,
where it attracted lecturers of the greatest eminence, including Ruskin,
always a major attraction.[37]

George Macaulay Trevelyan, who received his Cambridge degree
in 1903, had begun to teach history at the Working Men's College in
the summer of 1900. He too had inherited Clapham's tradition of
public service, and he threw himself into recruitment of teachers. He
was a man not to be denied; Forster once saw him climb 'a perpen-
dicular Border Wall, hanging on cracks by his fingers'.[38] By October
1901 nearly half of those teaching at the College were Trevelyan's
Cambridge friends.[39] Even before Forster returned from Italy in 1902,
Trevelyan said that he thought Forster was drifting, that it was high
time for him to find some real work, and that the Working Men's
College was the place to find it: 'England, with all its faults, working
England is a better place than invalids and tennis players in Italian
hotels.'[40] Forster offered to teach Latin and met his first class in
January 1903.

Almost immediately he was pressed into service as a substitute
lecturer, with signal success. On 21 February 1903, 'Mr. E. M. Forster,

B.A., our new Latin teacher . . . delivered a most interesting lecture on "Florence" illustrated with dissolving views, to a very full audience, many of the public being unable, for want of space, to gain admission to the Oval Room.'[41] In November he followed this with an illustrated Saturday evening lecture on 'The Renaissance at Florence'. He taught evening Latin classes at irregular intervals between 1904 and 1908 and spoke at least twice at the Debating Society. Some of the lecture topics suggest problems that arose while his novels progressed – or failed to progress. In 1906 the topic 'Is the Pessimism of Modern Literature to be Deplored?' surely worried away at him while he wrote *The Longest Journey*.[42] Was he making his point about life's supreme values, or would the common reader find the novel only morbid and self-defeated because the protagonist dies at the end? In 1907 he opened a debate, 'That the Sense of Humour should be cultivated with caution'. This touched a persistent concern of his own about his writing, for he felt that he was not at his best when he lapsed into facetiousness. In 1904 he had sent his story 'The Eternal Moment' to George Trevelyan's elder brother Robert, who indeed thought the style overly facetious. Forster asked him for specific examples of 'facetiae; . . . my taste doesn't guide me.'[43] Someone had once told him that he was amusing, and he was still trying to decide just what was meant and whether it was asset or liability. He still worried about this in 1905, when *Where Angels Fear to Tread* appeared. Again he begged Trevelyan to tell him where he had been 'unduly facetious . . . only you have warned me against it'.[44] Perhaps Robert Trevelyan, a classicist, was not quite a common reader, but Forster had to satisfy himself. He worried because he wanted his social comedy to make serious points that flippancy only vitiated. He had lost the College debate on humour by a vote of eighteen to twelve. 'Mr. Forster, in a delightfully humorous speech, argued that it was pernicious, that the sense of humour should be made to direct our lives; it was not capable of performing such a task; . . . '[45]

Lecturing sometimes helped him to sort out his ideas. In September 1907 he was embarrassed to discover that the two ladies who were to be his hostesses for an Extension Lecture at Ashtead knew more than he did about Dante: 'Must try and read all of Dante whom I cannot like.' The subject was already in his mind. In June he had listened to Dickinson and C.F.G. Masterman discussing Dante. Masterman had held that Dante 'saw everything', to which Dickinson had responded: 'He didn't. He never saw that there should still be cakes and ale.' Forster agreed with Dickinson.[46] So in November we find him reading to the College Literary Society a brilliant paper on Dante in which he examines reasons for his dislike and, on the other hand, for admiration. He connects Dante to the conduct of personal relations with those whom one knows best. Dante regarded those he knew, as the means to something improving, which was reprehensible above all when that other person was used as a mere stepping-stone to the divine. He used Beatrice as that stepping-stone. Indeed, she led him into the very presence of the Blessed. But was this use of her 'a true compliment to the woman herself?' No, and worse yet, Dante behaved badly to people he did not like. The twentieth century was far from perfect in its regard for personal relations, but there had been progress, for time had revealed the flaws in Dante's character. If his acquaintances did not inspire sublime thoughts, he treated them with discourtesy. 'He soared higher than we can, but he could sink lower.' Therefore his lapses were unworthy of him, for in his writings he had been able to reveal the wider range of the soul. Reading Dante can transport us also to the heights, but were he to materialise at that instant in the Working Men's College, 'we should make all haste to walk out of it'.[47] In short, Dante failed Forster's test for the right conduct of personal relations.

His lecture topics are often traceable to sources that have particularly moved him. In 1908, while casting about for a useful quotation, he turned to Walt Whitman, '& he started speaking to me. That the unseen is justified by the seen: which in its turn becomes unseen and is justified by the other.' Whitman convinced him that 'the spiritual world might be robust!'[48] Forster merely remembered what others had written, but Whitman entered into his mind and stayed as a part of himself, so that Forster felt on intimate terms with him.

In 1911 the editor of the College journal asked him for an essay on 'The Beauty of Life'. Forster chose Whitman as his subject, as a poet who speaks especially to those who know the life of work. He had worked with his hands; often, as in the Civil War hospitals, in conditions that might well seem hopeless. He knew from personal experience the darkest and most difficult aspects of life in both peace and war yet could continue to believe that 'beauty is manifest wherever life is manifested. . . . He went the "whole hog" in fact, and he ought to be writing this article.'

In fact, Forster himself did very well at speaking from the page. His essay is practical, colloquial, even evangelical. Working Men's College students knew all about the skills that Whitman glorified. Were they diminished if they could not glorify them in lines like

Whitman's? Not at all, for not everyone can be a Whitman. His circumstances were unique to his time, and his poetic voice unique in all time. His is the kind of voice that one needs to hear when one most needs spiritual encouragement and special guidance. But to try to be a second Whitman can only lead to frustration. Relax, is Forster's message: you have no time to waste in fruitless intellectual byways. Do not be discouraged if an understanding of beauty seems to come only in scraps, not in some dazzling vision. Scraps are a perfectly good way to approach beauty, which is timeless and omnipresent and waits patiently for our eyes and ears to be opened to it. Forster paraphrases Whitman's advice: 'Be cheerful. Be courageous. Do not bother too much about "developing the aesthetic sense," as books term it', for that will come, perhaps when it is least expected. He offers a rule: a workman's spare time is precious. Therefore, never force yourself on a subject that has become only a chore. Choose what appeals most and pursue that subject with all your mind and heart.[49] Forster has described perfectly the dilemma of Leonard Bast, the clerk in *Howards End* who slogs along at Ruskin because he has heard somewhere that Ruskin will tell him how to recognise beauty. He grabs at scraps of beauty but does so joylessly and therefore despairs of attaining the aesthetic sense.

When Forster joined the College in 1903 its pioneering days were history, and it had settled into its role as a London institution. It was still in Great Ormond Street but in the winter of 1905–6 would move to its present quarters in Crowndale Road, St Pancras. It was still 'pervaded by an atmosphere of the liberal Victorian culture of men like Tom Hughes, Ruskin, Westlake and Ludlow, who had helped Maurice in its early days. One of those veterans was still left, that amazing old bird F. J. Furnivall, the Shakespeare scholar, with a smile half benevolent half Mephistophelean permanently fixed on a red face framed in shaggy white hair; he was revered but not approved by the more responsible chiefs of the College.'[50] If Furnivall's day at the College had gone by, its inherent values had not. 'We studied and took exercise together,' he recalled, 'we were comrades and friends, and helpt one another to live higher, happier, and healthier lives, free from all stupid and narrow class humbug.'[51]

The College gave Forster a new angle on both 'class humbug' and the 'liberal Victorian culture'. Security and its blessings defined the difference between himself and his students. They were shop assistants, office clerks, artisans, mechanics, manual labourers. Their security depended upon employers' prosperity; Forster's was cushioned by an independent income. Their free time came at the end of long working days, and evening classes often meant hard battles with fatigue; his time was his own for reading, writing, visiting, travelling. For many, the College was their only source of intellectual nourishment; Forster's '"real" life went on in Cambridge still, and he was there as much as he was able, rarely missing an Apostles' meeting'.[52] The contrasts became an education in themselves, and they too became part of his 'copy', to be incorporated in his suburban novels.

A ROOM WITH A VIEW

To take the novels in conceptual, not publication order, the 'Lucy novel' was his first in mind. It went through several false starts, then was laid aside while he completed *Where Angels Fear to Tread*. Together they distil impressions from the Italian year and a visit to Greece in the summer of 1903. It struck him that many tourists were prisoners rather than citizens of 'that curious tourist state which tolerant Italy has allowed to grow up . . . '[53] The foreign presence dictated menus and meals, hours of trains and travel. It shouldered Italians out of the way unless they could be of service. Would England tolerate such a presence? Certainly not. Like all totalitarian regimes, the tourist state frowned upon eccentricity without at the same time recognising its own eccentricities. Its inhabitants followed prescribed circles, imitated the old tradition of the Grand Tour, understood less and less of its original purpose of cultural enlargement, and returned laden with 'bits from everywhere'.

Both abroad and at home, Forster felt himself increasingly crosswise to the currents of conventional suburban life. The Italian year, so much of it spent in the company of English tourists, focused his attention on the environment from which they came. His impatience with Suburbia increased, and 'he could not but feel, what horrors one encountered in a suburban way of life like his! They were his "copy" as a novelist; yet could one live one's life among them, and not be damaged? . . . He felt imprisoned among its genteel comedies and atrocities.'[54] And how terrible to contemplate, if he continued in this way, the possibility of being consumed by his own career. As he looked around Suburbia, he became convinced that it was the women who determined its social tone through nervous self-consciousness about their niche in that narrow society. At the same time, they were afraid to question it too much or too often. If there was a key to salvation, it was the ability to feel uncertain about the ordained rightness of Suburbia's classifying system. In *A Room with a View*, Mrs Honeychurch tries to justify to Freddy, her less-conventional son, Cecil Vyse's qualifications to be Lucy's fiancé: 'Well, *I* like him,' said Mrs. Honeychurch. 'I know his mother; he's good, he's clever, he's rich, he's well connected – . . .' She interrupts herself, for she knows that something is missing from this catalogue of admirable qualifications. All she can summon up is 'And he has beautiful manners.'[55] Still, she has been more perceptive than she realises, for Cecil's manners are superficially perfect but rest on the flawed foundation of self-satisfaction.

Mrs Honeychurch is one of Forster's many important minor characters who carry a major message. Her uncertainties suggest her virtues. She recites the litany of middle-class respectability, but her heart is not quite in it, for she is a natural person and is too honest to hide from herself. She has come up fortuitously from a lower level of the middle class, perhaps from a level lower still, but she has possibilities of which she herself is unaware and to which class is irrelevant. Her late husband, who lacked polish but had a keen eye for land development, had cleverly purchased on speculation a site beyond the most recent round of suburban expansion, had built a house and, unexpectedly, was ambushed by 'love for his own creation', so that instead of selling it at a profit he had made it a home for himself and his family.[56] He had had possibilities of perception out of the ordinary as well, for he fell in love also with the site and with its view over the Sussex Downs. He achieved a house that, although an economical box shape, is one with its location, unlike the grander houses that famous architects had built for grander clients after the neighbourhood became fashionable. Mr Honeychurch's eye for interiors had been less acute. The drawing-room furniture, his purchase, has 'the trail of Tottenham Court Road upon it'.[57] Mrs Honeychurch does not find it embarrassing until she views it through Cecil's condescending eyes; loyally, thriftily, she has preserved its freshness by keeping the curtains drawn, thus excluding the view and annoying Cecil, who values the view principally as relative improvement over the furniture. Mrs Honeychurch retains other habits from her humbler origins. She shouts. At moments of crisis she is more at ease in the kitchen-garden than on the terrace. She imitates (lapses into?) low-class accent and grammar. Pudding recipes, water for baths, the infirmities of water-boilers furnish her domestic landscape. She mistrusts genteel elderly ladies as tenants because they will keep canaries, which spill seed on the rugs, which attracts mice. She thinks women have no business writing books, is aghast at Lucy's notion of living alone in a London flat, and at once pictures her as a raging suffragette smashing shop windows.

But there is more to Mrs Honeychurch than puddings and water boilers. The migrating Londoners who came into the area assumed that the Honeychurches were 'remnants of an indigenous aristocracy', and honest Mr Honeychurch was alarmed by what might be expected of them socially, but his equally honest wife, who does not know how to put on airs, simply continued to be herself and did what came to her naturally. She called on all the newcomers, and by the time they learned the truth about her background she had made herself a part of the neighbourhood, and her antecedents were irrelevant.[58] She dislikes affectation, bombast, sentimentalism; and she dislikes herself when she falls into them while welcoming Cecil into the family. Instinctively she delivers others from their own social predicaments. Mr Beebe, the rector, ends in a conversational cul-de-sac when he blunders about Lucy's engagement. In desperation he begs for tea. 'You only asked for it just in time', cries Mrs Honeychurch. 'How dare you be serious at Windy Corner?' And Mr Beebe 'took his tone from her'. He drops all clerical unctuousness and gives up trying 'to dignify the situation with poetry or the Scriptures'.[59] Everyone is instantly put at ease. Mrs Honeychurch, in other words, was born gracious. Quite unconsciously, she routs the suburban assumptions about who is and who is not a lady. She floats through the Edwardian years as serenely as Marianne Thornton through the nineteenth century.

A Room with a View is more gently and more indirectly autobiographical than *The Longest Journey* will be. The characterisation of Mrs Honeychurch reflects pleasant memories of Forster's maternal grandmother, Louisa Whichelo; and George Emerson and his father could be wishful reflections of Forster himself and of the father who died when Morgan was not quite two. Lucy Honeychurch's younger brother Freddy and the Schlegels' sibling Tibby, who rebel somewhat tentatively against households of women, might be analogies for Forster's own domestic situation, but George Emerson possesses what Forster had never known: a sympathetic father who is friend as well as parent. Mr Emerson sets a steady, affectionate example of belief in Love as guiding principle, then lets George chart his own course in that direction. George makes Beauty his guide. Forster calls George 'a feminist with a sense of humour – by which I mean he sees how absurd pessimism is'.[60] In the film version of *A Room with a View*, George, exalted by the lovely May day and by love for Lucy, climbs a tree on a hill above Fiesole and shouts to the sky his affirmation of belief in Beauty. One cannot imagine E. M. Forster doing such a thing then or later. However, that invented episode does proclaim the point that he made so carefully in 1908, the year of this novel's publication, in his essay 'The Beauty of Life' with its advice to the Working Men's College not to strain after the aesthetic sense. It will grow if heart and mind get a chance to grow in the right way. Mr Emerson has given George the freedom to grow into the aesthetic sense, and Forster had found that freedom at Cambridge. But Cambridge could not be Mr Emerson to Forster's George and supply his ever-present loving confidence in the son. Even in his worries about the outcome of George's love for Lucy, Mr Emerson exudes serene confidence that his principles and George's are sound and right, and it complements Mrs Honeychurch's fundamental serenity. Together they create an atmosphere absent from Forster's daily life.

WHERE ANGELS FEAR TO TREAD

By contrast, Mrs Herriton, widow and formidable mother of the too-compliant Philip in *Where Angels Fear to Tread*, is unaware, uneducable, and in the final definition, unladylike. Where Mrs Honeychurch bestows sweetness and a saving uncertainty, Mrs Herriton projects classbound meanness and cynicism. The novel begins: 'They were all at Charing Cross to see Lilia off – Philip, Harriet, Mrs Herriton herself.'[61] If, after reading to the end, one returns to the first sentence, one finds that that word 'herself' has acquired a cluster of unattractive connotations. Mrs Herriton would have considered that she bestowed a signal honour by being at the station; she is there also to see that Lilia really does get off to Italy instead of taking it into her flighty head at the last minute to do something quite different. Directly or indirectly, Mrs Herriton has warped the lives of all the others on the platform: Philip and Harriet, her unmarried son and daughter; Lilia, her widowed daughter-in-law; Mrs Theobald, Lilia's mother, who has no one else in the world and has journeyed down from Yorkshire to say farewell and be snubbed by Mrs Herriton; and kind Mr Kingcroft, the Yorkshire farmer who hopes to marry Lilia but will not if Mrs Herriton can prevent it. Caroline Abbott is outside Mrs Herriton's circle except as she can be put to use as guard over Lilia while abroad, but her being thus separate will be the source of her strength when the others, who think of themselves as strong and wise, will display neither strength nor wisdom and will precipitate tragedy for the most innocent and defenceless character in the novel. Mrs Herriton classifies people according to her rule for determining which of them she can control inside her family circle, and outsiders whom she cannot control. Spinster daughter Harriet she has created in her own image. Son Philip too is her puppet. Son Charles has slipped the strings by dying, and daughter-in-law Lilia has been made his surrogate. Mrs Herriton has already appropriated their daughter Irma and has cut out Mrs Theobald, Irma's other grandmother. But Mrs Herriton will be wrong about Caroline Abbott, who is supposed to control Lilia during the year in Italy but instead encourages her to marry Gino, the Italian dentist's son. Mrs Herriton will try to appropriate their child as well. He too will escape only by dying.

Mrs Herriton, in her vanity and her rage for control, has isolated both herself and her family members as effectively as if she had built a wall around them – as indeed she has. Windy Corner, the Honeychurch home, bustles with guests and neighbours: Mr Beebe and his little niece Minnie, a self-assured social makeweight for the grown-ups; young Mr Floyd, Freddy's guest; the Emersons. Even the stuffier of those on the scene contribute to an impression of human activity: Cecil Vyse and the inept spinster cousin Charlotte; and even Sir Harry Otway, the local property-owner who is conscientious about his 'duties to the countryside' but finds to his sorrow that money alone does not necessarily guarantee an aesthetically pleasing house.[62] But Mrs Herriton's house at Sawston has no personality and no name, whimsical or otherwise. There are no friends, no guests, no neighbours who feel free to pop in on impulse. The family are Mrs Herriton's prisoners.

At Windy Corner the 'genteel comedies' of suburbia touch lightly and even affectionately upon the social 'atrocities'. At Mrs Herriton's house the social comedies are grim, and atrocities predominate. Snobbery too virulent to be mere stuffiness prevails, sometimes as a betrayal of the humane virtues. When Lilia had wished to settle in Yorkshire with her mother after Charles's death, Mrs Herriton had exerted all her 'kindness' to keep her hold on Lilia, whom she does not even like. It is her way to continue by proxy her hold upon the deceased Charles. That fraudulent kindness also squelched Lilia's incipient engagement to Mr Kingcroft. She returned to Sawston, cried, apologised, listened to Mrs Herriton's lectures on motherhood and widowhood but nurtured a small seed of revolt.[63] Philip Herriton, who has appropriated Italy as his aesthetic credential, suggests as remedy the year without Irma in that country. This enables Mrs Herriton to get on with re-making Irma, who has so 'improved' under Mrs Herriton's control that she is no longer 'that most appalling of things – a vulgar child'.[64] To Mrs Herriton, Italy too is only a 'thing', a mechanism useful only until Lilia meets and marries Gino. Mrs Herriton sentences her to suffer for the sin of insulting the Herriton family. She does suffer, but for the consequences of her ignorance of Italy and Italians, not for insulting the Herritons.

Mrs Herriton must now seize control of Italy, the mechanism that has dared to go wrong. In the most mechanical way – a letter from the family solicitors – she learns that the marriage has produced a child, in producing whom Lilia has died. At once Mrs Herriton concentrates on the disposition of Lilia's money, which she is convinced must have been the Italian husband's sole object anyway, and so far as she is concerned the baby is to be left 'quite beside the point'.[65] The baby remains beside the point until Italy slips the news to Irma by means of a postcard as from the Italian baby, her 'lital brother'.[66] As the news is certain now to leak out, only to avoid Sawston gossip Mrs Herriton despatches Philip and Harriet to Italy to fetch the baby. As she sends them out to do battle with Italy, her house seems more than ever a fortified place.

The expedition uncovers depths of English provincialism and Herriton arrogance. Although Mrs Herriton had first met Mr Herriton in an approved Chamonix hotel, Italians encountered in hotels, as Lilia is thought to have met Gino, are unacceptable. Philip prophesies war with Gino, whom he has never met. 'He's a bounder, but he's not an English bounder.'[67] An English bounder he could understand. He condemns Gino by association with all the difficulties and dislocations that Italy, and the Roman Empire in particular, has caused to the rest of Europe. The expedition to obtain the baby is loveless, and it never occurs to the Herritons that perhaps the baby's father loves him. From the moment Philip and Harriet abandon the idea of visiting that icon of literary love, Juliet's tomb in Verona, they become the most repellent kind of tourist, bickering, complaining, losing their belongings, hating the un-English climate, noise and smells. Harriet passes judgement: 'Foreigners are a filthy nation.'[68]

She refines it: Gino is unchivalrous, and a man who can be unchivalrous to a woman is no good. Philip rallies sufficiently to retort that Italians never have gone in for chivalry, and if that is Harriet's criterion, 'You'll condemn the whole lot.'[69] That of course is Harriet's intention. In Monteriano, within theoretical reach of the baby, she creates an impasse on the hotel stairway and refuses to budge: 'I'm English; . . . '[70] Shishing and shushing at the opera, she is conspicuously English. And when they do prepare to capture the baby, Harriet is in such a hurry that, if the baby can't accommodate himself to her haste, 'make him learn English ways.'[71] He will never learn her ways, for he dies when the carriage overturns in the dark and jolts him out of Harriet's English arms. The death of the baby upset many critics and readers, but only shocks sufficed to shake Forster's suburbanites out of their rigidities. This shock creates an atmosphere in which Philip, if he does not settle again in Sawston, may summon up courage to break away from his mother.

Mrs Herriton has barricaded herself against the possibility of shocks and it is impossible to imagine her among neighbours. Mrs Honeychurch, on the other hand, has brought her humane qualities with her to the suburbs. She is Victorian about oppportunities for women, but her innate possibilities need only the enlivening spark and a few benign shocks to bring them to life, as the Emersons bring Lucy to life. Mrs Honeychurch at the end of the novel has not forgiven Lucy for marrying George, but one may hope that her good sense will eventually prevail. She may be hesitant, but she does not rule out the possibility of change.

Cecil Vyse is a character in whom one is pleased to see at least a symptom of change. As Lucy says when she breaks the engagement, he has despised her mother's conventionality, but – more important – Lucy has recognised in him another of those who strain too hard after the aesthetic sense. He knows what things are beautiful but tries to make them exclusive to himself. She is afraid that by doing the same to her, he will cut her off from people, from the human scene. Cecil himself is conventional with respect to people, for he sees them as types instead of as personalities. Things – inanimate objects – do not betray him; it is different with personal relations, but, she says to him, 'when you come to people – '. She is afraid that he will use her as Dante used Beatrice, as a means to an elevating purpose all his own.

However, Lucy does not understand Cecil as thoroughly as she thinks she does. She 'had counted on his being petty', but he shakes her self-assurance by receiving her criticisms with genuine dignity. He admits that he is a conventional man and has projected onto her his conventional ideas about the ideal woman. He thanks her 'for showing me what I really am'.[72] Certainly George Emerson is the right man for Lucy, for Cecil is more ascetic than aesthete. Contemporary reviewers admired him rather tepidly for the way in which he took the shock, but they missed its importance as a possibly salutary influence. *The Spectator* thought that the 'element of nobility in the hour of his defeat' was 'a touch of fantastic humour, more surprising than convincing'.[73] But it *is* convincing, for Forster has made it plain that he believes in at least the possibility of improvement.

The point of *Where Angels Fear to Tread*, Forster told Robert Trevelyan, was 'the improvement of Philip'.[74] In fact, he is already improved. After Gino has nearly killed him but for Caroline Abbott's intervention, and when he realises with a shock that Caroline loves not himself but Gino, Philip makes a great discovery: he can be generous. Such an epiphany can promise him salvation, but it is also shattering, as a sudden religious conversion can be shattering, for it goes against all that his mother has gone to such pains to instil in him. He has discovered that 'there is greatness in the world' and has already begun to behave accordingly.[75] If he is really fortunate, he will turn out like the Emersons, another of society's eccentrics, crosswise to the main currents of convention, and he will enjoy Italy more because he will have ceased to appropriate that country to certify the genuineness of his aesthetic sensibilities.

Those who were distressed about the death of the baby in *Where Angels Fear to Tread* would be even more certain, after they read *The Longest Journey*, that Forster overdid the melodrama. He surely had both novels in mind when he opened a debate, 'Is Pessimism to be Deplored in Modern Literature?' at the Working Men's College in December 1906. His subject, he explained, was 'the pessimism *in* literature, not the pessimism *of* literature', and he cited Zola, Ibsen and Tolstoy as novelists unafraid of sombre endings, whose sombreness had carried over to English writers like Gissing, Hardy and Henry James. He intended to discuss pessimism's place and value in serious literature. Readers of novels are usually thought to prefer neatly optimistic endings such as marriage, but in real life marriage is a beginning, not an ending. A separation as ending stays with them longer, for it suggests possibilities still to be discovered. It is 'pernicious as well as inaccurate' to call books that end unhappily

'insane, or diseased, or continental rubbish'. Endings are more important in books than in life, and the reader does tend to remember
and judge a book by its ending.[76] What the reader takes away must
be the truth, however unpleasant that may be. The truth of Forster's
unhappy novels is that the most defenceless suffer most when sheer
humanity fails.

THE LONGEST JOURNEY

If *Where Angels Fear to Tread* is about the possibility of improvement
in Philip Herriton, *The Longest Journey* is about the education of
Rickie Elliot – and of E. M. Forster. Reviewers found it full of interest, but puzzling, pessimistic, even cynical. Mr Forster was a 'clever'
novelist (the word appears often in early reviews of his work), and
now he offered the story of 'an amiable failure . . . a fool of the nobler
type that is not far removed from genius, and he moves in a world
of fools less admirable than himself'.[77] But 'the commonplace people
in the book suffer from their author's hatred in some cases'.[78] He
sympathises, 'contemptuously though', with Rickie Elliot, but posi-
tively forbids readers to sympathise with Agnes and Herbert
Pembroke, even as he recognises the tragedy of their lives.[79] The
narrative explores 'that spiritual gulf which lies between two classes
of minds, viz., of the minority who have the instinct to think for
themselves, . . . and the majority whose valuations . . . are, in short,
those conventional soulless valuations, . . . '[80] Mr Forster may yet
produce a significant novel 'unless, unhappily, the "abnormality" of
his invention is constitutional and ineradicable.'[81] Everything is neatly
manipulated, but 'where are the connexions?'[82]

Forster himself had lingering reservations. A large part of the
problem was that the suburban mentality as portrayed in *The Longest
Journey* was that same hazard of which he was already aware: his
daily life was his literary 'copy'. His journal is replete with references to visits to cousins and aunts and uncles and his mother's
women friends. Of some he was genuinely fond, but the many calls
and duty visits often interrupted sustained work and could provide
an irritating surfeit of suburban copy. For relief, he had to arrange
and sometimes had to contrive rounds of visits to other friends
whose talk was about literature, philosophy, the arts, the condition
of England. He would visit Cambridge friends as often as he could,
in Cambridge and in London, particularly Apostles and others he

met through them, who would eventually be among those designated 'Bloomsbury Group': Virginia and Vanessa Stephen, Lytton Strachey, Clive Bell, Duncan Grant, Rupert Brooke, Maynard Keynes, Leonard Woolf. These people cared about the arts and about civilisation. They were good company, witty and stimulating, but, as time went on, Forster became wary of the flamboyance of their heterosexual and homosexual love affairs and uninhibited gossip, and he particularly disliked their habit of reading other people's private letters. His friendship with Lytton was 'tenuous'. He had much respect for Leonard Woolf and valued Virginia's criticisms of his own work, and she his, but she could be sharp and wounding. He was not out of Bloomsbury, but neither was he altogether in. He had been much the same when they had first known him as an undergraduate. They were baffled by the 'grave and modest sincerity of his manner, and his mild, implacable courtesy . . . Naturally withdrawn, even in his twenties, he seemed to combine the bashful demureness of a spinster with the more abstract preoccupations of a don'. But they valued his 'sensibility and subtle intelligence', and their enquiring minds and lively argument stimulated his own. In 1904 he told himself that he was destined to be 'a minority, if not a solitary, and I'd best make copy out of my position'.[83] Other people might not understand this; he does not mean it cynically. It is simply that he cannot pretend to be what he is not. He is fated to go against society's grain, and if making copy of it encourages others like him he will have been of service. Sometimes he was a minority and solitary as well; he liked to go on long walking tours in the country, sometimes with a friend, but often alone.

Both the satisfactions and the irritations of that situation went into the novel, along with old resentments about the unhappiness and indignities of his school experience. In Rickie Elliott's difficulties about vocation, Forster traced the difficulties of his own divided life. By contrast, the Rooksnest years shone as a time of consistent happiness and fulfilment. In 1942, when Arthur Koestler asked to see some of Forster's work he sent *Aspects of the Novel* and one other, *The Longest Journey*, whose theme and subject-matter he liked best among his novels, but was unhappiest about his working of them. He could reread it only with 'shame and rage' because he had come so close to attaining what he had had in mind. 'It is a door which I pushed open a little, and then it stuck, or perhaps I pulled it to, myself.'[84] Still, in 1960 it was nevertheless 'the book I am most glad to have written' because it came closest to the point where 'the creative impulse sparks. Thoughts and emotions collided if they did not always cooperate.'[85]

In 1907, however, Forster was particularly disappointed that reviewers missed his very personal point about the three young men at the centre of the narrative. They saw Rickie as a recognisable suburban type but thought that if death must be the outcome of his struggle to define himself, the reader was cheated. Stephen Wonham was 'only a kind of Tony Lumpkin not without his good points in an uncouth way . . . '[86] Stewart Ansell represented 'the pride of spirit of the philosophy-talking clique and their contempt for stupid physical robustness'.[87] Forster told G. L. Dickinson that he was disappointed that so few readers seemed to find Stephen, Ansell and Rickie really likeable. He did not try to view 'life as I write it . . . But I can imagine myself liking those three men, if they were alive'. In another part of this letter, Forster returns to the theme of his lecture on pessimism in literature and says, 'All I write is, to me sentimental.' He believed it a waste of time and talent to produce a book that does not 'add some permanent treasure to the world . . . '.[88] Like *Where Angels Fear to Tread*, this novel is about possibilities, some of them realised, others lost or rejected. That is one of the reasons why he considered it 'the one book of his . . . that had given more back to the world than it had taken from it.'[89]

It was too soon for contemporary critics to grasp that this was Forster's most autobiographical novel, but they seemed to miss the fact that it is about three kinds of education. The reviewer for *The Times Literary Supplement* dismissed the Cambridge–Sawston–Wiltshire framework as 'certainly a very skilful arrangement', but not as satisfying 'as the dexterity of the author seems to intend'.[90] But there is great satisfaction in following Rickie's educational pilgrimage. At each stage he has a mentor: the first and third of these are deliverers, the second a destroyer. Forster later recalled that in the Cambridge section he wanted to re-create the Cambridge he had known as an undergraduate, the Cambridge of G. E. Moore, unafraid of speculation and philosophical exploration. Even as late as 1960 that part of the novel was 'still romantic and crucial for me'.[91] Forster speaks to himself through Ansell, who says, 'There is no great world at all, only a little earth', alone and irreplaceable.[92] The choice of values is always between those of Cambridge, which represents the little earth, and those of the Great World, which are seductive but counterfeit. Rickie's soul is the prize in the battle between the two worlds. Agnes Elliott, neé Pembroke, thinks that she represents the great world that Rickie neglects. To remedy this she drags him into the meanly philistine world of Sawston School as an assistant master. Here Forster set forth all that he disliked about the public school system and its influence, as he described it in 'Notes on the English Character'. Its students try to remain lifelong Old Boys and indeed cannot imagine a world where not everyone is an Old Boy – preferably an Old Boy of their own particular variety. This becomes a disadvantage when they go abroad, and especially when they go with authority over non-English peoples. They emerge with undeveloped hearts, 'An undeveloped heart – not a cold one.'[93] In the Wiltshire section of *The Longest Journey* it is Stephen Wonham, who follows the lead of heart, who must repair the damage that Sawston has done to Rickie. It is true that Rickie dies tragically, but this ending is not unrelievedly unhappy, for just before it is too late he realises that he has seen through to an everlasting truth, that conventions 'will not claim us in the end'.[94] But the conventions, in the person of Agnes, have striven mightily for Rickie's soul. Like Mrs Herriton, Agnes appropriates places and people. At the beginning of the novel, when she and her brother Herbert, a master at Sawston School, arrive for a Cambridge weekend, Rickie has indeed forgotten that he invited them, but her manner of reminder destroys every possibility of graceful reparation. Her accusing voice precedes her into the room, followed by her accusing finger and a scathing catalogue of the inconveniences that are his fault. She appropriates the atmosphere by turning on the electric light, then appropriates Rickie's guests by appealing to them over his head about his rudeness. All but Stewart Ansell melt away in embarrassment. The space now belongs to Agnes – except for Ansell, who does not budge and ignores her proffered hand. But she considers even his rudeness unworthy of her indignation because he, like Rickie with his deformed foot, compares so poorly with her manly, muscular Gerald Dawes, who would have been happy to come and beat up Ansell on request. She does not realise that Rickie does not apologise for Ansell but pays him a compliment when he says that this draper's son and nephew of farmers is at Cambridge not on the strength of family pedigree or Old-Boy connections, but of intelligence. She is reassured by the thought that Rickie has become 'a terrible snob', but she has failed to understand that he has indicted her snobbery about education.[95]

Like Mrs Herriton, Agnes does not really like or want what she appropriates. She regards or rather disregards Mrs Aberdeen the bedmaker as merely a stock figure on the academic scene, but Mrs Aberdeen comments silently when she brings back Rickie's corrected shoes for Herbert, who arrives with wet feet and complaints about deterioration at Cambridge, for one of the students who had crowded him into the gutter actually wore an Eton tie.[96] He and Agnes then discuss careers for gentlemen. Rickie's idea of perhaps writing short stories is acceptable only if he will apply the middle-class work ethic, will 'work and drudge' from the bottom of the ladder. Rickie cannot yet cope with metaphors outside of fiction and is not quick with the telling argument, and it does not occur to him to say that 'art is not a ladder . . . '.[97]

Nor can Rickie cope with Agnes's appropriation of his private dell on the Madingley Road, a very real place that is Forster's metaphor for the possibilities of transfiguration at Cambridge. When Agnes returns for May Week after the death of the muscular Gerald, hers is the initiative that takes them along that road. On the way they discuss again the possibilities of Rickie's writing successfully – that is, profitably. (She does not imagine that that is different to being a successful writer from an artistic point of view.) Unfortunately, he introduces as example his dryad story of which his dell is the setting. Agnes wants to see it, but he has walked her past it on purpose, for he knows that its power and privacy will be gone if he enters it with her. She turns back, he sends her in alone, and she is immediately proprietary: she summons him in, and their engagement is the result.

Even before Gerald's death and Agnes's engagement to Rickie, Forster certifies the Pembrokes' middle-class credentials by ushering Rickie through a series of visits of the kind that characterised his own two lives. The first is a very happy one, to the household above Mr Ansell's drapery shop. He is a tradesman who is moving up in the local economy, who has 'what no education can bring – the power of detecting what is important'. Like Mr Emerson, he encourages his son to find his own measure of importance, and Ansell follows Philosophy. The living quarters are not tastefully furnished, and evidences of being 'in trade' are all around. Rickie finds 'a curious charm' in the commercial bustle of the shop, which belongs to a world that he now sees for the first time, as from the other side of the counter.[98] He finds a new kind of charm also in Mr Ansell, who has an unspecified amount of education and is certainly not a University man. Like Mr Emerson, he knows what people like Herbert will never know: that real education is a matter of leaving the mind free to explore. Like Mr Emerson and George, Mr Ansell and his son again suggest the ideal father-and-son relationship that Forster had never known in real life but idealised in his books.

Next, Rickie stops with the Silts, well-meaning but dreary relations who manage to live on the sharp edge of respectability. They harp on about Rickie's inherited money, which they respect because, like Forster's own, it is 'unsoiled by trade' (at least, by no visible evidences of trade). They ponder the future of Cadover House in Wiltshire, which belongs to Rickie's aunt Emily Failing, whose house and personality derive from those of Morgan's uncle William Howley Forster. In a defeated voice Mr Salt speculates that Cadover will probably follow Rickie's 'unsoiled' inherited money. He is happy to escape to Sawston and the Pembrokes.[99]

Sawston is not an escape but a trap for the unwary. Herbert Pembroke looks after the day-boys, which makes him feel inferior and unimportant. Agnes keeps house for him. Self-consciously, their small house seems to assert that it is not self-conscious about Culture but is the apostolic harbinger of 'the greater houses that shall come after me.'[100] But it is not so vulgar as to harp upon money as the means toward achieving them. Agnes's manly Gerald is there, of whom Rickie has only dire memories as the bully at his own school. Because of his deformed foot, Rickie has idealised athletes and thus has avoided compensating by 'despising the physically strong'.[101] But Gerald himself is despicable, a snob who 'can't stand talking to servants', unless he speaks to them first, unless they are pretty.[102]

Snobbery and exclusion are Sawston School motivs. In the seventeenth century it was a tradesman's generous idea of a grammar school for 'the poore of my home', but three centuries later those beneficiaries had been shunted off to a Commercial School well away from the original site. The remnant then expanded to accommodate gentlemen's sons. Thus Sawston is a debased version of an educational ideal. Herbert craves Old-Boy traditions but cannot define tradition. Rickie, with the naive honesty of the boy who observes that the Emperor has no clothes, suggests that perhaps the traditions had gone with the poor boys to the Commercial School. In Herbert's answer is all of Forster's repugnance for the social classifications of his own school and memories of himself as a day-boy. In Herbert's opinion, day-boys are a drag on tradition because they are isolated units and therefore easily suspected of disloyalty to the school. (They are also obstacles to his promotion to being in charge of boarding students, who he considers fully a part of the school.) He speaks of day-boys as if they are some kind of virus: 'They infect the boarders.'[103] Individualism is the trouble with them. They are no good because as schoolboys they are incomplete. But Herbert himself is incomplete, with the incompleteness that Forster saw in the English character: outwardly stiff and guarded against possibilities of spontaneous emotion. Herbert is neither wicked nor cold-hearted. 'It is the machinery that is wrong.'[104] The ladder of ambition is Herbert's machine. He teaches the boys what he had tried to tell Rickie: life is that ladder up which one must 'work and drudge'.

If Rickie had no ready answer to Herbert's metaphor of life as a ladder, Forster had a long answer in 1917 when his friend Florence Barger, the wife of a scientist friend from Cambridge days, had to make decisions about a school for her son Harold. She appealed to Forster, then in Egypt with the Red Cross. Herbert's ladder was still on his mind, and he hated it as much as ever. He still hated 'the "patriotism", the "good form", the snobbery of outfits – '. He was not even certain any longer about Latin as inspiration and intellectual discipline. Classics? The world at that moment was not behaving as if the classics would be of future use. Forster admitted that schools must have improved since his day – and indeed after the war the public school as an institution would be on the threshold of change, from the influence of new progressive schools like Bedales and Summerhill. But the war must end before that could happen, and Florence must keep Harold at home – presumably Forster meant, as a day-boy, which was the lesser of the evils. If for a time the light seemed to have gone out of him she must not worry, for 'it can only be temporary in his case'.[105]

Mrs Barger did not let Forster off so easily. He must give an opinion. She got it, in full, a recapitulation of his misgivings about the Sawston/Tonbridge method and its products. He hesitated to advise on such a subject, but he would like to protect Harold against the roughness and rudeness that he was certain to encounter from other boys at school, not by pouring his mind into the approved mould but by a means that Forster, looking back, thought might have made his own schooldays easier: some prowess at sports, not because games are the be-all and end-all of life, but because some bodily strength lends reassurance. The method chosen was not in question, but 'the iniquity of pressing such a child too hard whatever the method'. A nervous breakdown is the inevitable result, and here he had as evidence his own and others' unhappy experiences of school. He recalled an occasion when Harold had identified Ireland as the capital of Madrid, which had horrified his father. But such blunders would not be a worry once Harold grasped the rules of geographical classification. Forster approved of 'discipline, regulations, prompt and cheerful obedience' for Harold, for he was the kind of boy who would grow up to understand that such impositions are only that, useful in their place but not substitutes for things of the spirit. Harold will be all right *'provided he isn't overdriven'*, but if that happened 'one can't be sure he'll see through anything'.[106] While he was advising Mrs Barger, Forster wrote from Egypt to another friend: 'I suppose that England and the English character are altering terribly in one's absence. I love both, as they were just before the war, though I know it is correct to regard them as depraved.'[107] On the one hand, the good solid old virtues; on the other, the inability to express deep feelings. But English literature, and especially its poetry, which seems a paradox, proves that there is life at the core.[108]

When Rickie marries Agnes and settles at Sawston as a very junior Latin master, he resolves to be like Herbert and regard the school as a 'beneficent machine' that will re-fashion both himself and the boys. But really he knows that it is no good. Like Forster as Tonbridge day-boy, he knows that if the days at school are unhappy, a boy can flee at evening to 'his own dear home'.[109] He receives no help from Agnes, for she is a 'deadly debunker' of everything outside the system.[110] She must instil ambition. Rickie must write something more profitable than fantasy stories (so like Forster's own). At Cadover it is Agnes who invades the Cadbury Rings and interrupts the 'symbolic moment', a catalyst of experience that was all-important to Forster in life as well as in literature, when Rickie, who has just learned the family secret, might have told Stephen Wonham that they are half-brothers. Agnes interferes again when Stephen calls beneath the window and she refuses to let Rickie answer. She observes in the most detached and offhand manner imaginable that Rickie's symbolic moment has come and gone, and she is smugly satisfied that she has been the means of its going. 'It's not your fault.'[111] Stephen, an uncouth shepherd but a natural man in understanding, is inconceivably outside her system. Worse, being illegitimate, he is the evidence of family scandal. Mrs Failing, too, discards Stephen when it appears that the secret, no longer her idle amusement and device for manipulating both Stephen and Rickie, will become a social inconvenience. Both women leave Rickie to flounder until, in a scene of high melodrama, Ansell sets it all straight in front of the whole school at Sawston, which ends Rickie's career there. It is fitting that Mr Ansell's home above the shop should become for a time the shelter for both Rickie and Stephen. Its air of generous acceptance begins to heal the wounds that Sawston School has inflicted on Rickie.[112]

While he wrote his earliest fiction, Forster cast about for the best way to convey his truths as reality. In Italy in 1901 he had despaired about a novel later abandoned, 'Nottingham Lace', an early attempt at a suburban novel. He wrote to Dickinson about his unhappiness over that project. The problem was even more difficult of solution than that of style. He had intended to 'invent realism' by replicating in fictional form people and events from his own experience, but this turned out not to be real art, for 'by mixing two methods have produced nothing'.[113] Dickinson had assured him that he possessed 'the photo-graphic gift', but if that were true, he still had not figured out how to make the best use of it.

'The Story of a Panic', in which an English boy learns to be himself, was Forster's first experience of the disciplined imagination, a very personal as well as a literary epiphany. As Furbank says, 'something had shifted in his soul, and energies he had only half-glimpsed in himself were now in his possession.'[114] That story came to him as a complete vision, and *The Longest Journey* had come in much the same way, a visitation instead of a contrivance. For all the others he had had to 'look into the lumber-room of my past,' where he found useful things, but they had not brought him 'the magic sense' of reciprocal intimacy.[115] The puzzle was too close, perhaps, to that of the contradiction between his surburban and his literary lives.

HOWARDS END

Howards End is personal in a different way. It came out of the Rooksnest lumber-room. He will try to respond to that critic who asked of *The Longest Journey*, 'Where are the connexions?'

He will make England herself, for which Howards End the house is icon, the means of that connection. Midway in the novel, at Chapter 19, he makes that suggestion, just where Margaret Schlegel, the leisured and cultured Londoner, must decide whether to marry the businessman Henry Wilcox, whose late wife had been her friend. That chapter begins with the wonderful description of England and her rivers that flow from the countryside down to London and through Suburbia, to the cliffs of Freshwater and the Isle of Wight.

Not reason, but only imagination, can comprehend such a scene as the arrival of the rivers at the southern shore: 'the imagination swells, spreads, and deepens, until it becomes geographic and encircles England.'[116] Where the affections of the heart are concerned, reason alone is not enough.

While she tries to decide whether to marry Henry Wilcox, Margaret strives to remain reasonable. She tries to be rational about Love, which is an emotion whose complications she has never yet had to solve. She believes that Proportion, rightly used, will guide her past the hazards in Love's path: Property and Propriety, Family Pride, Theology.[117] One turns to Proportion only 'when the better things have failed, and a deadlock – '.[118] She cannot finish the sentence because she does not yet see that proportion and the better things must work together from the beginning. Her problem is Forster's own: it seems wrong to be scornful of those who labour to maintain the economic system that has made possible his literary life by assuring his independent income. Margaret finally decides to marry Mr Wilcox and lectures her sister about Proportion. But Helen intends to be guided by imagination, not reason, and retorts that she intends, if Margaret marries Henry, to dislike him thoroughly but to love her sister more than ever: 'tangible things – money, husbands, house-hunting' are their problems, and these cannot be allowed to interfere with a love that pre-dates Margaret's feeling for Henry.[119]

Forster wanted a settled home and place in which to read and write and think, but he hated the manifold bothers of property-owning. Here again he was smitten by contradiction. His mother's servant troubles caused interruptions and disruptions, but even when he rebelled he knew that it was the women's care of him that made it possible for him to work at all. He makes the Wilcox men react to property-owning by becoming cautious and suspicious. Because Charles finds Margaret's sudden friendship with his mother inexplicable, he suspects the unsuspecting Margaret, who knows nothing of the bequest, of plotting to get Howards End. He blames his inoffensive little wife Dolly for letting this information slip. He is convinced that Margaret has schemed from her first acquaintance with his mother, to get Howards End, 'and thanks to you, she's got it.'[120] They destroy Mrs Wilcox's pencilled note that expresses her wish that Margaret shall have the house. What Margaret does get is Mrs Wilcox's silver vinaigrette, given in sour atonement for the family's refusal to honour the wife and mother's last request. She had asked little of them while she was alive, but to her last request they had answered, 'We will not.'[121]

Henry's fit of suspecting Margaret is even more unworthy. Distrust seizes him when his earlier relations with the pathetic Jacky Bast come to light. Here Forster begins to undercut the Victorian stereotypes of male and female behaviour. Henry puts two and two together, gets ten, and suspects Margaret of digging into his past and producing Jacky in order to expose him. His response is a cliché straight from the code of the gentleman as set forth in romantic novels: 'I am a man, and have lived a man's past.' He tries to step out of the engagement as if there is nothing mutual about it, as if it is his alone to bestow or discard. Margaret's instinctive reaction to this insult and to the discovery that Jacky has been his mistress is to ignore romantic protocol. She neither weeps nor faints. She snatches the coat that a footman holds for one of Henry's guests and offers to help him herself. Henry, who feels safer when he is acting the gentleman, snatches the coat away from her. The 'playful little scene' provides the interval in which Margaret recovers to give Henry the response that he deserves: 'She left him without a word.'[122]

The following morning she disappoints him again by determining to go on as before, thus depriving him of the chance to carry on in romantic-novel style. He tries it anyway, wheedling for sympathy: 'I'm a bad lot, and must be left at that.' Margaret neither faints nor rages at him, and he tries the Victorian sheltered-lady line: 'women like you' cannot (and should not) understand the exceptions that must be made for even the strongest of men who contend with the temptations of the great world. When Margaret will not be drawn with such theories, Henry brings out the old Imperial rationalisation: the expatriate misdeeds of well-brought-up young men overseas and out of reach of English respectability. He has run out of excuses, and his dramatics fall flat, for Margaret perceives that he is neither a romantic-novel hero nor even a very strong man. 'He was a good average Englishman, who had slipped.'[123] His English character had betrayed him. One reviewer was pleased to note that Margaret 'does not develop as the romantic conventions would have her'.[124]

Noel Annan thinks that Forster 'hates the Wilcoxes'.[125] Certainly he does not like such people. But he writes in sorrow as well as in anger, and both are directed at the fact that the Wilcoxes, who have worked for England's material welfare, cannot summon up the emotional resources to make them responsive human beings. They have never recovered from that flawed Victorian education and its lesson that although it is bad form to talk about money, possessing it justifies all other actions.

Henry Wilcox, whose money flows from corporate competition in the marketplace, cannot bear competition with himself. He is defensive and angry when Margaret speaks kindly of the gauche and aspiring Leonard Bast and says that although he is 'vulgar and hysterical and bookish, . . . He's a real man.' Henry, who cannot analyse his own feelings, is humiliated by his jealousy of Leonard, not because jealousy is an unworthy emotion, but, worse, because that insignificant creature has glimpsed a kind of enlightenment that Margaret admires and Henry cannot understand. Feeling left out, he reacts with childish anger that persists 'long after he had rebuilt his defences'.[126]

Property-owning is the essential material of Henry's psychological fortress. The Victorian tag 'safe as houses' is never more appropriate than when he uses it. Wilcoxes collect houses, Helen says, as a little boy collects tadpoles. For them the personality of a place no more differentiates a house than it does tadpoles in a bucket. Market value separates one house from another. Their evaluations of Howards End are heavy with ironies, none of which they comprehend. None of them really wants, much less loves, Howards End, but they are outraged at the idea of its going to Margaret the intruder, 'who'd never appreciate'.[127] Charles 'wouldn't touch it with tongs', which suggests a withdrawal in distaste from something he has no intention of relinquishing.[128] For Henry it has 'endless drawbacks' – among which are the neighbours at the farm – whom Forster visualised as his old neighbours on the Rooksnest farm. Henry will let to some tenant not too particular about a neighbourhood that is rapidly 'getting suburban' as too many middle-class Londoners – like himself – rediscover the countryside.[129]

In city or in country, commercial value dictates Henry's place of residence. After Mrs Wilcox dies he tries to let his London house. He cannot admit his reason for wishing to be rid of it, which is that he is lonely there. He says that the neighbourhood is deteriorating; some 'operatic people' have taken the house across the road.[130] He praises Oniton, his Shropshire property, as a great acquisition, but it is really only a real-estate afterthought. When it has served its brief purpose as setting for his daughter's wedding, he discovers that it is damp and too far from London. He unloads it by letting to the proprietors of a new preparatory school, damp apparently not a consideration where small boys are concerned. In none of this does

Henry see the slightest contradiction; shuffling houses is business, pure and simple. Not without irony about his own reliance on an independent income from returns on investments perhaps control- led by other Henry Wilcoxes, Forster calls it 'a flaw inherent in the business mind' and alludes again to the theme that he will develop later in 'Notes on the English Character': minds like Henry's have masterminded England's power and prosperity, but one forgets at one's peril to be wary of that flaw.[131] Henry unloads this house also and begins to build one much grander at Midhurst, on the exclusive far fringe of Suburbia. A discussion at a Midhurst home where Forster stayed while lecturing there in 1909 may well account for his deciding to place Henry's newest house there. Conversation had turned to votes for women and the suffragettes who chained them- selves to the railings outside the Houses of Parliament. To the ques- tion of how it would strike one of those present if women of his own family were among them, the answer was,

> 'But think if your sisters or relatives chained themselves to the grille – *that* will bring it home to you.'
> 'I should mind it equally if men did it – they are bad citizens.'
> 'But so unladylike.'
> 'Yes – and the worst of it is, that may pay. Men never get anything by being gentlemanly.'
> 'Well perhaps not, but then so much less is somehow expected of them.'[132]

Such ideas about women would not have shocked Henry, with his antiquated ideas about how to manage them. But, even had all gone according to plan, Midhurst is not likely to be his abiding place. This John Bull has delivered the goods but cannot find a place in which to settle and enjoy the fruits of his labours. Charles, too, is on the move. He and his family have left a new house at Epsom for another at Hilton, the village near Howards End, ostensibly to be close – but not too close – to his father. Charles has probably found Epsom also deteriorating. It has not occurred to him that the motor car, the Wilcox family totem, is a chief agent of the decline. However, even Hilton seems to be going down, for undesirable local elements had tried to get into the Tennis Club. Like his father, he belongs to the 'civilization of luggage'.[133] As soon as possible, he will be packing for another move.

Neither Henry nor Charles comprehends the depth and strength of the deceased Mrs Wilcox's roots in Howards End, and Henry uses her to strike at Helen when Margaret tries to make him face the contradictions in his behaviour over Jacky Bast and in his refusal to allow the pregnant Helen to stay there for even one night. 'Straight from his fortress' he drags out the tired old clichés once more: a man's superior knowledge of the world, and its besetting temptations of a kind that a respectable woman cannot and should not understand, for if she understands them she is not respectable. He takes his stand upon consideration for his children and 'the memory of my dear wife.' It is worse than a cliché, for his respect for Mrs Wilcox's memory has not only been allowed to grow dim but has been openly insulted. Margaret counters with the contradiction between his relationship with Jacky, who had been one of his expatriate temptations, and his treatment of the pregnant Helen, whom he has forbidden to spend even one night at Howards End. Margaret has forgiven him; he refuses to receive Helen. He falls back upon yet another old formula for male control by condescension: 'You have not been yourself all day.' But Margaret, aided by his stubborn obtuseness, finally does know herself and Henry as well. She delivers her full indictment and connects the entire novel to its epigraph 'Only connect . . . ': 'Do you see the connection?'[134] Henry does not, and Forster has already laid the trail to this moment with his list of the Wilcoxes' own ironies about ownership of Howards End, none of which they understand.

Henry's ignoble response is ignoble suspicion that Margaret is trying to blackmail him, and he compounds the insult by wiping his hands as he walks away, a commercial Pilate. Only a great shock will finally breach Henry's fortress. Romantic and Imperial excuses will not save him. The shock is the family scandal that follows Leonard Bast's death at Howards End, when he goes there to find Margaret and confess – confess what? He does not know that Helen carries his child. (Contemporary reviewers assumed that Leonard is the seducer, for a respectable middle-class girl like Helen could not be actively attracted even briefly to the 'squalid' Leonard.)[135] Leonard knows only that he has done wrong in allowing himself to be drawn into this self-assured middle-class circle. When Charles rushes forward to thrash him, Leonard's fright, his undernourished heart, and the bookcase that he pulls over onto himself as he falls cheat Charles of satisfaction. The law, 'made in his image', finds fright, a bad heart, and a bookcase irrelevant.[136]

Leonard Bast's situation is even more disadvantageous than that of students at the Working Men's College. They have more specific skills. Leonard is one of the throng of office clerks who cannot climb the occupational ladder without a helping hand, and Henry Wilcox has refused him that. Forster has situated him on the brink of the abyss, which was how H. G. Wells habitually described the dumping-place for all the people he regarded as useless, society's throwaways. But Leonard is not useless, for he is honourable. His marriage is his honourable action to regularise his relations with the deplorable Jacky: as an Englishman, he will 'never go back on my word'.[137] This is the sturdy, virtuous side of the English character that Forster valued. Self-educated young men like him were legion, who tried without background or context to achieve a little of the advantage that the educational system gave to the privileged. But the Schlegel sisters are the wrong mentors for him. Their bookish brother Tibby might have been more suitable. Leonard has picked up 'scraps of beauty', but no one has ever given him Forster's advice to the Working Men's College, that those who come late to formal education should begin by studying only what gives them joy.

That College was founded for men like Leonard, and Forster learned from them, in much the same way that he has Rickie learn from being at Mr Ansell's shop. Alexander Hepburn, the bookbinder whose arguments had defeated Forster in the debate on humour, was a born linguist. During the Great War he was an officer who learned enough Chinese to interpret for Chinese labourers imported to the Western Front. E. K. Bennett, who became Forster's lifelong friend, was a clerk in Crosse and Blackwell's pickle factory and became President of Gonville and Caius College. Then there was a former navvy named Winter with whom Forster discussed religion. Winter believed in God because he thought he could not be happy otherwise, a belief so different and so much more attractive than what 'used to be shoved under one's nose like a plate of pudding', Forster wrote in his journal.[138] Just two weeks after making that diary entry he went to the Queen's Hall to the concert that included Beethoven's Fifth Symphony, which 'satisfies all sorts and conditions' and which he translated, with that echo from the Book of Common Prayer, into Chapter 5 of *Howards End* as the grand panorama of goblins and giants, gods and demi-gods.[139]

The failure to recognise Leonard's possibilities is everyone's fault. As time went on England would have to face the consequences of such failures. The theme of *Howards End*, wrote Lionel Trilling, is 'who shall inherit England?'[140] The Leonard Basts, one way or another, must have their share. At the end of the novel Margaret at last inherits Howards End, Forster's icon for the heart of England. The sisters are safe and have begun to give the house new life, but London creeps up on Hertfordshire.

Long before the BBC asked him to consider 'The Challenge of Our Time', Forster had been gloomy about the city's challenge to the countryside. When he talked to the Working Men's College in 1907 on 'Pessimism in Literature' he asked his audience to 'consider Box Hill', which had become an amusement centre but still escaped being swallowed by the city. What was its fate in the future? London will have absorbed it. Houses will be nondescript. Motor cars will pollute the roads and aircraft will scream overhead. The inhabitants will care more for manufactured consumer goods than for the fruits of the fields. A modern epic poem about Box Hill could only be pessimistic, but it must tell the truth, for truth might contribute to a balance and to some way in which the city as it spread might learn to complement the country places.[141]

However, that would not happen as long as the migrants from the city keep themselves to themselves, scorning the people and traditions of the countryside. In all four of these suburban novels, the only locals are servants or others whom the well-off consider in some way subordinate. Stephen Wonham, Rickie's half-brother in *The Longest Journey*, is only a farm-hand to those who consider themselves his betters. Mr Wilcox dismisses even the mention of Miss Avery, the old lady who lives at the farm and genuinely preserves the memory of Mrs Wilcox at Howards End. The 'dim bucolic past' only bores him.[142] He is not curious about Miss Avery's devotion to his first wife. Nevertheless, Suburbia had come to stay. For better or worse, urban migrants and locals were in it together. Forster believed that attitude toward the countryside is a reliable index to the character and morals of those who inhabit it. If those who really cared were prevailing, why were battles to save it so extraordinarily difficult? He did not have to wait a few hundred years to feel anxious about Hertfordshire and Rooksnest, which represented the stability, continuity, and connection that he missed in Suburbia. He wanted to see the house in the hands of someone who would give it loving care. In 1950, with his Clapham combination of generosity and banker's caution he helped its tenant, the composer Elizabeth Poston, toward purchasing it. He told Robert Buckingham that he would like very much to be of help but (remembering the Thornton dictum about debt and moral fibre) he disliked the idea and dreaded the mutual awkwardness that followed defaults. He could just manage to give the whole sum but decided to offer £500 'to be repaid, without interest, if they ever want to, but offered as a gift'.[143] Rooksnest became Miss Poston's much-loved home, and Forster kept the feeling that he could from time to time go home again.

Then in 1960 planners and developers again threatened the house together with 200 acres of fields around the church and the view across the countryside. Stevenage New Town was to increase from 40 000 to 60 000 souls, with twelve houses to the acre and, Miss Poston told Forster, 'not content with this, they want to increase their grasp, to comprehend the "view" country. This would mean obliteration of the entire countryside within sight.' The developers, she believed, wanted power and 'CBE's handed out for the millionth new house', while the Government were 'only too happy to have it off their hands'.[144] Local feeling ran high, and protests began. Forster reminded the Minister for Housing and Local Government that the house and its surroundings had been a lifelong influence on him, and that Rooksnest was Howards End. He trusted that a place 'so essentially English' would 'survive unspoilt' for 'the English people who come after me'.[145] Eminent authors and publishers wrote to the newspapers. Readers of *Howards End* wrote to the Minister for Housing. The National Trust and the preservation societies took an interest. There was an official inquiry. The planners and the developers were fended off. That had been a near thing, and in fact the fight to preserve the 'Forster country' goes on still. What happens to beautiful places that do not include the former home of a famous author?

Who then will inherit England? Will it be 'those who have moulded her and made her feared by other lands', Forster asks in *Howards End*, or those who have added nothing to her power, but have the ability to see England as a personality unique in its attributes, 'a ship of souls, . . . '.[146] Henry Wilcox, who tried to mould England in his image and did his best to make her feared abroad, never considered such a choice. He boasts that 'Concentrate' is his motto and implies that his success in business is due to his ability to rule out the wasteful distractions of sentiment and imagination, 'that sort of thing'.[147]

Because he ignores 'that sort of thing', 'telegrams and anger' control his life. He remains unaware of the 'panic and emptiness' at the core. Once Henry had begun to concentrate, 'there was no more to be said'.[148] Forster had a great deal more to say, and he summed it up in the novel's famous epigram, 'Only connect . . . ' England must in the end belong to those who have learned to connect 'the prose with the passion', and then the wearying conflict between materialist and ascetic would be unnecessary.[149]

Howards End, signifier of the ideal, will eventually belong to Helen and Leonard's son, whose childhood is to be like Forster's at Rooksnest, but it is Helen, the idealist, who points out that 'London's creeping' and 'life's going to be melted down, all over the world'.[150] But it is also Helen who had said that 'personal relations are the real life, for ever and ever'.[151] Forster has put readers of his suburban novels in the situation that is his own, which has been his intention all along. He wants them to recognise that there is a difference between a life of superficial passages and the real life of personal relations. Like him, they must decide which will be theirs for ever and ever.

3

The Indian Novel

Despite occasional puzzlements, critics judged *Howards End* to be not only Forster's best but 'the most significant novel of the year'. It was 'head and shoulders above the great mass of fiction now claiming a hearing'. It was 'a novel of high talent – the highest', 'a book in which his highly original talent has found full and ripe expression'. The *Standard*'s reviewer declared that Mr Forster had arrived, 'and, if he never writes another line, his niche should be secure'.[1]

At the time, Mr Forster was feeling as if he might not care to write another line. Creative weariness would not have been surprising; he had written four novels in five years as well as short stories and a very respectable number of reviews. The reasons lay much deeper, and it was a problem not unrelated to Clapham's moral influence: he could not be reconciled to the feeling that he had not measured up to his own high standard. Critics had generally approved of *The Longest Journey* except for its being 'jerky: "too many deaths" . . . Now what to do? Spent an unhappy day yesterday deciding.' The 'Lucy novel' did not progress, and although he liked much about it thus far, he felt that it lacked substance. As he told Arthur Koestler many years later, the literary flaws in *The Longest Journey* bothered him less than his conviction that he had failed to convey to readers the human values he wanted them to understand from his work. As for *Howards End*, supposedly his best novel up to then, years later he told Peter Burra that he still could not understand why he had perversely '*insisted* on doing things wrong there'.[2] Furbank thinks that his fears were both ethical and 'to a certain extent superstitious'. The fame that followed *Howards End* was so sudden; it might dissipate as suddenly. He tried to drive himself to work. If he began a book only for the sake of knowing that he had something, anything, in progress, would it turn out to be anything more than a potboiler? If esoteric paths of scholarship were to attract him, he had little faith in his own staying power in that direction. He had rejected fame as the spur. This left money as incentive, and there is much of Clapham evangelicalism, if little enthusiasm, in his rationalisation of money as more honourable than fame. Work of itself was virtuous, for it is one's Christian duty to improve the shining hour. Working for money was acceptable, 'for at all events it's of use to others'.[3]

In *Howards End* he had rejected asceticism. Now in his diary he came close to embracing it: 'Let me not be distracted by the world. . . . Henceforward more work & meditation,' and he resolved to devote himself more to those he loved.[4] Let him not be tempted either by the prospect of becoming a literary lion. A little later he chided himself for ingratitude, then shaded off into pessimism about his inability to remember his many blessings. His troubles, he told himself, were of his own making. He knew that he could not rely on good luck to bear him up indefinitely. He made a very Claphamesque assessment of his faults: idleness; stubborness about the rightness of his views and about criticisms of them; and envy, 'but the inevitable decline of my literary reputation will test that'.[5]

Of those whom he loved, his mother was most affected by his fame, for she felt left out of his life as it became busier and busier. Her own mother's health was failing, and Forster dreaded his grandmother's death, not only because he loved her dearly but because his mother's life would seem even emptier. The friend whose company he found most satisfying – when things went well between them – was Syed Ross Masood, another Latin pupil but one with a background entirely different from that of students at the Working Men's College. Masood, the grandson of Sir Sayyid Ahmad Khan, belonged to the intellectual aristocracy of India's Muslim community, and Sir Theodore Morison was Masood's link to Forster. Masood came to England in 1906 for admission to Oxford but needed tutoring in Latin. The Morisons, just returned from India, had settled at Weybridge. Lady Morison mentioned Masood's need to Mrs Forster, and Morgan Forster became Masood's Latin tutor. Thus the Morisons, by creating this link, put Forster in a position to view India primarily through the eyes of the Muslim Masood. He was also in a position eventually to write a book of a kind that in the days of the suburban novels he could scarcely have imagined.

Morison had gone to India in 1886 as Tutor to two very minor Maharajas; one of them was Chhatarpur, who would become one of Forster's important explicators of Vaishnava Hinduism. Morison's bias, however, was toward the Muslim community and its culture, and Sayyid Ahmad Khan was its inspiration. He was a product of the old Moghul regime in which Persian was the language of administration and of high learning and cultural refinement. He had limited command of conversational English, so that in his duties under

the British Raj as a legal officer and then as a judge he relied heavily
on translators. The British in India tolerated this unwieldy way of
doing business until 1837, when they made English the official medium. This followed logically upon Thomas Babington Macaulay's
prescription in 1835 for a literary curriculum on the English model
for selected young Indians, and after the Mutiny of 1857 Parliament
took control away from the old East India Company and from what
was left of the Moghul Dynasty at Delhi. As English education
became more widely available, Muslims began to fall behind, for
Hindus more readily embraced that new curriculum and its new
ideas. Too late, Muslims saw that their lack of English-language
education severely limited their opportunities. One cause of their
disability was their religious leaders' conviction that the new and
official English-language curriculum was inimical to Islam. Young
Muslims could obtain an approved education in the *madrasah*s, the
Islamic schools. Sayyid Ahmad Khan led the movement to open this
closed system to modern influences. He spent 1869–70 in England,
and in his request for leave from his duties he had said that he
wanted to observe factories, hospitals and commercial operations. A
private purpose, equally important, was research for the purpose of
refuting an influential English book on the life of Muhammad. 'By
all accounts,' writes David Lelyveld, historian of his career in education, 'Sayyid Ahmad's experience of England was a major personal
and intellectual crisis.'[6] He found British literacy, competence, efficiency and technical achievement utterly beyond anything young
Muslims could get in the *madrasah*s. He still thought *madrasah* education 'better than what the British schools [in India] had to offer, but
unlikely to lead India into a new future. . . . Indian Muslims were
drowning in the seas of decadence, with no one competent to save
them.'[7] From his English visit emerged the idea of a college to combine Western educational principles and Islamic traditions and at
the same time produce a new generation of Muslim leaders for
India. British-sponsored education had failed to widen Indian Muslims' world-view; therefore Muslims must see to it themselves, and
private individuals must take that initiative. They must open new
fields of thought, professional opportunity and entrepreneurship to
the new generation of Muslims. This is the predicament, with the
progressive Muslims' determination to remedy the situation, that
must be kept in mind as part of the background of Forster's Dr Aziz
and his Muslim friends in *A Passage to India*. Forster saw that predicament through Masood's and Morison's eyes and sympathised

heartily with that determination. He cannot be accused of unfair Muslim bias: he wrote of what he had come to know best.

Sayyid Ahmad attracted a circle of like-minded contemporaries who believed that Indians of their class and generation were 'educated to occupy positions of power. Now the equivalent education was confined to Englishmen in England.' Sayyid Ahmad demanded '"equality of rights with our European fellow subjects"' in order to 'make good the loss by establishing a three-tier educational system': basic vernacular literacy for working people, training for teachers, and institutions of higher learning for original research.[8] Sayyid Ahmad aimed at nothing less than intellectual renewal in the Muslim community.

The Anglo-Oriental Muhammadan College at Aligarh, some eighty miles from Delhi, was the result. It opened in June 1875. Theodore Morison arrived there as a professor in 1889, one of a chain of young men from London and Cambridge. 'These men,' says Lelyveld, 'carried to Aligarh a particular subculture of British intellectual life, one that suited the aspirations and priorities that Sayyid Ahmad considered appropriate to his educational efforts.'[9] He died in 1898, so that Morison had known him well for nearly a decade. Morison became Principal in 1899, and his own influence carried the College into the twentieth century. Sayed Ross Masood, the grandson, became Morison's ward at a time of family troubles and felt closer to him than to his own father. His coming to England in 1906 continued both a family educational tradition and an important friendship.

In India and in England Morison's name became a synonym for Muslim advocacy and Aligarh a Government byword for Muslim unrest. As a remedy for the latter, Morison argued for more Indians, especially Muslims, in Indian administration; but his most controversial proposal was a communal award: that is, separate Muslim voting constituencies at elections and legislative seats 'substantially in excess of their ratio to the general population'. When he died in 1936, *The Times'* long obituary began 'Sir Theodore Morison: Moslem Renaissance in India'.[10]

That renaissance was Janus-faced. One face looked to a future of strict equality for Muslims in the competition for the restricted range of opportunities open to Indians. The other looked back in nostalgia to the pre-British era when Moghul conquerors from Central Asia ruled India and Islam was the religion of power. Images and ideas out of the past pulled hard against a desire for dominance in modern India. 'Ah, that I had lived 250 years ago, when the Oriental despotisms were in their prime,' sighs Masood. Forster records this in his diary, to be translated much later into *A Passage to India* as Aziz's ecstatic imaginings about the reflected glories of putative ancestors who came down with the Emperor Babur from Afghanistan into India as conquerors in the sixteenth century: 'I take him as my ideal,' says Aziz. In that same diary entry Forster recorded Masood's retort to a remark (Forster's own?) to the effect that 'nothing is so interesting as thought'. Masood disagreed and argued that 'effects of thought are far more interesting'.[11] But no amount of the most intense thought could restore the Moghul Emperors or the privileged status of Indian Muslims.

When Forster reached India in 1912, official circles there were greatly agitated by the pressures for equality in employment opportunities, for Government was the major employer of Indians with Western-style education. In fact, its educational system had been devised to prepare Indians to serve as clerks and later, as lower-level administrators. By 1912 the gap between numbers of Hindus and Muslims qualified and employed for such positions had increased still more, and so had Muslim discontent on that score. The Government of India knew that all was not well in the educational establishment, but it had become so monolithic and so entrenched that where to take hold for reform was a question. In 1911, when Edwin Montagu, the Under-Secretary of State for India, urged the need for a Royal Commission to look into the Public Services in India, a principal question was whether *any* Indians, however well qualified, had an equal chance with Englishmen for appointments to the Civil Service. There had been no such inquiry since 1887, and it would be difficult to exaggerate the extent, as it appears in hundreds of official letters, to which India's administrators at all levels felt threatened by Montagu's idea.

The Government's guard over India had changed in 1910, when the Marquess of Crewe succeeded Lord Morley as Secretary of State for India, and Lord Hardinge of Penshurst became Viceroy. They were exact contemporaries, both born in 1858, both graduates of Trinity College, Cambridge, with friends and social experience in common. Hardinge had had diplomatic appointments in Russia and Persia, both of great importance to the security of India's northern borders. Crewe had been principally in London ministries responsible for overseas administrations but from 1892 to 1896 had been Lord-Lieutenant of Ireland. He was inclined to draw parallels between Irish Home Rule and Indian nationalism and the best ways to control extremists. He opposed absolutely self-government for India. 'I made it clear in the House of Lords last Monday that I will give no countenance even to the remote dream of a self-governing India, . . . ,' he wrote in 1912. 'I think it is much easier to be liberal in the extension of powers and responsibility if we are explicitly firm with the visionaries, even with such of them as do not wish to be thought revolutionary.'[12] He even thought that Hardinge went too far when he spoke of 'a larger measure of self-government' for Provinces in British India, even if the Government of India kept the power to interfere 'in cases of misgovernment'.[13] The two-tier system recommended in 1887 was still in effect: a Provincial Service recruited in India; and an Imperial Service recruited in England, the latter with more generous pay, leaves and pensions. In fifteen years past only two Indians had entered the Educational Service at the Imperial level. Requiring study and examinations in England was 'a very material consideration,' Montagu observed, and 'where the imperial branch is recruited by nomination, it is hardly a bare pretence of equality of opportunity. If it is a system under which we must either keep Indians out of the higher branch of the service altogether or approve Indians with qualifications inferior to those of members of the lower branch, it stands condemned.'[14] Those grievances would have been in the minds of everyone Forster met, Hindu, Muslim, Anglo-Indian; officials and civilians.

Montagu had no previous experience of Indian affairs but was a quick study. He had had the schoolboy's experience of British anti-Semitism. Now he tended to align himself with the disadvantaged. He believed in the validity of the Empire but wanted the system to be as advantageous as possible for Indians. His call for a Commission unsettled Hardinge, who wrote to Crewe, 'I am a little alarmed at the idea of a Royal Commission, which might be too drastic in its treatment and play havoc with a most distinguished and efficient public service.' The Government of India would be in an 'invidious position' if it declined to follow the Commission's recommendations.[15]

Some, however, thought the Civil Service neither sufficiently distinguished nor efficient. Sir Spencer Harcourt Butler, the Member for Education on Hardinge's Council, commenting forcefully on Montagu's Memorandum, observed that:

> we are on the brink of a new era in India. I have watched it coming for 15 years. . . . I am convinced by all my experience that Indians

are slow to complain and that, when there is general complaint, there is a real evil. In the case of the educational service, the evil amounts to a public scandal of the gravest kind.

Butler thought that the Civil Service had never been in 'a more unsatisfactory state. There is seething discontent among the younger men, and a phalanx of incompetence at the top . . . we must recognise that the world is falling into the hands of the younger men as the pace of progress quickens.'[16] Syed Ross Masood was one of those 'younger men' and, because of his important connections within the Muslim community, one whom Government would expect to shoulder national responsibility in future.

Robert Trevelyan and G. L. Dickinson were to travel with Forster. While they planned their Indian journey, a new Royal Commission prepared to begin hearings in India in the winters of 1912–13 and 1913–14. Lord Islington left his post as Governor of New Zealand to serve as Chairman. The selection process cast up all the issues that Forster would encounter and would later include in *A Passage to India*. He did not need two winters of residence in India to suspect that flawed personal relations were at the root of Britain's difficulties there. In fact, being 'too friendly with Indians' raised questions about Commission appointees. Lord Crewe proposed Ramsay MacDonald, who was sympathetic toward Indian political aspirations and kept in touch with groups from 'the educated classes', or 'advanced Indians', terms often used with overtones of ridicule and mistrust in both the press and the official correspondence. Hardinge strongly objected to MacDonald. But Crewe insisted, even though Parliamentary duties must make MacDonald join late. Crewe wanted him for 'his own qualities and because he is by far the most level-headed exponent of views that must be taken into account'.[17] Hardinge was not reassured. He then objected vigorously to G. K. Gokhale, the Hindu organiser of the Servants of India Society and a member of the Viceroy's Council. Gokhale advocated a middle road between terrorism and supine subjection to British rule, but Hardinge, who doubted his sincerity, felt that he would only seize the opportunity to put his case before a wider audience. There were complaints about Morison's Muslim bias. Montagu rejected them as 'simply ignorant', dismissed objections to Gokhale, and said that he would 'give way on almost all of them in order to secure Gokhale'.[18]

On education and university matters Crewe chose the historian H.A.L. Fisher of New College, Oxford, and considered the Commis-

sion lucky to get him, for he would 'represent the Oxford standpoint, which needs taking into serious account, . . . but will not do so
in too narrow or donnish a spirit.' Fisher accepted appointment as
'the greatest possible honour' although he too must join late.[19] Fisher's views became the basis of the Commission's recommendations
on education for India.

Since this was a Royal Commission, the King's views were important. He had only two: a Royal Commission would be unnecessary if
the Civil Service tried harder to send true gentlemen out to India.
And he was surprised to learn that Lord Islington possessed a Chairman's talents.[20]

One Service omitted from the Commission's agenda had direct
bearing on the professional difficulties and personal feelings of
Forster's Dr Aziz. This was the Indian Medical Service. It seemed
that no one had decided whether that Service should be principally
civil or military. The military got the great majority of the higher
civil medical appointments. A Civil Assistant Surgeon – which would
be the rank of Dr Aziz – got 'almost entirely' only 'inferior or minor
appointments'. It was the Indian doctors who had begun to bring
'the blessings of the modern medical sciences' to the masses, yet
Indian medical students found it very difficult in India, and even
more so in Great Britain – assuming that they could afford to travel
there – to get the necessary hospital experience.[21] Thus one easily
imagines Aziz's frustrations and resentments throughout his Indian
training in Western medicine. Forster would have easily understood
all that from Masood's friend, the Edinburgh-trained Dr Mukhtar
Ahmad Ansari. One understands also the tensions between Aziz
and Major Callendar, his less-competent superior. The Major has
been left stuck in the Civil Medical Service. Not only Indians dwelt
upon the idea of *izzat*: prestige. It obsesses Major Callendar.

The religious issue was ever present, with Muslims and Hindus
always on guard against slights and inequalities, real or imagined.
Forster certainly knew, from Masood and his friends, how delicate
was the communal balance in 1912. Muslims were particularly apprehensive; a 1906 reform had increased Indian representation on
Provincial Legislative bodies in British India. Hindus were a majority of the population; Hindus would have more political influence
than Muslims. 'For the first time, northern India began to become
interested in All-India politics. . . . Now the fear that Sayyid Ahmad
had enunciated in the 1880s was recalled: that a non-Muslim majority would use its power under democratic institutions to the detri-

ment of Muslim interests and sensitivities.' A Muslim deputation warned about 'the strong feelings of English-educated, Muslim youth, who felt that Muslims were losing out because they did not know how to agitate.'[22] One result was the Muslim League, organised in December 1906, the first durable and effective Muslim political association. All these events, electrifying for Muslims in India, would have been in Masood's news from home after he reached England in 1906. By 1912 tensions had only increased.

In *Howards End* Forster had stated his attitude toward imperialism through the Wilcoxes, whose rubber business had 'swallowed a helping' of Africa.[23] In his early acquaintance with Masood, however, the personal concerned Forster more than the political. Masood put the philosophy of friendship in a new light. Forster claimed that he had never read G. E. Moore's *Principia Ethica*, but he did believe in the possibility of an ideal affection. Its object must be 'not only truly beautiful, but also truly good in a high degree. . . . The bodily expressions of character, whether by looks, by words, or by actions, do form a part of the object toward which the affection is felt,' so that they 'heighten the value of the whole state'. Masood was truly beautiful, darkly handsome, a figure out of a Moghul painting, with great charm and the assurance of one born to rank. The imagination easily placed him among the Moghul conquerors riding down from Afghanistan into India. In Forster's eyes he was also truly good in a high degree, with the requisite 'great variety of different emotions, each of which is appropriate to some different kind of beauty'.[24]

However, Masood's great variety of different emotions rather baffled Forster. Masood said that he placed friendship above duty and casually added, 'Hence the confusion in Oriental States.'[25] He was full of contradictions. He had an extravagantly romantic view of Oxford as 'an Oriental radiance' populated by dionysian celebrants.[26] At the same time he thought Cecil Headlam's history of Oxford excessively romantic, a book that would have caused his mother great misgivings about her son's being there. He could be moody: 'a hearse hilarious in comparison', and self-centred: 'He's sensitive not responsive'.[27] Quite soon after making that observation Forster and he had 'very very happy evenings' while visiting Forster's Aunt Laura at West Hackhurst, and Forster felt that he was free of 'some frost that I even got when at Cambridge . . . .'[28] Then Masood had supper with the Forsters in Weybridge, and the frost emanated from him and from Mrs Forster as well, for the distance between herself and Masood was too great, and to Masood the world was 'a room full of secondary persons with himself feeling intensely in the centre'.[29] Perhaps in self-defence, Forster sometimes took up a tone at once proprietary and self-deprecatory. Masood might find better advisers in England but Forster would welcome his confidences, which would be 'a great pleasure to me'.[30] The tone was also self-protective, for he wished to say that he loved Masood but for a long time could not bring himself to say so. When he did find occasion to speak of that, there was no more to be said, and Forster had to be content with a friendship that was inspiring and warm, but no more than that. However often they saw each other, Masood remained to some extent a puzzle of cultural differences. Forster commented in his diary on '"Eastern" character. Unreliable – not in heart but in action. Sensitive but not accurate observer . . . *Perhaps* touched by display of emotion. *Probably* touched by kindness, . . . stronger sense of beauty than ours'.[31]

While Forster read about India and met Masood's Indian friends in Oxford and London, a visit to India after Masood had returned there became increasingly possible. *Howards End* was selling splendidly, and 'I shall probably make enough money by it to come to India', Forster told him near the end of 1910.[32] Masood encouraged this idea by telling Forster that indeed he did comprehend the Eastern character, and he hoped 'to get *you* to write a book on India'. Forster must not suspect this as Oriental flattery, for he was exceptional among Englishmen of Masood's acquaintance. He understood 'true sentiment . . . even from the oriental point of view'. Forster repaid Masood's confidence in him with the dedication to *A Passage to India* and, later, a memorial tribute in which he wrote of his unique personality and the debt owed: 'He woke me up out of my suburban and academic life.' *A Passage to India* 'would never have been written without him'.[33]

Thus, in an undefined sort of way, the trip to India was a personal literary assignment, details to be worked out later – much later. There was a pleasant air of scholarly seriousness about the expedition. Robert Trevelyan's classical interests would find parallels in Indian antiquity. G. L. Dickinson had a Kahn Travelling Fellowship and was expected to report his impressions of both India and China. Forster wanted to see Masood in his Indian setting. He seems not to have gone equipped with literary contacts, but in fact a broad and varied literary exchange with India barely existed at the time. Indian poets or novelists writing in English, or works translated from Indian vernaculars, had the most meagre and specialised audiences in the English-speaking West, for the supply of works was itself meagre. The general impression persisted that the Indian vernaculars possessed few serious works of artistic value, and that interest in Indian literature was the province of folklorists, Sanskrit scholars and other linguists. The painter William Rothenstein had been introducing Rabindranath Tagore to literary London in the summer of 1912, but Forster was not in Rothenstein's circle, and there is no evidence that Forster met Tagore often or at length, although he gathered information and advice from Rothenstein and others who had met him. Tagore's elegant English versions of his Bengali lyrics were then a novelty to English readers. Indian art, too, was thought to be of little account, and at Ajanta the wall-paintings, greatest surviving example of Indian painting, had been left to deteriorate in dark and damp. In the official view, India had handicrafts (those had commercial value), but no fine arts. This climate of opinion did not encourage intellectual exchanges about indigenous art and literature.

Forster's contacts in 1912–13, therefore, were mainly with members of the Civil Service and the Educational Service, made principally through Masood, Morison and Malcolm Darling, Forster's King's College friend who became an authority on the agricultural economy of the Punjab. Indian officialdom was then in an acute state of nerves. No one knew exactly how the Royal Commission intended to proceed, what long-established practices would come under its scrutiny, or what long-smouldering resentments and inequities might surface during the Commission's hearings. That anxiety would have had its effect on everyone Forster met. Every Anglo-Indian action acquired intensified political ramifications, and the political climate will be even more fraught when Forster returns to India in 1921. The political content of *Passage* exists mostly as overtones, but a careful reading in connection with contemporary events shows how sharp an ear he had for political as well as for literary nuance.

The winter of 1911–12, during which Masood prepared to go home and Forster prepared to travel, saw a marked compression in British–Indian relations. The change began with the death of King Edward VII on 6 May 1910. On 11 May King George V was declared Emperor of India, and he and the Queen would attend a great Coronation Durbar at Delhi; although the new King had visited India as Prince of Wales, no ruling English monarch had ever set foot there. The Durbar took place on 12 December 1911, and on Indian soil George V was formally crowned Emperor of India. He then announced two decisions kept secret from the public since August, and their political and cultural repercussions rumbled continually in the background of Forster's Indian journey. First, a new city at Delhi would replace Calcutta as the capital of British India; and Bengal, whose partition in 1905 as East and West Bengal had aroused angry and sometimes literally explosive protests from Bengalis, would be reassembled as a Presidency with its own Governor and Legislative Council. A Durbar presupposed Royal 'boons', but when this was first suggested to Lord Crewe, his response was 'Not practical politics, of course.'[34]

But then some practical aspects of removing the capital to Delhi began to emerge. The Durbar boon was a graceful way for the Imperial Government to get out of Calcutta and leave the Bengali problem to a new local government. The Government of India called upon all Indians to rejoice because their capital would now return to its ancient location. Delhi was still 'a name to conjure with', for the decisive battle in the Hindu epic *Mahabharata* was fought on the Delhi plains; Muslims would feel 'unbounded satisfaction' when they saw the Moghul capital still revered 'among the masses of the people' and 'restored to its proud position as the seat of Empire'. There would be 'a wave of enthusiasm' and general acceptance of the 'unfaltering determination to maintain British rule in India'.[35]

Enthusiasm was not quite universal. In fact, acute political and psychological anxiety prevailed when Edwin Montagu, the Royal Commission, and Forster with his travelling companions all reached India in the late Autumn of 1912. Calcutta box-wallahs – foreign businessmen – were dismayed by the prospect of losing their position as next-neighbours of the Government of India. To many Hindus the 'ancient capital' symbolised submission to the Moghul Emperors, for whom the British were only a replacement. The fleeting reference to the *Mahabharata* sank beneath the flow of rhetoric about past Moghul greatness; that emotional appeal to history seemed only one more example of British obtuseness. Many East Bengal Muslims feared that they were abandoned to their fate at the hands of Hindu Bengalis, and that nervousness communicated itself to Muslims throughout India.

In *A Passage to India*, Aziz, the Muslim doctor, and Cyril Fielding, Principal of the Chandrapore Government College, are both the explicators and the victims of these tensions. Elizabeth Heine, in the Abinger Edition of *The Hill of Devi* and others of Forster's Indian writings, identifies various analogues for those two characters.

Each contains some of each and perhaps of still others who suspected or wished that they too were among Forster's models.[36] But Forster avoided making the novel's people, places and time too specific. Irreversible changes were already under way when the novel was published in 1924. 'Assuredly the novel dates', Forster wrote in 1957.[37] Certainly it cannot fit calendar chronology. Between 1913, when Forster began *Passage*, and 1924, there intervened the First World War, the Amritsar Massacre of 1919, Gandhi's non-cooperation movement and intensified waves of Islamic unity.[38] The new generation of Muslim leaders seemed less cooperative, more demanding, less controllable than their fathers and grandfathers had been. Whenever Muslim unrest surfaced, Government turned its attention to the Anglo-Oriental Muhammadan College at Aligarh. It wanted full university status: specifically, a 'Muslim University of Aligarh'. Then Annie Besant's Hindu Central College at Benares would certainly demand official recognition, and Government would have to play the game of Hindu–Muslim tit-for-tat. There was also the prickly problem of affiliation, the system by which provincial high schools accepted the academic standards of a specific college or university. Increased enrolment and local influence were the advantages, but lowered standards often resulted.

At Aligarh, affiliation was much more than an educational or even a political issue. To progressive Indian Muslims, Aligarh was the keeper of a flame, a preserver of the best of Islamic culture and tradition. Whatever strengthened its autonomy and influence strengthened Islam. The Government suspected affiliation as a Muslim power play, which in a way it was, and as soon as he reached Aligarh, Forster was aware of the consequences of that suspicion. At about the same time Montagu, travelling to the Punjab, wrote to Crewe:

> I do hope you have not allowed Aligarh university [*sic*] to 'recognise' high schools. This seems to me an unnecessary feature of the new type of University. Let the schools earn recognition by the university successes of their alumni. I have no feelings about the name. We have sanctioned what I may perhaps call a sectarian university (I know you don't like the adjective and think it inaccurate when applied to so large a number) and whether we admit it by the title or whether we don't seems immaterial.[39]

Crewe's reply is significant, for it summed up the administration's kindlier thoughts about the 'educated classes':

No, don't suppose that I wish you to lose any sympathy with 'educated India'. I like personally most of its representatives that I know, and I hope they don't find me unfriendly. My only points of mistrust are that they will talk as though there existed no other India worth dealing with, or to be considered from any standpoint but theirs, and that they seem to take pride in swallowing whole, like a bolus, a political code which they conceive to be English Liberalism, without much reference to its particular applications. These appear to be the vices even of the best and cleverest of them.[40]

Montagu had never been secretive about his sympathy for 'educated India'. As the new Under-Secretary of State for India, he had said:

To a people so blindly obedient to authority the teaching of European and particularly of English thought, was a revelation. English literature is saturated with the praise of liberty, and it inculcates the duty of private and independent judgement on every man. . . . and the consequence is that a new spirit is abroad wherever English education has spread, which questions all established beliefs and calls for orthodoxy, either political, social, economic or religious, to produce its credentials.[41]

Montagu himself had broken with his father's uncompromising Jewish orthodoxy, and the pain of such a break made him sympathetic toward Indians who faced similarly rending decisions. His explicit sympathy for a more liberalised Raj and his explanations for Muslims' unhappiness over the defeat of Turkey in the Balkan Wars of 1912–13 would become principal obstacles to his succeeding Hardinge as Viceroy in 1915, an appointment that he wanted very much. In India in 1912 the situation was already so delicate that Lord Crewe had asked Montagu not to make any speeches there.[42]

Forster reached Aligarh on 24 October 1912 and quickly discovered that 'life at Aligarh showed many seams'. The campus was not very pleasant, and inconveniences caused inefficiencies. He found Muslim members of staff feeling psychologically and desperately involved in the Balkan War, the fate of the Ottoman Empire, and the implications for Muslims everywhere. The war had 'embittered them yet more against us' because Britain's sympathies were with the Balkan League and not with Turkey. Animosities sharpened by the affiliation controversy and Aligarh's drive for academic autonomy had exacerbated the daily relations of faculty, students and Trustees. Not surprisingly, the English staff felt that they were not trusted, that their missionary zeal was rejected, and they would be made redundant if the College gained autonomy and the Muslims got that opportunity to manage their own affairs. The English members felt out of touch with the Trustees and thought that their relations with the students were poisoned by the incendiary journalism of *The Comrade*, 'a forward-Islamic paper "which told lies"' and supported the pan-Islamic Khalifat movement in support of Turkey's old regime. The disunity, which 'is of recent growth', grieved Forster, who had thought of Aligarh as a reflection of Morison, of Masood and his grandfather, and as the centre of an Islamic Enlightenment.[43]

Montagu reached Aligarh a few weeks after Forster left with Masood for Delhi. Montagu cabled to Crewe that the Trustees 'want a guarantee that they will not lose a Muslim college and get a non-Muslim university', and they wanted 'to deal with a man and not with a corporation'.[44] Montagu's reaction was much like Forster's. He thought the situation 'highly dangerous because the controversy is leading to deterioration of the college and politics being substituted for its high educational tradition. If name they suggest were permitted the other two points could apparently be compromised' by allowing affiliation and having the 'Viceroy as chancellor act through the Education Member of Council'.[45] Muslim influence in North India came to be identified as 'the Aligarh movement'.[46]

Worrisome ramifications of Aligarh's demands seemed endless. Lord Crewe did not see how '"any race or creed can complain of us" if affiliation were denied to all *new* universities . . . .'[47] He was frankly unsympathetic with 'these quasi-religious institutions'. His Council had refused the title 'Muslim University'. It might let loose 'a sort of Moslem Maynooth or St. Bee's to spread tentacles over India though I thought the notion quite wrong; but if the Council were going to stand out for the local character, they must enforce the concomitant conditions. I think this is only logical.'[48] Hardinge, for his part, hoped to convince Muslim leaders that they 'gain nothing by agitation, and that the more they agitate, the more shall we harden our attitudes toward them. I hinted that, if they behave nicely, we shall look after the special interests, but I was careful not to specify any.' The Government would use improved education to conciliate Muslims so that they will not think 'we make concessions to them owing to the pressure applied'.[49]

At both Aligarh and Delhi Forster trod dangerous ground, for

Masood introduced him to Mohammed Ali, editor of *The Comrade*, and his no less militant brother Shaukat Ali. Forster admired Mohammed Ali's concern for the preservation of Indian antiquities but found him otherwise 'a most ~~offensive~~ untaking man' and *The Comrade* '~~somewhat~~ petulant though clever'.[50] Lord Crewe, sailing home from the Durbar, agreed about the cleverness but thought the editor not one to be trusted.[51] Indeed, *The Comrade* was a prime example of the kind of paper to which Government longed to apply the sternest restrictive measures of its Press Act, and Crewe so distrusted Mohammed Ali that in 1913 he gave orders that if Ali came to London no one connected with the Secretary of State and the India Office was to see him.[52] In Delhi Dr Ansari, host to Forster and Masood, was also under surveillance, not least because in December 1912 he took a Red Crescent medical mission to the fighting in Turkey.[53] Forster does not mention restrictions on his own movements, but it would be very surprising if Intelligence agents were not watching him despite his unimpeachable credentials of friendship with Morison and Darling.[54] Intelligence knew exactly what any unconventional tourists were up to. When William Rothenstein visited India in 1910 the India Office in London required him to carry special identification and to report to the chief British official at every stop. He wanted only to see Indian art and meet Indian artists, but that in itself struck the official mind as peculiar. The India Office was afraid that his reputation of having 'sympathy for Indians and for things Indian would encourage the Nationalists'.[55] Forster would have been particularly interesting to Intelligence because he had the very unconventional habit of staying with Indians – some of them emphatically the wrong kind in official eyes.

A PASSAGE TO INDIA

In that winter of 1912–13 Forster and a Muslim friend wondered why both Indians and English 'maximise their difficulties'.[56] The Government's efforts at control only contributed to that maximisation. Calculated fragmentation was its method of protecting the corporate *izzat*, prestige, of the British Raj and was also a means of dealing with Hindu–Muslim demands for equity, and with the uses and consequences of Westernised education and civil unrest. Forster made fragmentation the keynote of his novel, beginning with the geography of Chandrapore, which is Bankipore in Behar, where he visited

Masood, who had begun his Indian career as barrister. The city is jammed up against the Ganges but has no view of the river and is 'scarcely distinguishable from the rubbish it deposited so freely'.[57] It seems not even to remember its glory days as a port in the era of the Moghul Emperors. On the highest ground is the British Civil Station, geometrically functional, neither rubbishy nor beautiful, and trees screen it from the grubby city below. Between the two communities are the Eurasians, who might claim membership in either but belong to neither. They live near the railway station, another anomalous symbol of their position in Indian life and culture: many worked on the railways, but few made it from a ticket-collector's booth or an engine-driver's seat to the halls of power. Their loyalties were too likely to divide in times of trouble.

It was relatively easier for educated, England-returned Indians like Masood to enter the halls of power than to find full acceptance in Anglo-Indian society. Forster told his mother that 'Masood flourishes in the midst of this desolation amazingly', in spite of his social life's being very circumscribed.[58] Indians were excluded from the English club, and their own social clubs on the English pattern generated little enthusiasm. The pattern was too stiff and too foreign. For Indians who had begun to think about their identity as Indians, it suggested servile imitation. Cut off from the one, they stayed away from the other. Nor did social fragmentation always originate with the pettiness of minor officials. That no doubt happened, but the pattern existed also at the top of the Raj hierarchy. At times it reached heights of absurdity, as, for example, during preparations for the 1911 Durbar, a protocol nightmare under any circumstances, and it illuminated the tight little social corner into which the rulers had manoeuvred themselves. Should Indian members of the Provincial Legislatures be invited to stay in the official Camps at Delhi? Some winnowing seemed indicated. But by what criterion? One official suggested including those Indian officials who lived in European fashion – but how to define 'European-living' Indians? Some, by European standards, had achieved greater sophistication, others less, some little or none. Some dined in Anglo-Indian homes if invited but maintained Indian customs at home: could they be said to *live* in European fashion? Some would want to bring their wives, and what then? Some wives could cope with European customs while others remained uncompromisingly Indian. There could be separate messes for Europeans, Hindus, and Muslims, but space was limited, and Indians liked to spread out. Cooking odours would spread with them. Muslims would object to the Hindus' pork and Hindus to beef being cooked for Muslims. English ladies would object to both and would object even more to the false note that Indians would introduce into the social tone of the Camps. (Would they be expected to *entertain* the Indian ladies? Forster captured exactly this climate of snobbery, in Mrs Turton's social impasse with the Indian ladies at the Collector's 'Bridge Party' in *Passage*.) Above all, the Camps would lack *symmetry*; the President of the Coronation Durbar Committee was dismayed by the prospect of a camp part English and part Indian.[59]

Thus, instead of meaning a pleasing proportion of parts to one another, in the official mind symmetry meant exclusiveness and exclusion. Forster could not create true symmetry where none existed, but he examined three *possibilities* – remote, to be sure – of true symmetry: friendship between Fielding and Aziz; understanding between Adela Quested and Aziz; and, between Aziz and Godbole, religious toleration. In the first two, the lines become hopelessly tangled in the cross-tensions of cultural encounter. The third, from Aziz to Godbole, is the only one to even imagine a working model for India's future.

First, Fielding and Aziz. They have in common their education on the Western model, but they never discuss education as such. This is not surprising, for Forster was uninterested in its mechanics. He cared about the liberal learning that becomes a component of Culture. P. N. Furbank puts it thus: 'My own interpretation of him is that he believed in culture, but only half-heartedly believed in education. The half was enough to prompt him to spend a lot of his time and energy in teaching; but the other and sceptical half was enough to make him often use the word "educational" as a term of abuse.'[60] Fielding and Aziz must deal with the mass of contradictions that Western-style education had superimposed on India's cultural traditions, with manifold strains on personal relations. Fielding is a loner, a light traveller, an improviser. He has no missionary ardour except his 'belief in education', and he enjoys teaching anyone willing to learn. In the great crisis of the novel he takes a stand against the organisation, but in the end he tolerates it as long as it tolerates him. Aziz is alertly curious about the workings of the English mind and details of English living – he is surprised and delighted when the untidiness of Fielding's room contradicts his stereotype of the English with 'everything ranged coldly on shelves' – a characterisation so accurate that Fielding doubts it 'could be improved'.[61] But Aziz refuses to Westernise completely and insists upon the essentials of his Islamic-Indian culture. He is decidedly not 'European-living' at home. Nor does he dine with British officials; Fielding's is the first non-Indian home to welcome him. Had he been elected to a Provincial Council, Durbar officials would have been hard put to classify him, for his considerable professional skills, if not acquired in England, are literally essential to the well-being of the Raj. Yet professional skills count for nothing beside the one qualification that he cannot meet: a white skin. After the disastrous picnic at the Marabar Caves, while Chandrapore chooses sides for the prosecution and defence of Aziz, Fielding complains that Mr Turton, the Collector, had kept him from accompanying Aziz to Captain McBryde, District Superintendent of Police. Turton intended to spare Fielding embarrassment – but wished also to separate him from Aziz and thus avoid embarrassing the Anglo-Indian side. McBryde says, 'sentimentally': 'Sort of all-white thing our Collector would do . . . .'[62] The habit of racial classification is not surprising, since it existed also at the top of the official hierarchy. Its terminology was an unquestioned part of the Anglo-Indian vocabulary. While Forster was still preparing for his voyage, the Viceroy was expressing approval for an Indian considered acceptable because he came close to behaving like a white man.[63]

Close, but not *too* close. Too much Westernising encouraged Indians to presume, and Forster has caught the tone of official resentment of Indian presumption, alleged or real. Aziz's friend, the pleader Mahmoud Ali, presumed too much, to the detriment of his standing in court, when Ronny Heaslop as a new Assistant Magistrate invited him to smoke a cigarette with him. Indians are fine people, but 'we don't come across them socially', says Ronny, now initiated into the ways of officialdom. Rudeness, he says, missing the irony of his own remark, has become 'the educated native's latest dodge' and gesture of defiance – to which his mother replies disapprovingly that his standard of personal relations seems to have changed in India.[64] But Ronny ignores this, for he has embraced the code, which encourages Westernisation when it is useful but pounces and generalises upon imperfections such as Aziz's collar-stud kindly given to Fielding, which leaves Aziz's own collar unanchored and earns Ronny's derision at what he identifies as 'the fundamental slackness that reveals the race'.[65]

Misunderstandings and mythologies ensue when 'race' or 'white' becomes the defining word. Ronny accepts the mythology of race.

Mahmoud Ali accepts a relative mythology of British virtues: the higher up in the hierarchy, the more generous-minded they must be. He assumes that the Lieutenant-Governor of the Province, who to Mahmoud Ali (and perhaps also to the Collector) would have been as grand and remote as the Viceroy, had instructed Turton to give a Bridge Party. But it would have been an extraordinary thing for a Lieutenant-Governor to issue such an instruction. To a District Collector, as to Mahmoud Ali, Lieutenant-Governor and Viceroy would have been equally remote. Mahmoud Ali believes that high officials have only good will toward Indians. 'But they come too seldom and live too far away.'[66] He does not see the contradiction, for the officials at the top of the hierarchy seem sympathetic only *because* they remain at a distance. It was as well that none of the real-life Mahmoud Alis had access to the official archives, where unkind and scornful allusions to Indians are frequent enough to prove that Forster was reporting truth and not creating caricature. Yet it must be said as well that a real scoundrel seldom surfaces in those archives. The great majority of officials, higher and lower, were conscientious men committed to the service of the Raj, who had very little fun in life and worked themselves into exhaustion, ill health and sometimes an early grave. Their failings were the failings of their generation and more particularly of their class.

Forster knew this also. When Santha Rama Rau, in her stage adaptation of *Passage*, made a point of Ronny Heaslop's fundamental decency, Forster wrote on her script, 'Thank you for rescuing my poor Ronny.'[67] He is caught between his mother's and the system's standards of moral uprightness, but his moral sensibilities are of the 'sterilised public-school brand'.[68] He knows that he behaved badly when he broke up Fielding's tea-party. He almost redeems himself when he insists, for the sake of impartiality, that his Indian assistant Mr Das preside in his place at the trial of Aziz. But then Ronny knocks two large holes in that favourable impression. He wanted to show that 'my old Das is all right' and – surprising as it may seem – has 'moral courage of the public-school brand', which in turn will show Ronny's superiors that he has the right kind, the 'white' kind of Indian on his staff. And then he throws Mr Das to the wolves, for he finds it inconceivable that an Indian judge would dare to rule in favour of an Indian accused of raping a white woman. In any case there would be a row and perhaps a riot, but it would be less serious if an Indian pronounced sentence. Plainly, it is English fuss, not Indian fuss that Ronny cares about. But then, at the trial he supports

Das with 'devastating honesty'.[69] Ronny is well on the way to becoming a pukka sahib of the more rigid variety, but the fundamental
decency does not give up without a fight.

Forster has nothing good to say for Major Callendar, who poisons
the air by wanting to punish anyone who disagrees with him, or for
Mrs Callendar, in whom her husband's bitterness becomes virulent
hatred. Yet even for that there is explanation if not excuse: not only
is the Major stranded in the Civil Medical Service, but Chandrapore
is an administrative backwater. Mr Turton, as Collector the chief
officer of the District, also wants to see Indians punished, but caution holds him back. He too is stuck in Chandrapore, near the end of
a twenty-five years' career. Not to have achieved a more prestigious
post in all that time suggests a conscientious but unimpressive ordi-
nariness. It is too late to make up lost ground. Personal relations
make him nervous. He is essentially a public man, an exterior. 'He
was indeed always calmer' when he addressed a group or a crowd
than when with an individual.[70] The event at the caves – whatever it
was – drives him into a panic of irreconcilable contradictions. The
decent official side of him wants to be fair. The personal and emotional side of him wants to be Miss Quested's chivalrous defender.
Fielding and all the Indians he condemns together and would punish them publicly if he could, but if that were to start a riot he would
have to call for military assistance.[71] Damaged reputation is the Raj
official's nightmare. An appeal to higher authority for troops would
tell the outer world that he could not manage his District and would
call down upon him the stern attention of the Viceroy, the Secretary
of State for India, Parliament and the press. He would be criticised as
the Lieutenant-Governor of the Punjab was criticised when the Viceroy intervened after riots around a mosque in Cawnpore. The publicity, not his record of conscientious service, would then stick to the
Collector when he retires to some enclave of Old India Hands in
England. 'At Chandrapore the Turtons were little gods', but retirement was only a few years off, and a recurring official refrain was
that the English at home neither knew nor wished to know the
burdens that their Imperial servants carried in India.[72] For Turton
the episode at the caves is 'the worst thing in my whole career'.[73]
Still, while condemning Turton's narrowness, Forster credits the
genuine pathos of this limited man's position, so precarious at the
end of a life's work. Turton's administrative credo is a veiled appeal
for Fielding's understanding, and an apologia for his whole Indian
career. Hating Indians too publicly would be an admission of failure

in the 'civilising' mission of the Raj and an admission that his twenty-five years in India, six of them as Collector at Chandrapore, have been his personal failure. His entire argument rests on that panicky concern about familiarity, friendship and intimacy between Indians and English. In his experience familiarity has bred disaster, but he does not see that contempt is at the root of the trouble and leaves no space for the mutual courtesy that he persuades himself has prevailed as long as Indians and English avoided becoming friends. Outsiders ignore that hard-won tradition, and the reputation that he had assumed was established for the ages falls into the dust: 'It is the end of me.'[74] For Turton, 'outsiders' includes all who do not subscribe to the doctrine of separate communities. This includes Fielding, and his disagreement with the clan is all the more reprehensible because he belongs to that part of the India service that has been canonised in official despatches for generations as essential for 'civilising' India: the Educational Service. But Mr Turton is not really concerned now about 'civilising' India. He cannot think further than an India that he thought he had created in his own image.

What troubled Forster even more than the subtle and not-so-subtle discourtesies was the general atmosphere of distrust and the rulers' habit of self-protective refusal. Fielding says of Major Callendar that refusal is 'all he exists for'.[75] This attitude also has filtered down through the hierarchy. Cautious efforts not to give way or give away too much caused misunderstandings and resentments. The Viceroy believed sincerely that he was consistently kind and benevolent, but paternalism was the basis of such officials' professional training.[76] A Government of India Dispatch in 1911 had seemed to promise India Colonial status on the Canadian and Antipodean model, but on closer examination it proved to promise only a little more local autonomy – some day – *if* Indians learned to get along together without British soldiers to keep order. In the meantime the Provincial Councils would listen to what the people had to say: was not this autonomy? In any case, it was all they would get in any foreseeable future. Conscientious, conservative, stern but correct according to the rules, but also too often fatally cautious, humourless, and lacking in sympathies from the heart, the Civil Service made classifications and barriers the tools of its trade. *Passage* shows how clearly Forster perceived them. Adela Quested's distressed perception of unspecified barriers, not her effort to comprehend 'the whole of India', lies at the heart of her difficulties.[77]

The atmosphere of official refusal rebounds upon Indians in the form of officials' categories of the 'loyal' and 'disloyal', the 'contented' and the 'discontented', the amenable 'masses' and the 'educated classes' so often suspected of disloyalty and of instigating sedition and 'mischief'. When Ronny asks his mother whether Aziz in the mosque was 'well-disposed' she misses the point that that is Ronny's synonym for 'loyal'.[78] The word echoes and re-echoes in *Passage*, as in the official correspondence of that time, and Forster caught its resonances exactly. Ronny calls the Nawab Bahadur 'a real loyalist', for Bahadur is a minor title given to Indians for good behaviour and not infrequently for money to Government projects.[79] When the Nawab Bahadur sides with Aziz and reverts to being plain Mr Zulfikar, he will certainly be shifted to the 'disloyal' column. Even mild, inoffensive Professor Godbole had feared being thought 'disloyal' if he agreed when Adela criticised 'her race' and its fatuous entertainments at the Club.[80]

In Forster's experience, officialism tainted 'every human act in the East'.[81] It polluted personal relationships. When Ronny lectures his mother about the Raj he hammers away at his point that cultivating good personal relations is irrelevant in India. Force, not friendship with Indians and not even courtesy, is the key to control: 'We've something more important to do.' Mrs Moore is repelled by the 'self-satisfied lilt' of his words. Forster adds that 'one touch of . . . the true regret from the heart' might have redeemed both Ronny and the Raj.[82] Raj officialism infected non-officials as well. Jane Harrison, classicist and Fellow of Newnham College, met a relative who was

a retired Indian and such a *type* – only a bank clerk but with the true imperial outlook – puzzled that his Maker neglects to provide him with a troop of body servants – exquisitely deferential to his Mother and his Sisters and his Aunts – tho' they pain him deeply by earning their livings and airing their unfeminine views – really the dearest of boys but almost incredibly stupid, and with views that wd adorn the Ark.[83]

While Forster and Miss Harrison recorded their impressions, Montagu was writing from India in the very same strain:

The well-meaning of it is so pathetic. . . . An Indian official never explains; there are no rules to show him how. He does his duty and at that he is better than any man of any age – but to explain things and thereby to bring us and the people together in the light of humanity is to them impossible. . . . One sees in Lahore the type of what I fear exists in India, which, if it goes on, will lead us to disaster – the resentment of the educated Indian and his claims.[84]

The self-protecting officialism and the inability to explain complicated the work of the Public Services Commission. Anglo-Indians threw up barricades even before the English members of the Commission sailed for India in October 1912. Anglo-Indian resentments centred on this point: what could they who had never had Indian careers know of the day-by-day problems? Whenever authority seemed threatened, officials employed that man-on-the-spot argument: only the experienced insider knows the problems and how to solve them. Forster heard it often, and he made it serve many purposes. Turton uses it when he speaks of his years of service: the outsiders have imperilled his reputation. McBryde uses it along with his own shallow orientalism and the siege mentality derived from the British experience of the 1857 Mutiny when he harangues Fielding on the subject of crime in India and tells him to forget the *Bhagavad Gita* and read the Mutiny records instead, if he really wants to know how to manage India: 'The psychology here is different'.[85] Ronny uses it when he tells Adela that experience of India would be be useless to her 'because she could not interpret it'.[86] He uses it again after the trial when he decides that she will never make an Anglo-Indian wife, for she will never learn to be an insider, and that would be 'the end of his career . . . '.[87] Ronny has surrendered to the system.

How had all this come about? Many blamed the Oxbridge-model 'literary curriculum' that had shaped the Indian educational system since 1835 and was intended to introduce promising Indians to European arts and science and, not least, to improve Indian moral character. In 1838 Macaulay's brother-in-law, Charles E. Trevelyan, had stated that: 'the spirit of English literature . . . cannot but be favourable to the English connection. Familiarly acquainted with us by means of our literature, the Indian youth almost cease to regard us as foreigners. . . . they become more English than Hindus, just as the Roman provincials became more Roman than Gauls or Italians.' Political change, when it came, would be 'peaceably and gradually effected; there will be no struggle, no mutual exasperation; the natives will have independence, after first learning how to make good use of it; we shall exchange profitable subjects for still more profitable allies.'[88]

In 1912, however, the 'profitable subjects' still had not received passing marks in moral and political conduct, and that Western learning fuelled a great deal of struggle and mutual exasperation. It was too late to stuff back into the bottle the genie released through the study of incendiary ideas from writers like Shakespeare and Milton, Shelley and Coleridge, J. S. Mill and Dickens. By 1913 a move was under way to shift to the technologies that might keep India afloat in a changing world economy. Forster heard that mantra in Bombay and wrote, '"education needed but not literary education": then I see the results of technical and am appalled.' Perhaps there were intrinsic values he had not seen, but there was a suggestion of the Rooksnest water-tank in his question, 'why is the outside always so ugly?'[89] Education in India, whether literary or technological, seemed to have less than ever to do with Culture, and it seemed also that the closer the educated Indian came to the vaunted Western model, the more suspicion and caution he evoked from his rulers. Ronny Heaslop suspects an ulterior motive behind the Indian's every word. He will admit exceptions – but he does not suggest any. He is convinced that an exchange with an Indian, any Indian, always involves his attempt 'to increase his *izzat*,' by which Ronny means competitive prestige; for an Indian it means self-respect.[90] When the Indian ladies at the Bridge Party try their limited English on Mrs Turton, she panics and feels her own *izzat* is endangered, for she thinks that they know more than they really do and 'might apply her own standards to her'.[91] Ronny, who boasts that he knows all Indian types, has already classified Aziz as 'the spoilt westernized': he has got above himself because education has gone to his head.[92] Major Callendar, who thinks of Indians as one amorphous and undesirable type, never realises that educated Indians, who had been shut out of community life with Anglo-Indians, already constituted a community and, 'however painfully', were raising social barricades of their own against the British intrusion.[93] In that situation, Fielding, who has tried to ignore the artificial distinctions, is trapped in one of the Empire's fundamental contradictions: the Educational Service was considered essential to the 'civilising' mission, but a teacher with curiosity, imagination and, worst of all, an independent spirit, was regarded as a liability. 'There needs must be this evil of brains in India', Forster wrote, but the teachers who bear the responsibility for encouraging them also bear the blame when students act on the imported Western ideas about freedom of speech and liberty.[94] Too often, officialdom continued to view the educational system as a tool for making Indians useful to the administration and, as at Aligarh, for keeping them under control.

Forster talked with a number of teachers in Government schools. Their problems would be Fielding's problems as Principal of the Government College in Chandrapore, and they are perfectly described in Herbert Fisher's comments on the Educational Service. He agreed that, despite defects, many had acquired much useful knowledge and had learned 'to appreciate the beauties of English literature'. The system had produced 'a very large number of lawyers, government servants and doctors to use our tongue and to operate in varying degrees of skill and efficiency within Western categories of thought. This in itself is a great achievement.' But there were appalling shortcomings.

First, with one exception, he found 'no quiet disinterested pursuit of knowledge for its own sake. Teaching and learning are dominated by examinations. Knowledge is the last thing about which these young gentlemen are solicitous. They are out, frankly and greedily for marks'. Second, there was 'no real machinery for educating an intellectual elite'. Classes were so large that teachers had no spare time for outstanding students. A young economist at Bombay said that he learned nothing until he 'fell into the hands of Alfred Marshall at Cambridge, not that his Indian teachers were bad but that they were overworked'. Third, college teaching and learning were 'alike mechanical and soulless' because of a combination of stultified instruction and Indian society's patriarchal tradition. The 'prevailing ignorance of English' was extremely serious. Many who read English glibly could not follow the simplest lecture or write the simplest précis and were thus 'compelled to the deadly process of memorising (without intelligence) the notes of their crammer'. Fourth, the larger universities were 'the common property of educational theory'. Too many 'half-baked formalists' had 'never experienced the strict and bracing conditions of real scientific inquiry'. And finally, college libraries were *'terrible'*. It was 'vain to send good young Englishmen out to teach in India. As it is, they go to intellectual death'.[95] Fielding has not yet succumbed to intellectual death, but he will succumb to the system before the end of the novel.

However, many Indians cared less about the mechanised nature of the system than about their own lack of control over the machine. They wanted fewer teachers from England. Forster understood this resentment when he encountered it at Aligarh, and he created for Fielding a similar ambiguity in his relations with the community.

Even Aziz's friend Hamidullah, usually willing to give the English the benefit of a doubt, challenges Fielding about whether it is 'fair an Englishman should occupy [a position] when Indians are available?'[96]

Forster provides no details of professional life at Chandrapore's Government College, but Fisher's report describes precisely what Fielding, a dedicated teacher, would have been up against in daily duties. There is no hint that Fielding's staff is better trained or classes smaller than the dismal average. He does his duty and, evidently, more than his duty, and his fellow countrymen and women do not appreciate his popularity with both his students and their parents. He has declined to knit himself into the fabric of the British community. The men tolerate him, but the Anglo-Indian women disapprove of his independence. He refuses to flatter and dance attendance on them. His behaviour implies that he expects them too to be more independent, but in this society they are approved if they are dependent. Fielding had learned how to get along with Indians and with the Anglo-Indian men but had discovered that if he wanted approval from Anglo-Indian women he 'must drop the Indians'.[97]

Fielding not only does not drop the Indians but is hospitable to the two Englishwomen who do not fit the Chandrapore pattern. They are certain not to fit, for they ask questions, Adela Quested more persistently than Mrs Moore. None of the Anglo-Indian women in Chandrapore questions in order to elicit genuine information. If they offer information about India it is likely to be wrong and have disastrous results. Adela is conspicuous not only because of her questions, but because she doubts the desirability of becoming an Anglo-Indian wife, which the other women consider an aspersion on themselves. But Adela, the 'queer cautious girl', has come expressly to ask questions about India.[98] She does not realise that unattached women who made themselves conspicuous in India were not universally admired. The Irish Margaret Noble, who became Sister Nivedita at the Ramakrishna Mission in Calcutta, was well beyond the pale. There was the awful example of the fiery Annie Besant, half-Irish and fervently for Home Rule, who had left Church, husband, and children in England and ended up a Theosophist, a cohort of Gokhale and other nationalists far more radical, and in 1913 actually joined the Indian National Congress.[99] Miss Derek, who romps irresponsibly through *Passage*, gets away with it by being so conspicuously brash that criticism is useless. In fact, the more convention-bound ladies seem to envy her daring and independence.

Adela, however, does not know how to be brash. The courtesies are very important to her, but at every turn they trip over the cross-tensions of cultural encounter. As soon as she meets Aziz at Fielding's tea-party she asks him to explain the social contretemps with the Bhattacharyas. Her question is batted back and forth between Eastern and Western codes of courtesy, and this pattern will characterise each of her encounters with Aziz. Fielding foresees awkwardness and tries to neutralise the Bhattacharyas' behaviour as the result of a misunderstanding. But neither Adela nor Aziz leaves it at that. She fears that she and Mrs Moore have somehow been discourteous, although it was the Bhattacharyas who invited them but failed to send the promised carriage. Aziz the man of science pursues the facts but drops them hastily when he learns that the Hindu Bhattacharyas were the hosts involved. He tries to bury the wreckage of the discussion under a generalisation about Hindu slackness and unpunctuality. Adela is not satisfied; an invitation is a serious summons, and she dislikes mysteries, 'not because I'm English', but simply because that is a part of her temperament.[100] She does not see that in her case the two are the same. To be one-up on the Hindus Aziz invites everyone to his own house, then realises how dreadful it is and how embarrassed he will be, then grasps at the idea of the picnic at the Marabar Caves. That invitation too is ill-judged, but it is courteously intended. Aziz counters rudeness with rather hysterical courtesy when Ronny bursts in with his own invitation to the polo game and gives a peremptory order to Fielding's servant. Aziz offers to give the same order more idiomatically, which implies that Ronny is deficient in the vernacular. But Aziz is also trying to preserve his own *izzat*: 'His wings were failing', but his self-respect pushes him to go on needling Ronny.[101] Adela fails to catch some nuances of this exchange, but she knows that Ronny has been inexcusably rude. He will recover some of his English courtesy when away from the Indians, and his equilibrium is further restored when he averts a Hindu–Muslim clash over the Muslims' Mohurram ceremonies, which makes him feel competent and official; he 'had proved that the British were necessary to India'.[102]

Aziz and Adela meet next at the railway station on the morning of the Marabar picnic. Again Aziz, nerves all on edge, overdoes the courtesies. There is too much of everything – food, servants, transport, all intended as 'a stupendous replica of the tea-party'.[103] The result is a stupendous muddle of misconceived English menus and disorganised Indian service. Aziz's wish to honour English punctuality has taken him to the opposite extreme of spending all the previous night at the station. Even the level-crossing gates seem over-eager to be punctual in the English manner and close earlier than usual, thus cutting off Fielding and Godbole and setting up subsequent charges of their intentional tardiness. Aziz never really knows the extent of the ladies' genuine courtesy in submitting to the arduous day so as not to disappoint him. That part of their courtesy that he does comprehend is their simple goodwill in which he finds no taint of race-consciousness. He was unaccustomed to this from the English of his limited experience, and 'this moved him deeply'.[104] But India is pressing the ladies very hard. Adela's mind is on plans for marriage to Ronny, on Anglo-Indian family life, on servants. Mrs Moore, weary and unwell, contemplates an end to the life-stage that Indians would call *grihastha* – householder. She begins mentally to shed a *grihastha*'s responsibilities. Indians would understand her as approaching the fourth and last stage of earthly life: that of *sannyasi*, who has earned the right to retire to a private peace. She has had enough of the complexities of personal relations, which never seemed to bring human beings into harmony. She gives up on them, and the impulse to withdraw to a world of her own seems 'itself a person' drawing her away from her preoccupations.[105] Her state of mind on the Marabar train suggests an explanation for her subsequent Indian canonisation as 'Esmiss Esmoor'. The *sannyasi* is revered, and Mrs Moore is the only one of the older English who behaves in a manner appropriate to her age and stage of life. Forster may not have done so intentionally, but with Mrs Moore's domestic and spiritual meta-morphosis he touched upon a theme that applied in both India and the West, a theme very old and established in India and gaining momentum in the West: a woman's right at a certain stage in life to declare her domestic responsibilities discharged in full.

Aziz, who cannot know what is passing in the women's minds because they courteously keep their distractions to themselves, falls into his favourite imaginative state, which springs from his own and not from an imported Western culture; he becomes a Moghul Em-peror dispensing courtesies and gifts. To the ladies, however, he is 'again the oriental guide whom they appreciated' at Fielding's tea-party, which is so partial an impression of the man.[106] Finally both Aziz and Adela fall victim to Mrs Turton's partial knowledge of India. She is on-the-spot but ignorant and has assured Adela that all Muslim men *insist* on the four wives allowed in Islamic law, so that Adela, her mind revolving among quandaries about Ronny, asks Aziz the catastrophic question about the number of his wives. It is the height of discourtesy to ask 'an educated Indian Moslem' such a question.[107] His emphasis is on 'educated', *Western*-style education, and the phrase carries all the conflicts in Aziz's self-image as a new Indian, for he cannot yet reconcile pride in Islam and pride in his education, but like Masood he does have a new self-image. He gives Adela a quick short answer and plunges into a cave for a minute alone in which to recover the courtesy that is natural to him, but the whole tragedy of his trial and its bitter consequences stems from that question and from his instinctively civilised effort to keep his confusion to himself and not embarrass his guest. A cultural encounter becomes a cultural collision and a courtroom drama that puts everyone's good intentions in the worst possible light.

Forster may have found the germ of the cave and the trial episodes in an actual incident that would have occurred while he was in India. A Miss Wildman, a nurse in Indian Government service, charged that she was drugged and robbed on an Indian Railways train. The documents in the case made their way from the Railways Board to the Viceroy, by which time she had withdrawn the charge.[108] Forster could not have seen those documents, but news of such an incident would travel in a hundred ways along the Civil Service grapevine. He simply followed such a charge to a logical conclusion. *Something* had terrified Miss Wildman, and *something* terrified Adela in the cave, although we get no explanation for either. Forster, weary of being asked what *really* happened in the cave, said ten years later, '*I don't know*.' He had used 'an unexplained muddle' as analogue for India as 'unexplainable muddle'. Perhaps, in hindsight, that was a fault in the novel's form.[109] However, there is no doubt about the speed and completeness with which an Englishwoman's real or imagined predicament could become the manipulatable property of a nervous bureaucracy. Adela's situation is almost worse than Miss Wildman's, for she is neither officially in nor yet entirely out of the Anglo-Indian community. Mrs McBryde, following her husband's line and abetted by the irresponsible and intrusive Miss Derek, manipulates Adela's situation so adroitly that no one, least of all Adela herself, knows how to break the cycle of 'hard common sense and hysteria' that has taken hold of her.[110] Adela's tragedy is that she comes out of her Indian interlude feeling that she has caused irreparable damage and that she is 'not fit for personal relationships'.[111] She sees Aziz only once again, from across the courtroom, and it is part of the tragedy of both that under the circumstances he cannot understand that a crucial battle rages between her desire to recon-

struct the precise truth and the determination of Chandrapore officialdom to make her its public demonstration of the condescending
chivalry that so efficiently threw up barriers between Englishwomen
and 'the real India'. Fielding does understand. He tries to explain to
Aziz what courage and integrity Adela had shown, even though she
knows that the Anglo-Indians have made her into a cause instead of
allowing her to be an individual, 'the entire British Raj pushing her
forward' toward a statement that would confirm its dire prophesies
about the dangers of friendship with Indians.[112] But Aziz has his own
kind of chivalry, which is emotional and cultural, not political, and
he reserves it for his memories of Mrs Moore, to whom as *sannyasi*
legalities and political appearances had become irrelevant. Then it
becomes Fielding's turn not to understand. When he says that Aziz
overdoes his emotions, Aziz counters, 'Am I a machine?'[113] He is
already withdrawing into his own real India. Fielding, for all his
goodwill, cannot follow. Aziz will now be more concentrated within
himself, more focused in his opinions, more cautious in friendship.
Consequently, he will have lost some of the charm that had made
him so attractive but also had made him so vulnerable. He is himself
a victim of the widening distance between twentieth-century India
and twentieth-century Britain. In the last analysis, everyone's troubles, personal, professional and Imperial, derive from flawed personal relations.

Aziz withdraws from British India both geographically and psychologically. At Godbole's suggestion he goes to the Hindu Princely
State of Mau, where professional demands are less rigorous. Godbole
is already there as Principal of a projected new high school. Forster
called this section 'Temple', and many readers and critics thought it
an anti-climax to the trial scene that ends 'Caves', the second section.
In 1957 Forster said that he had been told that the novel should have
ended with the trial, to which 'one can but bow and smile a little
wanly'.[114]

In fact, 'Temple' has crucial importance, and not only because of
the two religious sites. It turns the reader back to 'Mosque', the
opening section with its perfectly balanced pair of icons of the cultures of Hinduism and of Islam: the workable balance that is achieved
in 'Temple' between the Muslim Aziz and the Hindu Godbole. Those
icons are Godbole's song at Fielding's tea-party and Aziz's recitation
for his own friends of the poem by Ghalib. Forster's use of them
proves that it was possible, even with his informal and very personal
preparation, to grasp the essentials of Indian cultures.

First, Godbole's song. Fielding has intimated that the professor may perhaps sing for the tea-party guests. Instead, he puzzles everyone with his inconclusive explication of the Marabar Caves' significance. The party becomes a muddle of social signals sent, missed, extinguished. On the surface the conversation is 'light and friendly', but the disturbing 'underdrift' is Aziz's attempt to bait Godbole.[115] Then, when Ronny's rude entrance shatters the social charade of non-connection, Godbole suddenly sings his song that implies love as the imminent power of divine connection and completion. Thus the 'Mosque' section establishes the Hindu theme of the novel, and 'Temple' will fix it firmly in the *bhakti* or devotional tradition of Vaishnava Krishna-worship.

The term Vaishnava derives from Vishnu, one-third of the Hindu Trinity: Brahma (Creator), Siva (Destroyer and also Renewer), and Vishnu (Preserver). Hinduism offers *dharma* (duty), *yoga* (discipline), and *bhakti* (devotion) as ways to eventual union with the Divine and release from the bonds of mortality. Krishna himself preferred *bhakti*, and Vaishnavism sprang from a great devotional movement in centuries corresponding roughly to the European Renaissance, with even earlier roots in medieval popular movements that reacted against Brahmin monopoly in South India. But *bhakti* presents a paradox and a dilemma: release from earthly desires is both means and end. Release must not come through selfish ambition. That is the point of Godbole's song, which is a Vaishnava lyric of invocation. Krishna refuses to come until the suppliant understands that he has no monopoly on the god's attention. Then Godbole begs Krishna to multiply himself by one hundred and send the ninety and nine to others, and the remaining one to him, but the god still refuses. When Mrs Moore suggests that perhaps Krishna comes in some other song, Godbole replies with perfect equanimity that Krishna will not come. The idea of prayer so obstinately unanswered is disturbing to Fielding's other guests, who remain baffled, and 'only the servants understood it'.[116] Godbole's song, which contains a highly sophisticated theology, speaks only to the most unsophisticated persons present, which is satisfyingly consonant with its origins as a popular movement.

Forster did not incline very much to religious mysticism, but he found Krishna, the Preserver and eighth avatar of Vishnu, particularly congenial. During the First World War, Vishnu was a recurring motiv in his letters. While debating whether to join an ambulance unit in Italy, he told Malcolm Darling that he felt he might cope with the traumas of battlefields and hospital wards, if at the same time he were able again to be a creative writer, but 'when creation fails one starts thinking of Vishnu.'[117] When he finally went as a Red Cross searcher to interview the wounded in Alexandria hospitals he told Florence Barger, 'Preservation is my cry, I worship Vishnu.'[118] He simply wanted decency, loyalty, kindness, honesty, all the solid old virtues that coalesce as love.

The Vaishnava Krishna is he of the sixth-century _Bhagavad Purana_. Love is his keynote, and song is the heart of Krishna-_bhakti_. The Vaishnava poet speaks through a persona and identifies himself in the closing couplet. There is an established iconography: monsoon rains, peacocks, nightingales, flowers; blue as the colour of Krishna's skin, the result of his swallowing poisons that Kansa used to pollute the oceans; the sound of Krishna's flute or footsteps, fading as Radha wakes just too late to greet him; the jingling of her jewellery as she goes out into the night to find him. The whole vast complex of lyrics about the delays, progress, and meetings of the lovers became an allegory of the relation between God the Divine Friend and the soul, which waits, pines and grieves, and once in a very long while achieves a meeting all too brief. Vaishnavism belongs to the worldwide tradition of metaphorical religious mysticism.[119] Vaishnava themes, images, vocabulary pervade Indian literature, art and even everyday conversation. Forster was one of the more unusual English tourists at the time, in his ability to catch those nuances.

William G. Archer, in _The Loves of Krishna_, explains Krishna's dual character: 'Krishna is God, yet he is also man. Being a man, it is normally as a man that he is regarded. Yet from time to time particular individuals sense his Godhead and then he is no longer man but God himself. Even those, however, who view him as God do so only for brief periods.'[120] Krishna's round dance with the milkmaids explains Godbole's god who 'neglects' to come. Each passionately desires him as her lover, but vanity causes each to think that he is hers alone, so that he teaches them a lesson by leaving with one chosen girl. This in turn is the lesson of Godbole's plea for humility and generosity. The milkmaids seek Krishna until he relents and points out that he left in order to test their devotion. Thus Godbole's explanation: when he begs the god to come to him only, Krishna is deaf to calls that spring from selfishness and vanity.

Krishna's combination of gaiety and moral admonition lends itself to mime, which is how Forster first encountered Vaishnavism, at the court of the Maharaja of Chhatarpur in 1912. Both Forster and William

Rothenstein, who had preceded him at Chhatarpur in 1910, recognised at once the hieratic nature of the 'mystery play', as Rothenstein had called it, for he immediately recognised its similarities to medieval church plays and the parallels between the story of Krishna's birth and that of the birth of Christ. Forster described the cumulative effect of the drama, which combined music, dance, mime and ceremonial. The Hermit who suggested the Magi in the Christ story danced 'with elaborate and dignified little steps'. And there we have Godbole in the temple at Mau, leading the Vaishnava celebration of Krishna's nativity, 'clashing his cymbals, his little legs twinkling' as he dances alone or with groups of celebrants. This is Vaishnava *kirtan*, song and dance joined in an ecstasy of praise. Forster wrote in detail about the mystery play at Chhatarpur because he knew that he had seen 'something very uncommon'.[121] The attitude with which he and Rothenstein apprehended the event also was uncommon. Neither had an academic acquaintance with Vaishnava faith and practice, but they recognised a strain of Indian thought that few officials and even fewer tourists ever encountered. Both realised that they had been uniquely privileged, for the Maharaja brought his court players only before visitors who would receive them sympathetically.

Next, Aziz and his recitation of Ghalib's poem. Throughout the 'Mosque' section he ricochets from one social or political or professional group to another, always hoping for approval or affection. There are ten such encounters, and they resonate in Forster's Indian letters and diary. Aziz first appears with fellow Muslims who speak for three stages in the evolution of the modern Indian view of the English. Hamidullah reminisces about Cambridge at the turn of the century and before Indian students in larger numbers made them less welcome. He insists that friendship with Englishmen was possible then, because imperial machinery had not yet ground down their native kindliness. Mahmoud Ali still smarts from Ronny Heaslop's snubs. Aziz, youngest and most ebullient, can still shrug off the old controversy. While he is with his friends he does not care about trying to be friends with the English: 'Let us shut them out and be jolly.'[122] But that they cannot do. Almost at once Major Callendar summons him to an assignment that begins with Aziz's arriving late and finding that Callendar himself has taken the call, so that Aziz must deal with the Major's supercilious Hindu servant. It ends when Mrs Callendar and another memsahib comandeer Aziz's tonga. These ladies, shrilling an offensive pidgin English, are a repellent inversion of Mrs Moore, and his resentment flashes out at her when he stops to rest at the mosque. Her thoughtfulness deflates his anger, but this third encounter ends with a reminder that Indians are excluded from the Club.

Aziz's fourth and fifth encounters occur the following day. Callendar, mistrustful and antagonistic, calls him to account, but he knows – but cannot admit even to himself – that Aziz is the better surgeon and that patients are safer in his hands. Callendar storms away after a long and unworthy wrangle, but Aziz is armoured by the knowledge that he is 'competent and indispensable'.[123] Later that day, buoyed up by that confidence, Aziz cuts the Collector's ill-conceived Bridge Party and goes instead to the maidan on Hamidullah's polo pony to practice that game derived, like his own ancestors, from Central Asia. There he meets a stray British subaltern, and their skills with mallet and pony prove nicely complementary. They practice shots and then leave the maidan in mutual respect, each thinking, 'If only they were all like that.' (That subaltern, who later never imagines that the Indian polo player and Aziz the prisoner are one and the same, will betray him at the crisis meeting in the Club.)[124]

Aziz's sixth encounter is with his Hindu colleague, Dr Panna Lal, who leaves the Collector's Bridge Party in a foul mood and sees Aziz tap a wandering bull with his mallet in order to deflect it from a group of Muslims at prayer. Another unworthy wrangle ensues. Later in the day, 'breathing the prevalent miasma', Aziz becomes uncertain. Instead of thinking in terms of personal relations he begins to calculate balances of power.[125]

That frame of mind revives at Fielding's party, the seventh encounter, where Aziz tries to bait Godbole. But he is more subdued at his eighth encounter, with the Muslim Nawab Bahadur, his grandson and several hangers-on. Aziz observes, but only in a whisper, that Muslims must rid themselves of superstitions 'or India will never advance' – implying that Muslims share the responsibility for India's future.[126] Still, this humbled reflection is a kind of atonement for his conversational excesses at Fielding's party. He goes home and falls slightly, or more likely psychosomatically, ill.

The ninth encounter is the one most pertinent to the Hindu–Muslim theme. Muslim friends gather around Aziz's bed and gossip suspiciously about Godbole and Panna Lal. Aziz is the better physician: why was he not called instead of the Hindu Panna Lal? Aziz interprets the negative comments about Hindus as praise of Islam, falls into a beatific mood, and begins to recite an Urdu poem of a kind that Forster knew through Masood and his friends. It soothes whatever ruffled feelings Aziz and each of his friends has accumulated during the day. It reassures them 'that India was one; Moslem; always had been'.[127]

The poem is by Mirza Asadullah Khan, known as Ghalib, who was born in 1796 and died in 1869. His life spanned the period when English rule, which ended Moghul domination, and English education, which deprived Persian of its official status, became consolidated in India. Ghalib led a rather feckless life and his work fell short of its promise, but none of that matters to Aziz and his friends.[128] Ghalib's poems are their bittersweet symbol of Moghul ascendency and decline. Aziz is not yet a political creature. Causes that had become rallying cries for radically-minded Muslims – communal voting, autonomy for Aligarh - to Aziz are relevant but still remote. His own poems are elegaic, about 'the decay of Islam and the brevity of love'.[129] The political passion will come when he feels that English friends have betrayed him, but for the moment the poems are enough. Again, Forster has caught the nuances of a literary genre and a tradition whose influences reach to the most intimate levels of a culture.

Ghalib is most celebrated for the *ghazal*, or love lyric. Like the Vaishnava lyric it deals with romantic longings, separated lovers, happiness lost or delayed; and some of these also may be read as metaphors for the soul's search for union with the Divine Friend. Aziz's own poems imitate Ghalib's. For both, the romantic melancholy invokes the pathos of Muslim history in India. Ghalib, says Forster, belonged to the past along with Moghul greatness, and through his poems Aziz feels his kinship with all the Muslim countries, the 'sister kingdoms of the north,' the link that makes 'ridiculous Chandrapore' bearable.[130] For Aziz the message is that he is a stranger in a strange land, and it is important that *he* not appear ridiculous there. By the 1920s new Urdu poets like Muhammed Iqbal would take up new themes of Muslim identity and Muslim nationalism, but for the time being the *ghazal* speaks to Aziz's spiritual condition.

Thus song and poem, both standing as metaphors from deep in the pre-British past, introduce us to the pre-trial Aziz. That trial will jerk him violently into the political realities of the twentieth century, and belatedly his emotions of cultural solidarity will turn political. 'The Muhammadans', Morison wrote in 1899, 'are in some ways the most definite and homogeneous political unit in India; they are heirs of a common civilization and common traditions of glory, and they are conscious to an extent unsurpassed in India of their corporate existence.'[131]

When Forster returned to India in 1921 for a stay of six months at the Hindu Princely State of Dewas Senior, Masood had left the squalid Bankipore/Chandrapore to be Director of Public Education for Hyderabad State. His visit to Forster at Dewas was also his first to a Maratha court, and it became a delicate diplomatic encounter. Forster did not at first realise 'how dramatic the occasion was'. Dewas was muddled, medieval and relatively inconsequential. Although Hyderabad was a Princely State predominantly Hindu, it had a Muslim ruling family and participated in the outer world of political involvement. Muslims prided themselves on the fact that Moghul rule, once it had settled down in India, had set an example of administrative efficiency. The muddle at Dewas did not worry Forster, but to Masood it was 'an extreme example of his country's inefficiency'.[132]

Masood's visit to Dewas simply confirmed the cultural discomforts and uncertainties that Forster had already begun to weave into his Indian novel. When uncertainty threatens, as at Fielding's party, Aziz's habit is to snatch at bits of Moghul grandeur and fancied evidence of Moghul efficiency; he fantasises about the water in Fielding's pool supposedly flowing from the tank at the mosque. Forster lets him down gently, for 'no Emperor, however skilful,' can defy gravity, for the pool was well above the mosque.[133] When Aziz reassures his Muslim friends by reciting Ghalib's poem, he does not realise that he responds unconsciously to Godbole's song, which has its own aura of an even more ancient Indian history. Quite apart from arguments about whether Forster saw all of the real India, the inclusion of song and poem confirms his intuitive understanding of those histories. Both song and poem speak to the human condition, to 'our need for the Friend who never comes yet is not entirely disproved'.[134]

Aziz, Godbole and Fielding reassemble two years later at Mau, which as a princely state is right out of British India. Its setting and details derive from Forster's sojourn at Dewas as described in *The Hill of Devi*. At Mau Aziz's Persian poems and Godbole's *bhakti* exist in a spirit of live and let live. Aziz's poetic themes are elegaic, all about oriental womanhood and Islam's faded glories. But in the poem that the Hindu Godbole likes best, Aziz redefines Islam. He goes 'straight to internationality', and Godbole identifies that idea as true *bhakti*, wants to translate it into Hindi and even – mixing ancient and modern - into 'Sanskrit almost, it is so enlightened'.[135] Aziz finds Gokul Ashtami, the festival of Krishna's birth, its hubbub and Vaishnava *kirtan* irrelevant and rather boring, but all is relative, for when Fielding and his wife (who Aziz assumes to be Adela but is actually Mrs Moore's daughter Stella) insert themselves awkwardly into the ceremonies on the lake, Aziz finds that their ineptitude reminds him of the mishandling of human relations that has characterised both his personal and official relationships at Chandrapore, and he becomes pleasantly tolerant of the Gokul Ashtami celebrations with all their mess and muddle. English courtesies are fraudulent by comparison. 'This pose of "seeing India"' was only that: a counterfeit of friendship and of courtesy, and he had allowed it to seduce him.[136] Fielding and Aziz 'laughingly' resume the interrupted friendship, but the laughter is hollow.[137] The something that happened at the Marabar Caves had made everyone wary. The English had 'permanently frightened' Aziz, and Fielding has become official and now says that bad manners are not sufficient reason for doing away with the British Empire.[138] Thus he too is one of the novel's tragedies, for the distance between his mind and Ronny Heaslop's has narrowed.

At the same time, the distance between Fielding and Aziz has widened, for they have changed too fundamentally. They have confronted the Empire's most fundamental problem and, unfortunately, have retreated from it and from each other. They are frank at last in their new position, 'perhaps because they were going to part', and their last ride together turns into a political row. Fielding, who has lost his faith in courtesy, does what he never did at Chandrapore: he mocks and jeers at Aziz's flights of nationalist aspiration. Aziz's political emotions are not yet coherently organised, but he has hit upon the line that in the end will bring Muslims and Hindus together in the concerted effort that will make possible their independence from the British Raj: 'We may hate one another, but we hate you most . . . .' The last and greatest of the tragedies in *A Passage to India* is that reliance on hatred as the only key to a future in which Fielding and Aziz can be friends at last.[139]

Forster's dilemma, while he wrote his suburban novels, was that his 'copy' was all too close and enveloping. The 'Indian book' dealt with an environment that began to seem distant and unfamiliar as soon as he left it behind. Two sets of impressions jostled together in the memory, and those unmarked by a familiar kind of beauty faded first. This happened even before he left India. In the five days between seeing the Hindu and the Buddhist caves at Ellora and entering the description in his journal, memory had carried on its work of selection. The Buddhist caves with their figures of the Enlightened One were benign, but he found the Hindu caves threatening, satanic and altogether uncongenial, for 'I do not believe in the devil'.[140] Fielding experiences Forster's own sense of separation and selection as he travels westward, but when he reaches Venice he has a sense of completeness and homecoming. He greets the architecture and landscape of Venice with an appreciation that he knows he could never explain to his Indian friends, nor they understand, for 'the Mediterranean is the human form'.[141]

Then there was the actual form of the Indian book to be determined. At first he had thought of it as a description of travel, for that was what travellers to India usually wrote; library shelves were crowded with travelogues and Anglo-Indian memoirs. By the time he began to write, probably in July 1913, his own book had crossed over into fiction, and subject influenced tone. In a manuscript of the 1950s, Forster explained that although the general public read it as a political tract, since contemporary events had made it seem particularly timely, its real theme is that of Godbole's song and Ghalib's poem: the search for the everlasting Friend. *A Passage to India* is about 'the search of the human race for a more lasting home, . . . It is – or rather desires to be – philosophic and poetic.'[142] The fundamental truth of the book is that the politics of that time contaminated the sources of philosophy and poetry. One of the worst indictments is that in a political climate so invasive and interfering, an occupying government found it possible to use its system of education, once grounded with the best of intentions in English literature, that treasure-house of philosophy and poetry, to manipulate Indians to make them 'behave nicely'. The same political limitation and the resulting wariness curtailed the possibilities of friendship, if it did not wreck them outright. By including Godbole's song and Aziz's recitation of Ghalib's poem, Forster declared the existence, despite politics, of that 'something wider'. Philosophy and poetry were alive, but unfortunately, in the atmosphere of hatred and suspicion, they had gone underground.

In 1913, however, his emotions about India had been still unsettled. He had had experiences that never came to the tourists who made the rounds of the standard sights and sailed away feeling that they had seen the real India, but when he looked back from the 1950s he realised how much pain had been mixed with the pleasure. His impression, then and later, was that he had been accompanied all the way by 'the sense of racial tension, of incompatibility . . . '[143] If he were to be honest about that experience, and if he were to fulfil Masood's desire that he write a book about India, that darker side must be a part of it. He had drafted a few chapters after he returned to England, then had laid them aside. This hiatus was disturbing because at least two fragments of novels were already on the shelf. One was 'Nottingham Lace', about which he had confided his doubts to Dickinson in 1901. Another was 'Arctic Summer', which he began in 1911; it concerns young Englishmen in Italy and the concept of gentlemanly behaviour. It is not an early *Room with a View*, for it implies problems of sexuality more deeply buried than Forster felt able to explore at the time. Just before he left for India he put 'Arctic Summer' on the shelf, where it stayed until 1980.[144] His dissatisfactions with the state of his literary life only increased when the Indian novel too became stalled, but later in 1913 those lightened somewhat when he paid a visit to Edward Carpenter, and Carpenter's friend and lover George Merrill touched Forster affectionately, a moment that he remembered as a psychological epiphany: Merrill's touch had entered 'my ideas, without involving my thoughts'.[145] A draft of the novel *Maurice* was the result, an exploration of a homosexual relationship. In one way it was a release, in another a major frustration, for it too had to go onto the shelf, not only because he was dissatisfied with it, but also because the practice of homosexuality was still a criminal offence, and there was no possibility of publication in the foreseeable future.

World events then took charge of everyone's lives, Forster's included, in the form of the First World War. It sent him to Egypt for service as a Red Cross 'searcher', to interview wounded soldiers and compile information about others dead or missing. Islamic Egypt was in that respect a familiar environment, but he liked Egypt less than he had India. He made some 'copy' out of Egyptian history for articles and reviews, but like everyone else he could only slog along through the war years. Then, however, he met Mohammed el Adl, a young tram conductor. He was an attractive personality characterised by simplicity, gravity and great courtesy. He and Forster became lovers, and Forster realised what it was that he had been trying to say in *Maurice*. 'My luck has been amazing', he wrote to Florence

Barger, to whom, day by day, he confided the history of this friendship.[146] At the war's end, Mohammed had married. A grateful Forster saw him comfortably settled, then returned to England and the problem of what to do with his life: more particularly, what to do about the Indian novel.

India came violently to the world's attention with the event in the Punjab city of Amritsar that became known as the Amritsar Massacre. On 13 April 1919 General Reginald Dyer ordered troops to fire without warning into an unarmed crowd of several thousands, women and children among them, as they listened to speeches in a confined area called Jallianwalla Bagh. The firing continued for ten or fifteen minutes, at the end of which 200 were dead and some 1200 wounded. The massacre set unquenchable flash-fires of hatred, bitterness and suspicions of conspiracy on both sides. It was the climax of many festering resentments. The Rowlatt Acts of 1918, which gave Government permanent powers to crush suspected seditionists, had set off storms of protest throughout India, and Amritsar was the spark to the powder-keg.[147] It determined the direction of Gandhi's non-cooperation movement, and the Indian National Congress closed ranks behind him. Edwin Montagu, now himself Secretary of State for India, found himself virtually alone in Parliament in his public condemnations of Dyer's action and the humiliating penalties imposed on Amritsar Indians. For many months Montagu was pilloried in the Commons for being too friendly with Indians, most especially with Gandhi. One Member said that if Montagu 'is Mr. Gandhi's friend he has no right to be Secretary of State for India.'[148] He was never to become Viceroy, an appointment that he wanted more than any other. He was censured, his political career was ended, and we cannot know what he might have thought of *A Passage to India*, for he died in 1924, lonely, embittered and greatly mourned in India.

Amritsar and its consequences upset Forster profoundly. The Indian novel might become a kind of sympathetic atonement – but he could not finish it. He took the drafted chapters with him when he returned to India in 1921 at an invitation to be private secretary to the Hindu Maharaja of the Princely State of Dewas Senior. Some of Forster's friends thought the idea of his being anyone's secretary more than a little amusing, but his duties turned out to be few and perfunctory. Dewas Senior was something of a comic-opera state, but Forster developed both fondness and great respect for its Maharaja, to whom he referred ever afterward as Bapu Sahib: roughly, 'respected parent'. However, being in India again did not help the Indian novel forward in 1921. Six months later he brought the chapters home in much the same state as when he had left. Thus they remained until Leonard Woolf took him and them in hand. Leonard's experience as an administrator in Ceylon had enabled him to know the eastern Empire from the inside, and he saw that Forster had something both important and salutary to say about it.[149] Part of his difficulty came from the fact that his attitude toward India had changed subtly. To some extent he blamed himself for falling out of touch with his own sense of that country, and there is a touch of imperial mission in his feeling that he had a responsibility to 'call out the best from an Oriental, real or imaginary.'[150] In any case, his more sombre view provided a psychological distancing that he needed in order to write to the end. When he finally finished it and he began to feel that the work and the worry were really finished, 'I think it good.'[151] It came out in June 1924. In September he told Darling that although personal relations 'still seem to me the most real things on the surface of the earth', he had learned something about their successful conduct. Friends, to remain friends in the most rewarding way, 'must go away from each other (spiritually) every now and then, and improve themselves'. This was the moral at the end of *A Passage to India*. What happened next, he could not yet say, perhaps would never be able to say, but he understood that the concept of 'the multiplied Krishna' had shown him how 'loneliness and intimacy . . . might be combined. The King's [College] view over-simplified people: . . . We are more complicated, also richer, than it knew, and affection grows more difficult than it used to, and also more glorious.'[152]

4

The BBC Broadcasts

It would have been expecting too much for critics to agree about a novel as complex and as close to the Imperial bone as *A Passage to India* was in 1924. Forster understood Muslims and misunderstood Hindus. He understood Hindus but misunderstood Muslims. He was drastically unfair to Anglo-Indians. Or, he had skilfully balanced their devotion to duty against their shortcomings. Or, he was scrupulously fair to both Anglo-Indians and Indians. There is a good deal about 'the Indian mind' and India's eternal mysteries. The Indians in the novel were 'children of Nature', or they were 'all miserable creatures', or they were 'neither primitive nor uneducated'. The novel left one with 'a sense of disappointment' because it was difficult to know 'what it is about; . . . all the details are good but the ensemble is fuzzy, or wuzzy.' Or, on the other hand, there is 'no silliness, no lapse, no wobbling.'[1]

Individual characters attracted the same kind of contradictions. Adela is 'rather stupid', without real 'capacity for sight'; or she is 'an achievement . . . a queer, unattractive, civilised, logical, intellectually honest girl.'[2] Mrs Moore's 'mystical apprehension is finely conceived'. Or she is 'sinister, obscure, horrible'.[3] Godbole is generally baffling; Forster's notion of his Hinduism is called 'purely fanciful', and Gokul Ashtami is the 'only feeble part of the novel', or it is 'a virtuoso passage of the finest'.[4] Aziz is condescended to as 'a simple-minded, almost childish person' but also a 'very decent little fellow'.[5] Or he is 'the victim of an hysterical woman and an equally hysterical society' and also 'the hero of the story'.[6] E. A. Horne, an experienced Anglo-Indian in the Educational Service, wrote from Patna – whose suburb Bankipore was Forster's Chandrapore – to chide him for telling too little about Aziz: '("Touched by Western feeling" is the most that we are told on the subject.)' But Horne, with fourteen years of service in India, cannot tell more. He can '"place"' the Cambridge-educated Hamidullah; he cannot place Aziz and is 'left groping'.[7]

None of the reviews included in the Critical Heritage anthology gives Fielding concentrated attention. He is the 'liberal Englishman, eccentric in India', or 'the unconventional Anglo-Indian schoolmaster' with 'pro-Indian proclivities' and therefore not pukka.[8] There are passing references to the Indian 'educated classes', and the novel is a 'finished study of the psychology of Educated India'.[9] It deals with 'transmission of ideas . . . between one race and another' that has resulted in 'a smattering of Occidental science upon Oriental metaphysics'.[10] But few enquire further into that psychology or ask what ideas were transmitted, or what they had done to or for Aziz and the other Indians. Aziz is only the 'Europeanised Oriental, drifting, emotional'.[11] 'An Indian' who signed his review 'A.S.B.' made one of the few specific comments on the kinds of Western ideas transmitted from race to race and on the conditions of transfer: 'For who would not sympathize with the . . . fervent educationist who is busy devising pedagogic methods in order to inculcate a taste for Milton and Shelley amongst a people who he is certain would be immensely the better for it?'[12]

A few critics noted anachronisms, such as allowing the Superintendent of Police instead of a Government Prosecutor to conduct Aziz's trial; and the use of 'Burra Sahib' (head man) as a form of address from the Anglo-Indians to the Collector.[13] Forster made a few such corrections after the first edition, but in general he put the novel behind him. He had had his say on India in novel form. But he felt for a time at loose ends. 'I have no faith in my instincts after forty, though much in my increasing idleness', he told Malcolm Darling after he had turned down an appeal to return to Dewas, which would involve him in a palace crisis.[14] His attitude toward India had changed even more during the writing of *Passage*; it was harder-edged (but not harsher) and less romantic. He now knew that the problems of British–Indian relations were more intractable than he had imagined. He told Masood that he no longer thought of his book as 'a little bridge of sympathy between East and West, . . . I am not interested whether they sympathise with one another or not.'[15] He did not mean that he did not care. He meant that he saw no further way to treat the subject as fiction; his caring would, in future, be expressed journalistically. Certainly the aftermath of the war was not a good time for Anglo-Indian friendships, not because friends could not rely on one another, but because irresistible political forces drove them apart. As the rocks seem to rise up at the end of *Passage* to force Fielding and Aziz to pass them in single file instead of side by side, even then the issue was whether Britain and India would proceed together or singly into the future.[16]

A feeling of being emotionally unsettled coincided with the completion and publication of the novel. Mohammed el Adl died in May 1922. Forster's feeling of bereavement was only a little mitigated by the knowledge that his money had made Mohammed's last months of life more comfortable. Then in April 1924 Forster's Aunt Laura Forster died, so that he felt unable to take full pleasure in the publication of *Passage*. She left him her house, West Hackhurst at Abinger Hammer near Dorking, Surrey. His architect father had built it for her, and this brought a flood of emotions and some practical problems similar to those at Rooksnest. Forster told his Irish friend, the novelist Forrest Reid, that the house had 'no gas, no electric light, no hot water, no main-drainage. Close to a station but no trains, when you get to it.' Ought they to take on so many problems? The stresses of sudden decision-making were hard on both of them, but Mrs Forster wanted West Hackhurst because, in addition to having lovely surroundings, 'the house was built by my father . . . '[17]

As at Rooksnest, indecision siezed her. She wanted to keep both West Hackhurst and the Weybridge house and talked of 'retiring' at Weybridge while Forster settled by himself at West Hackhurst, 'but of course nothing of the sort will happen'.[18] He even considered disposing of West Hackhurst at once. At last he delivered an ultimatum and set a deadline of two weeks; by then she must decide. Just at that time he had to pay £400 in death duties on his aunt's estate, a daunting sum but in a way the timing was fortunate, for his mother became conscience-stricken about the extra expense of keeping on two houses. It was actually 'the thought of action' that upset her.[19] At the beginning of 1925 she was still 'upset and upsetting', and everything was at sixes and sevens, but the move to West Hackhurst began. Forster exclaimed to Joe Ackerley, 'Philosophy! hither, hither, thou legless & aimless deity.'[20]

There were less tangible concerns. He told Florence Barger that he still did not know how he ought to regard the fame and the money that had followed *Howards End*. They made him uneasy, although he still insisted that 'I am not an ascetic'. The details of life at home did not make for a rewarding existence, 'and there is no one to fill it emotionally.'[21] New friendships helped to some extent. Among them were T. E. Lawrence; the South African journalist and novelist William Plomer; Joe Ackerley, who had begun a career with the BBC as a Talks Producer and would become Literary Editor of *The Listener*; and Charles Mauron, whom Forster's French publisher had engaged to translate *Passage*. That last stirred anew Forster's worries about the effects of money on friendship. He considered both Mauron and his wife 'a great find' but wished that the business element did not enter in, even though no money changed hands between them, for he was 'terrified at it overgrowing the affection'.[22]

By the end of 1925 the Forsters had settled finally at West Hackhurst, where Morgan discovered that suburban property developers – as at Rooksnest twenty years later – hovered nearby. He forestalled them by buying Piney Copse, the freehold adjoining wood. The purchase stirred up a round of ironic reflections on Suburbia and the psychology of property-owning, which he described for Malcolm Darling with amused objectivity. He found himself as possessive, as boundary-conscious as any suburbanite who had for the first time acquired a piece of property by purchase. He had all 'the emotions of property, and very amusing they are. I hear a stick crack and dash out of the house trembling with rage, as I think someone is spoiling My wood'. But the intruder is only a bird, with a very natural absence of scruples about boundaries and property rights. These sentiments almost verbatim went into his essay 'My Wood, or the Effects of Property upon Character'.[23]

In fact he had long had a somewhat druidic attachment to woods, trees, groves and copses, and, like the dell on the Madingley Road in *The Longest Journey*, he used them as settings in his fiction. After one tree-planting he described himself to Malcolm Darling as 'an intellectual writer who has no faith in the future of civilisation, kneeling in mud and squashed fern roots while he carefully spreads the fibres of a one and six-penny tree which mayn't be as tall as him until he's dead'. Many people had doubts about the future, and now it seemed that few planted trees as small as his, 'a sign of the times, and a sad one.'[24]

The plentiful sad signs of the 1930s made him pay more attention to things that last and to the feeling that he himself was not among them. By the 1930s, the prospect of old age, his failure to produce more novels, and 'the death of trees' became increasingly interconnected in his thinking. Between himself and trees there existed a moral reciprocity, and he suffered pangs of guilt if he betrayed it. He confessed in his *Commonplace Book* the chagrin he felt because he had cut for fuel an oak that might have lived decades longer, 'the oldest living thing I have ever owned, . . . Yet my crime was a young man's'.[25]

Worries about himself expanded to include doubts about the nature of civilisation, which 'except when it develops the heart & the mind – does seem so useless'.[26] By the 1930s, says Furbank, Forster was 'now convinced that he would write no more novels, [and] felt the urge to exert himself more on the public scene'.[27] About that time, an opportunity of considerable importance presented itself in the form of the British Broadcasting Corporation.

The BBC was born in 1922, just after Forster returned from Dewas, as an association of businessmen interested in wireless communication and development of the necessary equipment. By 1928, when Forster broadcast his first talk, radio was well on its way to being an essential part of both public and private life. Asa Briggs, historian of the BBC, says that in its first four years, from 1922 to 1926, 'something happened both to British society and to British government. Broadcasting itself ceased to be a toy, . . . it became an institution. It affected people's ways of thinking and feeling, and their relations with each other. No history of the BBC – not even a history of the Company – can be a business history alone.'[28]

On 16 July 1928, Forster broadcast a talk with the title 'Of Railway Bridges'. He did not think that he had distinguished himself. However, the eccentricities of early microphones and accoustics did not affect his delivery. Jean Rowntree, who produced many of his talks, recalls that he was 'a natural broadcaster, who combined the rhythms of informal speech with a pattern of thought that made them easy to remember. His actual voice was against him, as it was rather high and easily became squeaky; but the substance of his broadcasts was so good that it did them no harm. Listeners used to say that you went on thinking as soon as he had stopped talking.'[29] Forster described for Darling his first performance:

> 'What a flow of language!' writes the village schoolmistress to my mother, but the general feeling, with which I agree, was that I didn't do it well – and yet everything's organised to the nines, your artless cries written out and typed beforehand, exquisite young men in dress clothes bending over you or flitting over the felt carpet.[30]

He calls this 'a rag-tag letter', but it is important. It suggests that, although he would soon begin to see broadcasting as a platform from which to speak out on his convictions about Culture, his broadcasting career began as a stopgap to time that he did not know how to fill. He told Darling that he was 'rather casting about for decent work to do. I am afraid that anything first class in me is now dried up.' His life was so comfortable, on the surface 'so civilised; yet perhaps for want of faith in civilisation itself – a faith I lost during 1914–18, if ever I had it – I cannot turn the life I lead into creative literature. Decent work rather presents itself as an alternative.'[31]

THE BRITISH BROADCASTING CORPORATION

'Of Railway Bridges' set Forster to thinking about the connections between wireless broadcasting and civilisation. 'Wireless etc. abolishes wavings of handkerchiefs etc. Death the only farewell surviving.' Human relationships would be compressed by the new technology. What then becomes of our control over that essential going away from each other, the sense of distance between ourselves and others, the privacy and solitude that are essential balances to successful personal relations? A relentless proximity will give rise to barriers of other kinds than geographical distance. 'Opposed to wireless etc. are passports etc.'[32] True, the wireless can be turned off at will, but it creates a new set of cultural common denominators. Unless one were to become a hermit, there would be no escaping them.

In structure and in spirit the BBC was the creation not of its businessmen originators but of J.W.C. Reith, the Scots engineer who became the Company's Managing Director, then was Director General when the Company became a Corporation. He was totally dedicated to the work and expected the same from his staff, and the early BBC was an operation run on improvisation, ingenuity, enthusiasm, and overwork. Reith had the Scotsman's drive for education and self-advancement. He distinguished between schools programmes specifically designed as 'educational' and 'the educative influence, potential or actual', which was more difficult to classify because it blended with the audience for entertainment.[33]

If the BBC was to win and keep audiences it must be interesting. Being interesting often caused controversy, and the 1927 licence to broadcast commanded avoidance of '"statements expressing the opinion of the Corporation on matters of public policy"' and from '"speeches or lectures containing statements on topics of political, religious or industrial controversy".'[34] Reith protested, arguing that 'a halting, inconclusive and even platitudinous manner . . . involves the neglect of many opportunities in forming public opinion in matters of vital importance.'[35] The ban on 'editorialising' remained, and it fell with particular weight on the new Talks Section. For six crucial years Hilda Matheson was its Head. Her view of the function of the talk 'left a very powerful imprint on the BBC'. She 'saw that the Talk – it began to get a capital letter – offered a very special opportunity in broadcasting.'[36] It was 'rediscovering the spoken language,' she wrote, 'the impermanent but living tongue, as distinct from the permanent but silent print.' The trick was to 'avoid the pitfalls of impromptu speech and yet retain its atmosphere.'[37] The constrictions that bothered Forster during his first broadcast gradually relaxed to fit individual temperaments and styles of delivery. He submitted carefully crafted scripts but often asked permission to broadcast without rehearsal, which he felt diminished his chances to sound spontaneous. He also disliked recording: 'I like talking live much better because it keeps me alive.'[38] George Orwell, his producer at the time, advised John Arlott, who was a producer before he became the BBC's great authority on cricket, 'Forster is no work at all, but don't try to change him.'[39]

He did not broadcast again until February 1930. In the meantime his influence filtered into the Talks Section by way of Joe Ackerley. One of Ackerley's first ideas was a series on Indian arts. Forster said that he himself was 'too much out of touch with India' to take on the assignment, but he suggested others to assist and cautioned against the kinds of cultural references that could easily tumble over into political controversy. He reminded Ackerley of the connections between Indian music and the traditional dance that many in the West thought unacceptably erotic, and it was not helped by the fact that, also traditionally, prostitutes were its exponents. Indian public opinion generally forbade it for respectable girls. Ackerley's adviser's point of view on these points would be all-important. The least suggestion of sniggering condescension would be fatal. At the same time Ackerley must 'keep it free of uplift – it is the constant intrusion of higher matter that makes the peninsula such a crashing bore. Allow no Englishman to talk about his country's duties and no Indian to mention his country's hopes.'[40]

Life in Talks in the early years was a daily scramble. Lionel Fielden, who joined in 1927, remembered that 'we had one aim and one aim only – to find Voices to fill the Hours. If they were distinguished Voices, saying what we thought should be said, so much the better: but if not, programmes had to be invented to support poor voices. The first objective was to avoid silence.' This was not always easy, for there were 'no financial carrots to dangle, and many distinguished people fought shy of risking their reputation on the unfamiliar microphone'. With special gratitude he remembers 'best the trinity of E. M. Forster, Desmond MacCarthy and H. G. Wells, who all gave us freely of their time and wise counsels'.[41]

Miss Matheson worried less than did Reith about conflict between entertainment and education in broadcasting. If no one had yet defined the 'educative influence' that Reith wanted to encourage, neither had anyone yet defined 'entertainment value'. So far as she was concerned, it was useless 'deciding what people ought to learn without at the same time considering how it may be made interesting – without, in fact, an unremitting study of human psychology'.[42] She envisioned a number of audiences: children, adults and the rank and file of the labour movement, certainly its leaders, who knew from hard experience the handicaps 'imposed by an education which ceased at fourteen or younger'.[43] The BBC could serve that audience, or it could 'with such fatal ease encourage the native laziness of the human race'.[44] Her definition of education pleased Forster more than Reith's, which he thought limited and dangerously puritanical. The really splendid opportunity belonged to the BBC, and Miss Matheson's concern for a more democratic approach to radio audiences spoke directly to his long interest in the Working Men's College.

What was clear was that, willy-nilly, broadcasters were educators, but if they fell into a lecturing tone of voice, wouldn't they lose a voluntary audience? Forster sometimes thought educators their own worst enemies, for he could not escape the thought that '*education* must have a bad effect upon the educator'. Was education a help or a hindrance to creative work? And did he fool himself into thinking that as an educational broadcaster he would improve the public mind and contribute to the sum total of Culture? 'We creatives are never sincere here and always imply that good work corrects public abuses – at all events ultimately.'[45] But 'ultimately' could be too late.

Miss Matheson's was the kind of supervision that Forster appreciated. Fielden wrote that she was 'never preoccupied by power, never lectured, never laid down the law: she ran her department on a loose rein, encouraging, helping, sympathising, and yet keeping herself firmly in the saddle. She was in the saddle because she was usually right.'[46] But Reith did not think that Miss Matheson was usually right. Fielden's analysis was that for all his enormous abilities and virtues, Reith's 'presbyterian cast of mind is not wholly at ease in the artistic world' so that 'his influence did tend to hold the BBC back

from all things provocative, or even bold.' He 'sent sharp little notes
to Hilda suggesting that so-and-so held eccentric or subversive or
atheistic or anarchistic views and was not a suitable person for the
microphone.'[47] Reith, who had once defended the rightness and
necessity of controversy, now wished to vet the controversialists,
and Miss Matheson resigned in 1931. Briggs says that Reith was
'very glad indeed, however, to see Miss Matheson go.'[48]

Her replacement was Charles Siepmann, who came from the Adult
Education Section in 1927 and became Director of Talks in 1932.
Forster feared that he represented education institutionalised instead of a broader, more comprehensive education for Culture. After
a talk over lunch, Forster decided that Siepmann was 'a dark horse,
and prone to that division between creative and uncreative careers
which I have learnt to dread . . . .'[49] The 'uncreatives' merely accumulated knowledge for the sake of accumulating, which led to cram-
ming and examination-worship of the kind that blighted education
in India. That approach, as Forster had warned Mrs Barger on behalf
of her son Harold, kills the ability to connect facts with ideas; and he
kept to his dire opinion that another friend's son was the victim of
her supposedly progressive theories, which 'almost looks like Nature's revenge on her . . . I write as a retrograde'.[50] Retrograde he
remained, and if his BBC editors and producers occasionally thought
him a bit stubborn and old-fashioned, they recognised also that he
attracted and kept an educated audience that might be a minority
but had significant influence on public policy.

In Talks, empathy between speaker and producer was crucial.
Perhaps the ascendance of Charles Siepmann had something to do
with a Forster diary note in 1934, that his skills as speaker had
declined, and that he now felt himself to be 'no creator. But [I am] a
good journalist'.[51] Not only the mechanics of broadcasting but the
atmosphere inside the BBC began to bother Forster as it bothered
Fielden; they saw it becoming less flexible as it grew larger and more
institutionalised. The BBC, 'with its growing influence, was coming
under fire from all sides for suspected favouritism of one kind or
another: too Tory, too Labour, too Red, too Reactionary, too many
symphony concerts or too few, too many talks or not enough, nep-
otism on the staff, bad coverage: any old stick would do to beat this
huge Aunt Sally.'[52]

Forster was happier when George Barnes, who had been a Talks
Producer since 1935, became Talks Director in 1941. Barnes too was
a King's College man, which sweetened Forster's association with

him. He too wanted education to be much more than Reith's instrument with which 'to build up knowledge, experience and character'. Forster respected Barnes's care for the technical details of broadcasting and his strictness about scripts and timing. Jean Rowntree, who assisted Barnes, recalls that when Forster finished a broadcast he would ask, had he done well enough? Had he been convincing? She suspected that some academic speakers thought Forster's method and diction, partly developed for the Working Men's College and largely the product of his temperament and writing technique, were a come-down.[53] However, he was content to let academics talk to one another as much as they wished. In effect, he had already served notice that he intended to continue at the BBC along his accustomed lines, when he delivered the prestigious Clark Lectures at Cambridge in 1927. They became *Aspects of the Novel*, his analysis of novelists' methods and readers' responses, which has been quoted ever since then by earnest academics and literary critics. Eighteen years later he adapted some of that lecture material for a BBC talk on 'The Art of Fiction'. It has the same easy colloquial, conversational tone. The text is bright with the same characteristically unexpected turns of phrase and imagery, and imaginary but typical voices speak up for this or that attitude toward the novel as story or prophecy or fantasy. He neither talked up to the Cambridge audience, nor down to his radio audience.[54]

Forster and Barnes both regarded broadcasting as 'the sower'. The function of a broadcast talk was 'to communicate ideas/stimulate their circulation/report experience/describe what men think and feel'.[55] In this spirit, Forster carried on with his book talks, and his convictions about their importance were sharpened by the knowledge that on the Continent an evil censorship was condemning books to be burned. He talked about books about ideas, and he talked about ideas about books. Inside and outside the BBC, he was following the line that he had laid down for himself in 1928, that year of his first broadcast. He had appeared for the defence at the trial for obscenity of Radclyffe Hall's lesbian novel, *The Well of Loneliness*. That effort 'had given him his line. From now on he would often be heard on the censorship issue, and, by extension from this, on civil liberties generally'.[56]

In 1934, although he was anything but a joiner he became President of the National Council for Civil Liberties. It was not a good year for civil liberties. An Incitement to Disaffection Bill, otherwise known as the Sedition Bill, was aimed at Communists and made it an offence to own or to distribute literature 'liable to seduce soldiers or sailors from their duty or allegiance'. Enforcement would be awkward. What if a soldier or sailor interpreted passages of the Bible as incitement to pacifism? The Bill became law in November, but the Council's protests had helped to dilute it so that it became virtually unenforceable. Forster saw no reason to gloat. He had addressed a large meeting in the Central Hall Westminster but 'the wireless and press scarcely noticed us, they want opposition stifled. . . . enthusiasm – and then silence.'[57] As a personal protest he sold off his holdings in Imperial Chemicals, which manufactured poison gas. He knew that that was not all there was to it. However much he wanted to 'wash my hands in innocence', it was useless to try to play Pilate. 'There's nowhere to wash.'[58]

The Sedition Bill, a nasty straw in an ominous wind, connected uncomfortably with BBC nervousness about controversial topics and speakers. Even if libel insurance were practicable, lawyers would have to pass the manuscripts. Words and phrases would fall out of context, for a lawyer would necessarily be cautious: 'he would never have passed Bleak House e.g.' Forster blamed the official timidity on both the libel laws and a lack of regard for English literature, which is 'an important matter, not to say a national asset'.[59] The dismal prospect was that authors too would become timid, and for future generations there would be fewer and fewer books like *Bleak House*. His argument that literature is a national asset is the line that he continued to take throughout his work and personal associations with the BBC.

Therefore Forster's book talks, which comprise the great majority of his 131 broadcasts, took the line of appreciation and, when necessary, the defence of English literature as a national asset. A 1937 talk that introduced a series for sixth-form students is an excellent example of his method: the talk is educational, to be sure, but he will establish connections from the factual to the creative. He promises the sixth-formers that he will not talk over their heads, that he understands and even shares some of their misgivings about his subject. So he begins with facts, then employs guileless-sounding understatement to persuade toward the ideas that he wants his listeners to remember. He says, quite simply, 'I am going to talk about books.' Books are not the only or the most important things in the world, but he will talk about them because that is the subject that he knows best. He will not prescribe a reading list, but is it not worth considering why books have been around for some 3000 years?

Books are 'an old and well established institution', and he has three reasons for these students' not only becoming readers, but also for reading in the right way. First, if the facts are wrong a book is worthless, whether it is a railway timetable or a biography of Gladstone. Facts are useful. We come to grief without facts.

But facts are not enough. Is *Macbeth* useful? There is historical fact in its background, and we know some facts about Shakespeare, but *Macbeth* deserves study because it is a new creation, and not only new but unique because Shakespeare's mind was uniquely creative. Such a book 'is good because it seems itself to be alive'. It is *imaginative* literature. He makes a long leap forward, to Arnold Bennett, who, in *The Old Wives' Tale*, had re-created for us Victorian lives of a kind increasingly remote. Then Forster makes a sharp turn toward T. S. Eliot and 'The Wasteland', which stirs imagination and should stir a questioning attitude that makes us examine the world 'as it seems to have become'. Forster likes this kind of imaginative writing 'better than any, and if I didn't I should not have taken up literature as a job, or talked this afternoon'.

Third, one reads because one needs help. The world has become more dangerous. Can books help us to survive in such a world? Not if they are confusing instead of useful. Forster cites Samuel Butler's *Erewhon* as a useful book, which he says woke him up early in the century, for reading it had made him feel as if he had 'touched something alive'. Indeed he had. That something was 'Samuel Butler's mind'. His final word to the student audience is that from whatever they read they demand first, accuracy, and second, imaginative creativity. He could promise that the two together would 'wake you up and strengthen you'.[60]

His advice presupposed freedom to range freely among ideas. The dangerous new world had added one more impediment to freedom of speech and thought: a Ministry of Information, outlined provisionally as early as 1935. By 1939, when Lionel Fielden was considering appointment to the BBC, he was informed that that Ministry *'shall have close and constant contact with the BBC, who will remain constitutionally independent, but will naturally act under Government instructions . . . so far as may be necessary, in matters that concern the national interest and the conduct of the war'*.[61] Fielden's response was profound scepticism. Forster understood that it was difficult in wartime to draw a clear line between propaganda and information, but he felt extreme discomfort. On 5 October 1939, when the Anglo-French declaration of war against Hitler was exactly one month old, he set forth his position in a letter to Mrs Robert Trevelyan, who seems to have raised the pros and cons of trying to come to some kind of understanding with Hitler. Forster saw no advantage at all. He was certain that any accommodation with him now would gain no more than a little breathing-space that he would use to prepare for total war and the destruction or theft of every Briton's possessions, and worse, the end of individual freedom under law. For Forster, worldly goods 'don't spiritually matter, anyhow to me'. It was true that the British Government in its present dire anxieties was multiplying the restrictions on its own citizens, but Hitler's restrictions were infinitely worse. The spectacle of crowds of refugees fleeing the Continent, 'which is always before me', dispelled any idea that Hitler intended anything other than a totalitarian Britain.[62]

His own anxieties intensified as the war continued. He resisted intimidation, for he saw that the censorship he abhorred would be the outcome, no matter how benign the Ministry's intentions. Authors could not always know why their scripts were refused. J. B. Priestley complained vigorously to Barnes after his informal and enormously popular 'Sunday Postscripts' were terminated. He realised that 'you no longer have much of a free hand'. Still:

> What is wrong is that most of your people in authority are not creative-minded radio enthusiasts but administrators who wish first and last to avoid trouble. They would thus always prefer a mediocre contribution that aroused no antagonism to a first-class one that aroused enthusiasm but also some opposition. . . . And all this is very undemocratic. There can be no doubt that when my postscripts were cut short the M[inistry] o[f] I[information] and your people deliberately went against the wishes of the vast majority of the people of this country, thousands and thousands and thousands of whom have written and spoken to me about it, always with suspicion of the government, for they knew this was a most undemocratic move.[63]

From the very beginning of the war, the Society of Authors had been concerned about all of war's effects on writers. Denys Kilham Roberts, its Secretary, asked Forster to suggest ways to keep the public's attention on books and their importance.[64] Forster volunteered to suggest to the BBC, among other measures, the resumption of the weekly book programmes 'which it supplied some years ago'.

(That he deleted the word 'offered' and substituted 'supplied' is in itself a comment on wartime climate, for Talks thought of its programmes as *offerings*, not *supplies* sent on order.) He wanted two reviewers, 'one of the extrovert the other of the introvert type', who would broadcast in stints of three or six months, then would be replaced by others of the same general types.[65] He knew that the BBC would not be keen about making such an arrangement; for one thing, it would require additional negotiating and arranging at a time when staff were already overburdened. For another, the censors would have to adjust at regular intervals to new sets of ideas. However, Forster pleaded on grounds of 'the desperate situation of contemporary culture'. The BBC was created to educate and inspire as well as to communicate, and its facilities were 'ready to our hand'.[66] If more air time for books could not be obtained through Barnes, Forster was prepared to go higher in the chain of BBC command.

Nevertheless he continued to press Barnes, who he thought put too much faith in Audience Research and Listener Panels – in which Forster had very little, for he thought it impossible to evaluate the *quality* of the listening. He also thought Barnes too apprehensive about threats of criticism from authors with grudges who might complain to higher authority in the BBC or to a Member of Parliament, or even to a Cabinet Minister. He did, he assured Barnes, see the 'basic bother', for literature 'is on the one hand a national and traditional glory, and on the other hand a trade, and up to all the trade tricks.' When the churches wanted radio time, they could make a stronger claim because they were a national establishment with subsidies from the State. But no one subsidised writers. Forster thought that the average listener would not miss either church or literature if it were omitted, but surely the BBC must have 'a conscience towards either'.[67]

Forster made the paper shortage, which worsened as the war grew longer, his own crusade. Government departments got most of the available stocks, and English classics were going out of print. He estimated that of Dent's Everyman's Library of approximately 1000 titles, 'half have gone out of print', and literature of that quality, in volumes of that handy size, ought to be standard items in packages to prisoners of war. He repeated his argument about literature as a national asset and pointed out that Churchill had agreed on this point, which gave the BBC a sound predecent for considering Forster's ideas about paper allocations.[68]

At last Barnes could not resist mounting a mild counter-offensive, which Forster took in good part. Miss Rowntree one day entered Barnes's office and heard this exchange:

G.B.   What's the good of giving you paper, Morgan? You never write anything on it. . . . And there are so many other things you should be talking about; this paper business is a bee in your bonnet.

E.M.F. Well, perhaps a little mosquito.[69]

Many of his wartime broadcasts were for the Eastern Service. George Orwell was a Talks Producer for its Indian Section, and he and Forster worked well together. The Indian Section was extremely important politically, for the leaders of the Indian National Congress remained bitter because England had taken Indian troops into the European war without consulting Indian political leaders, and Berlin radio capitalised upon their resentment by broadcasting 'books by English authors which had attacked the British presence in India, notably E. M. Forster's *A Passage to India*', about which Orwell later remarked that 'so far as I know they didn't even have to resort to dishonest quotation.'[70]

Forster's mild radio voice and even tone would have been a contrast, to say the least, to Berlin's hysterical rhetoric. His technique in the Indian talks was much like that for the sixth-formers, not because he wished to talk down to either audience, but because simplicity and gentle persuasion were his more effective ways of making strong points. As in *A Passage to India*, his oblique references touch upon current issues of which informed Indians would have been aware. An exhibition of photographs of Hindu architecture and sculpture in November 1940 inspired a broadcast talk typical of his approach to Indian listeners. It begins with an echo of the more unhappy relationships in *Passage* and ends by explaining what that exhibition had done for him personally.

In the political background of this talk was a serious stand-off between the Government of India and the two major Indian parties: the National Congress and the All-India Muslim League. In 1940 the Government of India made an 'August Offer' to enlarge the Viceroy's Executive Council, thus allowing more Indian representation at the top, and promises of several postwar rapprochements. Neither Hindus nor Muslims were interested. The suggested cooperation was so transparently intended to benefit the war effort about which

India had not been consulted. Gandhi called for a peaceful campaign of civil disobedience. The Muslim League wanted political equality; it was willing to enter an enlarged Executive Council – but not as a minority; it must enter on equal terms with Hindus. Indian moderates wanted a compromise of some kind, but nothing came of it. A group in the House of Commons wrote rather plaintively to *The Times* and wondered why everyone could not just get together and solve their differences in a friendly spirit.[71] But Indian leaders had had enough of the old 'reservations' that invariably meant less than independence. The London Government's response to Indian intransigence was a new BBC Central Transmission, of which one part was an expanded Eastern Service for India and the Far East. It opened on 6 October 1940. Forster's talk on the Indian photographs at the Imperial Institute was one of the early broadcasts for that new Service.

What could his musings on the philosophy of Hindu temple construction and decoration contribute to that most untranquil and intractable situation? In a way, his talk was more than a little subversive, for he slipped past the censors a subtle appeal to Indian pride in indigenous art and architecture, a communication with the many Indians who were discovering or rediscovering through their arts a new sense of national pride and identity. Listeners aware of the history of British attitudes toward Indian art could adduce evidences of British denials, by word and deed, of the value and even of the very existence of fine art in India.[72] Forster had tried in 1913, he said, to purchase photographs of some ancient temples and mosques that he had visited. It was possible, he said, to get photographs of the Taj Mahal and the Angel of Cawnpore and the Victoria Terminal at Bombay, all standard tourist attractions. He had thought that he had another chance at photographs when he met a Public Works official and asked whether the Government had taken photographs of Indian antiquities, and whether he might buy some. Obviously the official was not accustomed to such a request, for he 'administered a severe official snub'. The Government's photographs were for official purposes only, not for '"any Tom, Dick or Harry".' Forster, silenced, pictured Government of India cabinets stuffed with photographs and marked 'Very Secret' for no explainable reason – at least, for no reason that he could imagine – and considered 'too terrible to contemplate'. In fact, many British in India and at home still regarded Indian temple sculptures as too terrible to contemplate, scandalously erotic and grotesque, one more proof that Indians were not ready for civilised self-government.[73] (It is quite possible that those photographs of temples could have been caught up in some panicky general order from Intelligence, for it was the Indian pressure for more self-government that was truly 'too terrible to contemplate'.)

Forster remembered that Public Works official very well. 'I even remember his name. I did not like him.' But he mentions the episode not to air an old grudge but to say that the photographs at the Imperial Institute represent a change for the better. The exhibition is officially sponsored, and the Secretary of State for India had opened it. It is beautifully mounted; there is no admission fee; and everyone is welcome.

He explains why he thinks this exhibition is wonderful – not as a romantic display, but as an aid to his understanding. This is the key to his audience appeal. Thoughtful Indians were tired of one-way cultural traffic, and Forster spoke of true exchange. He calls it 'a spiritual exhibition', for it dealt not merely with architectural and archaeological objects, but with the Hindu tradition. Then he tells what he has learned, as a Westerner who has visited some Hindu temples but had seen them only as 'impressive buildings, very or-nate outside, and rather poky inside'. Now he knows that the Hindu temple is an analogue for the world-mountain; that the ornate out-side, which struck so many non-Indians as a vulgar sculptural jum-ble, represents the universe; that the interior that had seemed so dark and poky belongs to the individual worshipper, who pen-etrates the world-mountain to be alone with divinity in the undistracting gloom. How he wishes he had known all that when he visited the Khajuraho temples thirty years ago! Now, with 'relief and joy' he understands all this. He wishes that his Public Works ac-quaintance might see this exhibition, for it 'might do him a world of good'.

Forster has made it plain that he wishes not to be as the man from the Public Works Department but still tries to avoid implying that he alone knows best what Indians need to know or not know. He does not presume to tell Indians about Hinduism; he is only telling them 'what the exhibition told me'. The talk is a gracious invitation to India to continue instructing the West. It is also a graceful apology for that long-ago restriction on photographs, and for his own thirty years of non-comprehension.[74]

Forster's genial tone did not match the working atmosphere inside the Indian Service, which was soon in a state of civil war. Briggs says: 'India had been such a cause of contention in British politics during the 1930s and its political future was so uncertain during the early years of the war that these personal struggles behind the scenes had more than local significance.'[75] They involved Lionel Fielden, on loan from the radio service of the Government of India; Zulfikar Bokhari, trained in the BBC, recommended by Fielden, and seconded from All-India Radio as adviser; and Malcolm Darling, the Editor. They were instructed to keep India informed, appeal for and keep Indian goodwill, and counter the German propaganda broadcasts. The *New Statesman* observed that Indians preferred the German broadcasts because the Germans 'had made a special study of India' and therefore 'understood how to meet Indian tastes and susceptibilities better than the English'.[76] With all their on-the-spot experience of India, the English were outmanoeuvred, for the Germans knew too well how to manipulate British talk of freedom and free choice against British failure to grant those to India.

What should have been an ideal team to salvage this situation began almost at once to fall apart. Between Fielden and Darling a rift was inevitable; they disagreed fundamentally in temperament and in attitude toward India. Fielden thought it 'urgently necessary that some sort of bridge of understanding should be made between the British Government and Indian nationalists.'[77] Broadcasting could be that bridge-builder. But Darling believed in 'firm political control of the Service'. Fielden, who had initially hoped to be appointed Editor, left after six months and angered Darling by publishing an article in which he said that the entire propaganda broadcasting effort was 'swamped by the mass of the mediocre' and hobbled by '"Committees"' instead of being 'the responsibility of producers'.[78] Forster told Darling that if he were in charge he would 'sack you both and appoint an Indian', and although Forster found Bokhari 'pleasantly fizzy to work for' he did not especially like him.[79] Darling did not get on well with Bokhari and was even more unhappy when Professor Rushbrook Williams, of the University of London School of African and Oriental Studies, became head of an Eastern Service Committee that, in effect, hobbled Darling's policy- and programme-making.

Forster, who thought that Darling's being in the BBC at all was the waste of a valuable resource, believed that he should resign at once or at least threaten to resign. If the BBC thought Darling so influential that they had brought him back from India for this assignment they owed his complaints serious consideration. Punjab agriculture and cooperatives, not office administration, were the field of his expertise. Darling had been on the verge of resigning for some time. Forster thought that he ought to make his threats more urgent, for 'your desire to protect [your staff] has surely carried far enough'. Darling carried on until 1943. Bokhari stayed until 1946, although he had serious questions about whether the BBC really trusted Indians.[80]

Nor did the genial tone of Forster's broadcast on Hindu temples represent his own mood in 1940. Just preceding the talk on temples, he gave three sombre talks that served to get him onto the Nazi blacklist of those to be rounded up after Britain fell. They comprise his wartime credo of Culture. In the first talk, 'Culture and Freedom', he says that everyone's trouble sprang from the fact that Germany had allowed its great culture 'to become governmental'. English culture is national, not governmental, and an understanding of English thought and English attitudes was the beginning of protection against its becoming similarly governmental. In the second talk, 'What Has Germany Done to the Germans?', Forster reminds his audience that England, in her own anxieties, must not forget that the German people and their culture had been betrayed. In his third talk, 'What Would Germany Do to Us?', he projects Nazi controls onto English society and culture. In view of the Continental example, England had no choice but to fight for the total defeat of totalitarianism. Any terms based on a Nazi victory would 'kill the impulse to create. Creation is disinterested. Creation means passionate understanding. Creation lies at the heart of civilisation like fire in the heart of the earth.'[81]

Through the spring and summer of 1940 Forster's outlook became increasingly sombre. It was difficult to settle to any kind of sustained work. Spy fever infected the Guildford area. The Borough Surveyor was arrested, and Forster noted in his diary that Sir Oliver Lodge 'was suspected by Lady Farrer', who did not recognise him when he came asking directions to West Hackhurst, and that Mrs Trevelyan and her nephew, being Dutch, were considered questionable.[82] All of this was deeply disturbing and discouraging. Earlier he had written to Mrs Trevelyan: 'Yes, like you I am courageous by fits and starts.' The only thing that kept him going from one day to the next was the knowledge that this was a momentous point in history, and that 'one can usually be of a little use to someone'. But these were really psychological makeshifts. 'And endurance is not an adequate substitute for hope.'[83] Most of all he hated the breakdown of the courtesy and human decency that define the level of a nation's culture: 'Deeper than the cruelty and the deceit, the vulgarity.'[84]

Belgium and Holland had fallen by mid-May, and Forster expected Hitler to be in England by June. He had written: 'IT IS TOO MUCH TO THINK ABOUT FOR LONG.'[85] On 24 July the first air raid forced him to think about it. German bombers' route to London crossed over the Home Counties, and he knew that 'the danger is great, but the sense that it is waxes and wanes'.[86] In September there was a nasty report that Canadian soldiers had captured a German parachutist nearby, had cut off his hand and nailed it to a tree. Apparently, they claimed that the hand was already nearly off. It was a low point for Forster, who until then was 'mildly pursuing my broadcasting', but the distance was too great between the BBC with its civilised atmosphere and the world in which such atrocities could happen. It was difficult for him not to feel 'half-hearted' about everything that he did.[87] Culture is a matter of passing on the best of the past and the present, but how to 'select – provided one gets the chance – what is worth passing on?'[88] He could not be sanguine even about victory and told Mrs Trevelyan that he foresaw England too weakened and worn out at the end of the war to create that brave new world some talked about. He could hope for no more than 'mutual exhaustion out of which some good, at present unimaginable, will spring'. Again he saw two possible courses of action: 'withdrawing into oneself' or 'dispassionate recording'.[89] Again he had little faith in either. For one thing, he was not one to withdraw from such a momentous concern, and for another he was by nature a *passionate* recorder of events.

One thing he could do: he continued his campaign for more BBC literary programmes. If books had been around for some 3000 years, they were important during this war and, one had to hope, afterwards. For Forster, the quality of the programmes, not mere quantity of hours filled, was crucial. When invited to be one of a series of writers interviewed, he replied that, in view of the BBC's laggardly attitude to literature as national heritage, such a series would be so inconsequential as not to be worth the trouble and expense. His impatience with what he considered the BBC's neglect of books and writers finally boiled over: had the BBC even tried 'to treat our national heritage in letters seriously?' It had no right 'to invite authors to chat!' – for surface chat was what it would expect.[90] Eventually, however, although the BBC never included as many book programmes as he thought literature deserved, his efforts actually bore fruit as more literary programmes of substance began to appear among the war broadcasts. Not that he was ever satisfied, but he had made the BBC make a beginning toward improvement.

If the BBC had taken a small step forward, it took a long step backward in 1941 when it began to blacklist persons who had expressed opinions hostile to government policy. This ban was aimed especially at pacifists and those who subscribed to the 'People's Convention' proclaimed at a Communist-sponsored rally in London. It demanded separate peace proposals and a home government policy more responsive to working people. The National Council for Civil Liberties stood by its formal statement of 1940 that recognised the necessity for certain restrictions in wartime but maintained also that 'the essence of democracy consists in the actions of all authorities being guided by a balanced and well-informed public opinion.'[91] Forster joined Ralph Vaughan Williams and several others to protest the BBC's action. Vaughan Williams cancelled permission for performance of his compositions, and Forster cancelled three talks. These were particularly close to his heart: one on Masood, who had died in 1937; one on Indian writers; and the one on George Crabbe that begins, 'To talk of Crabbe is to talk of England'. 'Poor Crabbe! what would he have thought of all this!' Forster wrote to Malcolm Darling, 'and what would the Empire [have] thought of Crabbe, too!'[92] After Forster submitted his official notice of the cancellations he told Darling that it had occurred to him that his letter would become part of an official file, and he added for the record that he was neither 'a member of the People's Convention nor a Communist, nor a Pacifist and that I believe in the prosecution of the war'.[93] On 20 March the Government backed off and on 21 April he signified his willingness to return. But he added a caveat to the effect that if the blacklisting were to be resumed he would cancel again, 'little as that individual protest is worth'.[94] In fact he had demonstrated that individual protest was worth a good deal.

INDIA ONCE MORE

When at last hostilities ceased and people could begin to think about putting their lives in order, Forster's fell into disorder. He still felt that he *ought* to write another novel, and Bob Buckingham repeatedly urged him to begin. A principal reason he could not was that he feared, as a result of the war years and his prolonged self-reproaches for writing-time wasted, that he would slip into cynicism. His home life seemed all 'trivialities', and even the National Council for Civil Liberties and the BBC seemed 'unimportances' beside the problem of the novel not written. It was the old problem of 'copy'. The life that he knew best, the suburban subject-matter that in the mind of the general public had become his trademark, rested on a foundation too flimsy to carry the weight of more serious work. There was also 'the old artist's readiness to dissolve characters into a haze.'[95] They may be read poetically, but they sacrifice the weightiness that makes an effect outside the book itself. He was now sixty-four, and the prospect of old age was more troublesome than ever. It only curtailed the possibility that he might yet prove to himself that he could write another influential, publishable novel.

In March 1945 his mother died, and he was devastated. When he received an invitation to be the honoured guest of the all-India P.E.N. Club Centre, at a writers' conference in Jaipur, his friends urged him to accept. Within twenty-four hours he exchanged dull, cold England for Indian sunshine and warmth. 'Profound thankfulness filled me,' he wrote, for India was 'the country I loved . . .' Despite the war's interruptions, and in good measure because of his book talks for England about Indian writers and for India about English literary affairs, literary exchange between India and the West had begun to flourish in a way that was impossible in 1912. Forster's visit was an event, for his broadcasts had created a special following among Indian intellectuals. He saw some old friends and would have liked a little more time for his own explorations of familiar places, but just being out of England was a salutary experience. At Delhi he chanced to overhear scornful comments about the waste of scarce air accommodation for a useless visit by an old writer at a time when India needed to make the best use of every resource. Forster begged to differ. He was not useless. Just his desire 'to be with Indians' was 'a very little step in the right direction'. Still, there was a nagging concern that the direction of postwar India was not exactly right. His fellow conferees were all Indian intellectuals, all products of the upper reaches of the educational system, and all obsessed with politics. For them, every other problem, artistic, social or economic, must await the political solution. They were even more certain of this than when he had last been among them. The mechanics of political strategy absorbed them. Later, they told themselves, they would worry about everything else. Forster still thought their attitude not only shortsighted but also dangerous, for to those with eyes to see, an independent India was more inevitable with each passing day. When he spoke about 'form in literature' and 'individual vision', their attention wandered although they listened politely, for literature must be the servant of politics, at least until India had gained independence. But Forster was convinced that the concern for literature, which makes one's life more than a political passage, must inform and illuminate independence. At the conference he admired a speech by Jaipur's noted city-planner, Sir Mirza Ismail, who had a well-earned reputation for utilitarian organisation, but important as that was, 'his indifference to art for art's sake' was all too evident.

Was this, at last, the 'real India'? Forster disowned the phrase, for it can be applied to either change or changelessness. His final verdict on India in 1945 was mixed. Rules of purdah had relaxed a little in the Muslim centres. English was widely, but less correctly, used. Cinema flourished in Bombay but produced rubbishy romances and did nothing to cultivate the critical spirit. Book production was active, but authors were poorly paid, and there were no poets to compare with the deceased Rabindranath Tagore and the Muslim nationalist poet Muhammed Iqbal. In the end, Forster despaired about India's political future. He closed the circle begun with *A Passage to India*: personal relations were still the key to solutions of political problems. Mere goodwill, at such a juncture of history, was of little use. Only genuine, disinterested 'affection or the possibility of affection' was of any real use, and 'that can surely do no harm'. On the contrary, where it is trusted it can do a great deal of good.[96]

When he returned from India he suffered another blow: he must vacate West Hackhurst. He had known that it was not a freehold property. It stood on land that belonged to Laura Forster's friends the Farrers of Abinger Hall. The sixty-year lease, already twice extended for Mrs Forster's lifetime, would not be renewed again; the Farrers needed the house for one of their own. It was still notoriously inconvenient and difficult to keep; now none of its drawbacks figured beside the fact that Forster's father had built it, his mother had died there, and he was homeless. Now *he* was one of those postwar people who needed houses. All his own theories about the deleterious effects of property-owning on one's character now rebounded upon him, and his loss became an obsession that embittered him and annoyed his friends. He thought of Stevenage, where he could be close to Rooksnest, but news of the projected Stevenage New Town blighted that idea. He made a token effort at house-hunting and thought about some prolonged travels, when King's College gave him, as an Honorary Fellow, a room in College and arranged for lodgings in the home of the Senior Tutor. At first he felt miserable and out of place but then began to settle in and make new friends, although still subject to recurring fits of sorrow because he did not have a house as home. In time, King's would become his only residence. In fact, in his circumstances King's was the best solution; domestically he was a dependent person and badly needed someone to see to the daily details of living. He also needed occupation and new interests, something that might get him writing again. Within a few years after the war ended, two new opportunities presented themselves. One was the BBC's Third Programme. The other was the ascent of Benjamin Britten in the world of British opera. Forster's involvement with both demonstrated how radio and the arts could work together.

'THE THIRD'

The Third Programme began on 29 September 1946 and continued until 4 April 1970. It came out of the postwar need to think things out anew, to make a new beginning, preserve and pass on the cultural values so desperately threatened during the war. Kate Whitehead, historian of its considerable literary contribution, calls it 'the first ever broadcasting station to be wholly devoted to "minority interests", with the specific goal of "promoting excellence" regardless of the demands of the mass audience.'[97] No one doubted that the Third's audience would be a small segment of that mass audience; it was designed for those who would welcome the higher culture in the form of talks, music and features. The idea of something like the Third Programme had been around from almost the beginning of the BBC. In 1924 there had been a proposal for two kinds of programmes, one for 'high brow education and better class material' and another to be 'popular'; even for 'two opposite types of programmes each night'. This was dismissed as a 'drastic and expensive change in our present programme'.[98] Reith considered the BBC primarily an educator, but he thought specialisation as limited and expensive as that for a programme like the Third was outside the BBC's constitutional mandate as public-service broadcaster to all levels of British society, each at the standard of the best *in its own class*.

In 1943 Harold Nicolson, a Governor of the BBC who by his own admission felt no enthusiasm for popular broadcasting, had written to George Barnes: 'How is one to explain the unfaltering instinct of the B.B.C. for the second-rate?' He charged 'lack of unity . . . unity of purpose, . . . We never seem to know whether our aim is to educate, to inform, to entertain, or merely to avoid trouble.' This was understandable in wartime, but there was 'lack of self-confidence' due in turn to 'lack of inspiration at the top and resultant over-sensitiveness.' Broadcasting was excused as 'either a debased form of expression or at least an invention which has not found its own creative formula'. He concluded:

> Whatever we may say, we do not really care for mass production. The higher enjoyments are always private enjoyments and the B.B.C. is so horribly public. . . . But until there is some mind at the centre, permeating the whole organization, which feels some sense of mission and regards the B.B.C. as something more than a public utility corporation I do not see how unity, courage or enthusiasm can be born.[99]

At the war's end, when a Third Programme – in planning stages called the 'C Programme' – at last became possible, the mind at its centre was that of George Barnes, who left the Talks Department to be the new Programme's Head (later Controller) during its first two years. He had the full support of William Haley, who came from Reuters in 1943 to be BBC Editor-in-Chief and was Reith's successor as Director General when the Third began. Reith, who had retired in 1938, continued to say that he thought such a programme 'objectionable', the 'waste of a precious wavelength' for material 'too limited in appeal'.[100] Haley and Barnes, however, regarded it as an opportunity for experiment and the preservation of a cultural tradition. Barnes wanted excellence with no halfway measures. Miss Rowntree recalls that Forster had considerable influence in discussions with Barnes about possibilities, ways and means, and most particularly whether a general or a specialised audience was the goal. Miss Rowntree recalls:

> I got the impression that this was not the relevant question. [Barnes] was certainly not interested in esoteric programmes by or for academics – those began to creep in after his time. What I remember most clearly was his purpose of making good things generally accessible – ('*All* the piano concertos of Mozart and *all* the histories of Shakespeare') – and if it is objected that the idea of good things must be based on a value judgement, I have to agree: some value

judgements are unavoidable, especially in any form of communication that is not open-ended – subjects and syllabuses of education, for example. It is our responsibility to see that we get them right.[101]

How to get them right? Miss Rowntree quotes from the broadcasting gospel of Barnes and Forster when she says,

Not, I am sure, by imposing definitions that coming generations would reject. Standards of excellence must change from time to time, even if there remains a hard core which has been accepted by educated opinion in different times and different places. . . . A world with no peaks and no masters – old or new – would be a very grey and meaningless place. You cannot be egalitarian about greatness.[102]

As soon as he could book a passage, Barnes set out for America, to educate himself and to learn how the BBC was regarded across the Atlantic. He travelled as far south as Atlanta and as far west as Denver. He became rather depressed when he discovered how generally the BBC was thought to be government-controlled and government-operated. He talked with politicians, government officials, clergymen, academics. Justice Felix Frankfurter said that 'whatever happened Britain must avoid commercial radio'. At the University of Chicago Robert Hutchins warned him not to 'mistake surface-culture and the goodwill of fashion-followers for liberal thinking'. Henry Wallace thought the BBC 'an important and unique world experiment', even if programmes were sometimes inferior. Barnes said that he wanted thinkers who would influence each other in argument. How 'typically British' was Wallace's comment.[103]

Back in London, Barnes assembled his notes and ideas as a detailed plan. The BBC had already created a public for serious listening. Now for 'a sense of discrimination and a critical attitude to standards of performance'. Educated listeners want 'Reflection not excitement. The need to ponder/Contemporary relevance essential/ Linking up of ideas, facts, moods'. Half the time should be given to music, one-quarter to 'presented speech' and one-quarter to 'straight speech'. Even at the risk of overcrowding, the first year's schedule must set the standard. Busy people would comprise this new audience; they would be willing to plan their time and pay attention but would be resentful if that time were wasted.[104] On the other hand, the new Programme must not alienate those who were wary of Culture with a capital 'C' but might be attracted by the 'educative influence' that Reith had valued but could not define. Above all, programme planners must think nationally. 'Never forget', Barnes told the critic Basil Taylor, 'that you are broadcasting to a national audience, not to Londoners.' Taylor, when he talked about art, must include news of the provincial galleries.[105]

Barnes and Haley received enthusiastic support in the more liberal quarters of the press, but they also expected – and received – complaints that the new Programme was elitist and undemocratic, an appeal to snobbery. Cartoonists had a rich new field for comment; a typical example has the caption, 'They're nice people – definitely third programme.'[106] But Barnes and Haley held to the position that the Third took nothing away from the BBC's other domestic programmes, the Home Service and the Light Programme; in their view the Third *completed* the range of BBC offerings.[107]

Ten years before the Third Programme seemed even a possibility, Forster had composed an essay that was in effect a brief for what would become the Third Programme's reason for being. He asked, 'Does Culture Matter?' 'Culture' he defined as 'the various beautiful and interesting objects which men have made in the past, and handed down to us, and which some of us are hoping to pass on.' Not only objects such as paintings and sculpture, buildings and mosaics, books of poetry and music scores and recordings, but also the intangibles that follow along with them: ideas, aesthetic enjoyment, inspiration. But even then, before the war with Hitler, Forster's prognosis for Culture's future was gloomy. Science's new inventions were so plentiful and ingenious and arrived at such a rapid rate that they crowded out the legacies from the past. 'Broadcasting and cinema have wiped out the drama', and it was only a matter of time until the next wave of inventions disposed of them too, and civilisation would be obliged again to adapt in both thought and habit. (In fact, television was already more than an inventor's idea in 1931, and the video-recorder would become television's inevitable competitor.) Inventions made entertainment so easy that we would forget that mere entertainment is not always the stuff of culture. He intended to use his literary talents to combat this tendency, 'without too much attempt at fairmindedness'. He will not pretend to be fairminded because belief in Culture is a faith, and total faith does not compromise. 'Faith makes one unkind: I am pleased when culture scores a neat hit.'[108] Thus, when German bombing began, the lunchtime concerts that

Dame Myra Hess initiated at the National Gallery particularly pleased him. They were not only proof of British ingenuity and pluck, but an instance of Culture scoring a neat hit while literally under fire.

When *The Listener* announced in January 1946 that the Third Programme would begin in September, it diffused the snobbery issue a little by shifting the emphasis from capital-C Culture, that 'forbidding word', and stressing instead the national inheritance of culture that belonged to everyone. The Third would be 'in the broadest sense, "cultural" – not a word which trips very smoothly on an English, as compared with a Teutonic, tongue . . .' And was it not curious that the home of so great a literature 'has always lacked a generic expression for "things of the mind" capable of making its way in ordinary speech'?[109] In other words, the listener to the Home Service or the Light Programme need not feel closed out; even intellectuals had difficulty defining their own key term. The proof for everyone would be in the listening.

Forster's allegiance to the Third is plain from the record of his radio appearances. Between August 1947 and December 1958 he broadcast twenty-two talks, the great majority about books and authors. Seventeen of these (and possibly eighteen, for the script of one has not been found) were originally for the Third or were rebroadcasts from the other services.[110] He did not change his diction and style of delivery for this more specialised audience. Nor did he modify his conviction about the function of the Third Programme. On its fifth anniversary, he read out the Gospel of Culture according to George Barnes. The Third was equally obligated to old and new. It 'was Janus-faced, two faces, one of them gazing with tranquillity into the past, the other with ardour into the future. One of them reflects, the other explores.' The Third's function, in addition to preserving the best from the past, was to present to a discriminating audience whatever seemed worth preserving from the present and establish it firmly in the cultural memory. Listeners like him – and he knew it was an anomaly – were 'a vulnerable aristocracy in the midst of a democracy'.[111] This definition led to a mass of difficult distinctions, but he stood by it.

He had misgivings about the Third after Barnes left in 1948 to be Director of the Spoken Word (News, Talks, Religion, Education). His successor was Harman Grisewood, who had been in Talks for a year but resigned in discouragement over a Department that he thought had become arid and over-organised. Barnes invited him into the Third as his assistant. Grisewood liked its atmosphere and variety of

controversy: 'The rest of the B.B.C. mostly felt that the Third Programme was self-admiring and eclectic. It was "highbrow" where
the rest of the output was, in varying degrees, "popular".... Combat
on behalf of the Third Programme, though strenuous, was for me a
health-giving exercise.'[112] Grisewood and Barnes were an interesting
contrast. Barnes was 'musical and romantic' (these, in particular,
among his virtues for Forster). Grisewood was 'literary and classical'.[113] Barnes was Cambridge and Grisewood was Oxford. He thought
that the 'Cambridge people I met felt they understood the modern
world with more certainty than friends I could think of at Oxford.
. . . Oxford was "worldly" for George', while for Grisewood Cambridge was a 'world of emotions and ideas'. He tried to keep himself,
'with George as an example, from slipping into a settled attitude
moulded by previous inclinations'.[114] But Grisewood too had difficulty over a definition for the Third. 'Everyone agreed that the Third
Programme was "cultural"; the trouble started over interpretations.
I had to be quite clear what I meant by "culture" and not only about
what others meant by it.' Interpretation caused some friction between him and Forster. Grisewood settled for the anthropologist's
meaning rather than the educationist's – even though 'instinct warned
me that I should never be drawn into a definition. You cannot define
the purpose of culture except in terms which describe the culture
itself.'[115] A definition of the Third would be 'far too controversial for
the B.B.C.'[116] Forster certainly rejected the educationst's definition,
but he could not accept Grisewood's anthropological definition, and
their difference came to a head over light music. Grisewood wished
to demonstrate with a series of concerts that 'good music could be
light-hearted and gay and many of the great composers thought so'.
However, the publicity made Forster think that Grisewood 'was
letting down the high standard which his friend George Barnes had
set'. When he objected, Grisewood thought of him as '"high-minded
Cambridge" voicing its suspicion of "worldly" Oxford'. They met
for lunch, and among Forster's supposedly surreptitious reminder
cards was one that read 'Temper! Temper!' This was unnerving,
since Grisewood was anxious to prove himself to Forster as 'not
a barbarian. I did not feel as I left him that I had been a great
success.'[117]

Forster was unhappy again after John Morris became Controller of
the Third in 1952. Morris, another King's College man, had studied
social anthropology there. His Asian experience included military
service in India and teaching English in two Japanese universities. In

1943 he became Head of the Far Eastern Service of the BBC, so that he and Forster had already worked together. Forster's unhappiness was the result of Morris's rejection, kindly but firm, of a travel report on Chinese prison reform by their mutual friend W.J.H. Sprott, who was Professor of Philosophy at Nottingham University. Morris, and others who read the script, felt that Sprott's experience of China was too limited. He did not know the Chinese language, had been a guest of the Chinese government so that he had seen only what they wished him to see, and he had no other first-hand knowledge of China. Morris thought also that Sprott lacked 'a sense of *audience*', most of whom, Morris believed, would sympathise with the anti-Chinese forces then fighting in Korea.[118] To Forster, the rejection rang alarm bells of censorship. He had read Sprott's manuscript and knew that it would not be well received just then outside of England, but he did not see why it could not be accepted for the Third Programme, where discussion of controversial subjects was supposed to be welcome. Why did Morris think that Sprott showed 'no sense of engagement' with a prospective audience? That phrase was new to Forster, and he objected to its 'totalitarian tang'. He thought it a sell-out of both Sprott and the Third Programme, a sell-out to 'the alleged opinion of the majority of listeners'.[119] Was this how the Third, so valiantly begun, was going to end? Morris tried to reassure him and argued that its well-known standards did not necessarily imply carte blanche for every speaker, except in a very few special cases such as the lecture series established in Reith's honour. He would not surrender his right to the kind of editorial discretion that Forster, if editor of a journal, would wish for himself. He invited Forster to talk the matter out with himself and Grisewood, for they had no wish to slight his concern about the Third Programme.[120] When they met, Morris wrote that Forster was in 'his most puckish mood' and laughed a lot, but Forster told Florence Barger that he thought the incident 'disgraceful', and he was convinced that he had had the last word. To their objections that Sprott had failed to give a '"general picture" of China', he had demanded '"a general picture of England." There was silence.'[121]

Part of the difficulty was that Forster had long had a somewhat proprietary attitude toward the Third Programme. With Barnes, he had been present at the creation, and he wanted everything connected with it to measure up to Barnes' high standard. Another difficulty was that by the early 1950s the pressures on the Third had increased and had changed in character. The range of criticism had always been wide, from faithful advocates like Rose Macaulay, who thought that it engendered 'increased admiration for the grandeur, riches and versatility of the communicable human mind', to the radio critic of the *Evening News*, who wrote that it 'inclines to bore the pants off me'.[122] But in the 1950s change came too fast for assimilation. Miss Rowntree thinks that the disproportionate expense and the relative smallness of the Third's audience were not really the problem, but the influence of American broadcasting, the explosive growth of the BBC itself, and competition in the form of new radio channels, local radio and, above all, television. In broadcasting, 'everything happened too quickly, and there was no time – and perhaps no desire – to make use of the principles on which the BBC had been built up. Any re-examination was done piecemeal and took place in a permissive society which was afraid of paternalism and dazzled by the power and possibilities of the new medium.' Thus 'there was no defence against competition when it made its first impact', and constructively conservative opinion had less and less influence.[123]

THE ALDEBURGH CONNECTION

Music was extremely important to Forster, and the Third Programme's music offerings added a new dimension to his life. After its first evening's broadcast he told Barnes that although he took exception to 'a bounder of an announcer' who he thought had garbled Zoltan Kodály's name, he was thrilled by Monteverdi madrigals, the Goldberg Variations, and *Comus*, and again he could only hope that 'an even firmer line will be maintained against vulgarity'. During the war he had been thinking 'more seriously about music than other things', but he needed a mentor to tell him whether he was 'thinking in the right direction'.[124] Music on the Third Programme, carefully planned within both historical and critical contexts, gave him that something to check up against.

The Third's contribution to music is incalculable. Its programmes fulfilled all of its obligations to both past and present and to the future as well. It rediscovered forgotten works and gave performances and encouragement to new composers who would have had great difficulty in getting a hearing in concert and recital halls. The Third could take chances with its audience that would have frightened away both the impresarios and many in the typical concert-going public. It also began to commission new works. Many years later the mezzo-soprano Nancy Evans (Crozier) looked through her appointment diaries from those years and was delighted and also astonished when reminded of the range of opportunity, of a kind never before available, that the Third had given to composers and performers.[125]

Forster's Third Programme talks connected him with one of the most important developments in modern music, a new direction in English music history that would have an international influence. In 1948 he was still engaged in his long and sometimes puzzling task of sorting the huge accumulation of letters and other family papers that his mother and aunt had left at West Hackhurst. The process was a symbolic marker; it signalled that a new phase of his literary career was at hand and that he was ready again to look forward instead of dwelling on the past. 'How difficult the past is!' Forster wrote to William Plomer. 'How great is one's responsibility in deciding on it!' Should he, for instance, 'confer temporary immortality' on a Mrs Stainforth who had died in the 1880s and had left seven children, 'no money, many debts, and some goods in a warehouse'.[126] Even the fact that the warehoused goods were jams and preserves from the 1860s, and bonnets and trousers from the 1830s, was not irrelevant. Was Victorian thrift her virtuous motive? Had she become miserly, so that thrift had lost its point? Had she been asking the Thorntons for assistance? Now one who had never known her must decide how much of Mrs Stainforth should pass on into tradition, a Victorian vignette. There is always a price for forgetting. Among her debts was £100 in arrears for storage. Solidified jams, and bonnets and trousers no doubt moth-eaten, do not rank with Monteverdi madrigals and the Goldberg Variations and *Comus*, but those too would languish in limbo, while society's arrears steadily accumulate, if no one cares enough to pass them on. The Third Programme was that passer-on, that spreader of the Gospel of Culture.

A few months later he began again to feel genuinely a 'creative'. In 1937, through W. H. Auden and Christopher Isherwood, he had met Benjamin Britten, then twenty-three years old and composer of the incidental music for the Auden-Isherwood play, *The Ascent of F 6*. Forster had reviewed it favourably when it appeared in book form in 1936.[127] From 1939 to 1941 Britten had been in America, intending at first to settle there permanently, until a copy of *The Listener* came to hand, with Forster's 1941 postponed radio talk on the eighteenth-century poet George Crabbe, an Aldeburgh man. Britten had grown up in Lowestoft, a few miles to the north on the Suffolk coast.

Forster's evocation of those distinctive places – 'To talk of Crabbe is
to talk of England' – had a powerful influence on Britten. That essay
had played a large part in turning him back to England.[128] Then in
1944 Forster had been greatly impressed when he heard Britten and
the tenor Peter Pears perform Britten's *Michelangelo Sonnets* at a
National Gallery Concert, and they met more frequently thereafter.

In 1945, at the very end of the war, Britten set the seal on his return
to Suffolk with his opera *Peter Grimes*. Eric Crozier, then producer at
Sadler's Wells Opera, perfectly remembers its genesis.

> One day Ben came to me and gave me a script and said, 'Look, I'd
> like you to read this. I want to write an opera, and I've got a
> commission from Koussevitsky in memory of his wife.' . . . Would
> I criticise frankly and say how it could be improved? A very
> delicate position to be in, particularly with a young composer . . .
> the danger, by over-criticism, by being too punctilious, of pulling
> his creation down; the same with the librettist. Anyway, they liked
> my *kind* of criticism, I think, because from then on we met regu-
> larly, to get the thing into its final shape.[129]

'The thing' was Montagu Slater's libretto based on a vignette from
The Borough, Crabbe's long poem of 1810 drawn from Aldeburgh
and its people. The collaborators – Britten and Slater; Pears, then a
rising young singer of thirty-three who would create the role of
Grimes; and Crozier as producer – felt from the start that this could
be a turning-point in English opera, perhaps the most important
since the death of Henry Purcell in 1695.[130] Unlikely as it seemed at
the time, there was a new audience for opera. The war had forced
London theatrical and opera companies, bombed out and drastically
reduced, into touring the provinces. Sadler's Wells had been 'playing in towns that had never had opera, of any kind, and gradually
they built up an audience for themselves . . . *but* – it was a real
struggle'. Younger singers were away at the war, and quality depended on 'a good dramatic spectacle rather than a display of great
singing, and in this way we gradually built up a company which was
capable of inspiring a composer like Britten in an opera like *Peter
Grimes*, and capable of doing a performance in 1945 that was I think
a very high standard indeed, a completely new, original modern
work. . . . There couldn't have been a bleaker or less promising time
to tackle a major artistic work in a form of art that had not succeeded
in England for the past two centuries.'[131]

They set to work. Slater had been writing film documentaries for the Government and had never written a word for opera. Britten, along with music for theatre, film and radio, had recently composed works for orchestra and voice but had never composed an opera score. Nevertheless, their discipline in timing and dramatic effect proved invaluable. 'It was a great event,' Crozier says, 'because *nobody* believed that an English composer *could* write an opera. It had not happened for so long.' *Peter Grimes*, the story of a Suffolk fisherman, bitter and alienated from the community and haunted by the successive deaths of two apprentices, scarcely seemed the kind of tale to cheer up a London audience in 1945. But the result was quite otherwise when the opera had its première at Sadler's Wells on 7 June 1945. Crozier says:

We had lived through four years of war. We'd struggled every night through the blackout. We had slept in cellars and garden-sheds. We'd gone fairly hungry. We'd seen bombing, . . . wherever [Britten] went at that time he had the score with him in case he should be bombed. And such things happened. And suddenly on that first night the drama that he presented of this curious, tor-mented visionary fisherman Peter Grimes, and the people sur-rounding him, who were at loggerheads with him, and antagonistic – somehow their conflict expressed the extraordinary frustration we'd all felt during those years of war – the audience arrived in the theatre not knowing what they were going to see, but they went out wiser, profoundly moved, exhilarated but shaken by a musical experience that hadn't occurred in English music in the lifetime of any of them.[132]

An interest in George Crabbe was only one of the connections between Forster and Britten. Philip Brett suggests that when Forster's talk on Crabbe in 1941 drew Britten back from America, he 'had decided to exchange uncongenial freedom abroad for unknown peril at home', not only in the form of society's strictures against homo-sexuality but also as the 'Forsterian sacrifice' – the constriction of artistic powers in the conflict between society and his own homo-sexual nature.[133] Paradoxically, it was Britten who gave Forster the new opportunity to be once again a 'creative'.

In June 1948 Forster lectured on Crabbe and *Peter Grimes* at the first Aldeburgh Festival, which Britten, Pears and Crozier organised on a foundation that originated with their English Opera Group.[134]

At that time Britten asked Forster to consider whether he would write the libretto for an opera commissioned for Covent Garden during the 1951 Festival of Britain. This production would be prepared in circumstances altogether different from the hardscrabble conditions of the 1945 *Peter Grimes*, and it would draw international attention. Forster hesitated, for he had no experience of writing for the stage, but novice librettists had not daunted Britten earlier, and Forster's misgivings did not daunt him now. He promised Crozier's help as consultant on dramatic problems, but soon Forster insisted that cooperation be collaboration. First, however, they had to find a narrative. Forster, a devoted Wagnerian, wanted something grand and elevating. 'Literature, &^{ct} stirs me when it wakes me up to the greatness of the world,' he told Crozier.[135] *Peter Grimes* did that for him, and this was a large part of the attraction in the new collaboration. Finally they settled on *Billy Budd*, Herman Melville's parable of the conflict between goodness and unrelenting evil. Forster had discussed the story in *Aspects of the Novel* twenty years before, and in 1947 he had reviewed the new edition by William Plomer in one of his BBC book talks. In *Aspects* he had written that in *Billy Budd* 'evil is labelled and personified, instead of slipping over the ocean and round the world, and Melville's mind can be observed more easily.' In 1960 Britten was uncertain whether it was that reference or William Plomer's new edition of *Billy Budd* that had suggested the story for a possible libretto.[136] In 1948 it seemed especially timely in view of the totalitarian evil that had so recently slipped 'over the ocean and round the world'. Crozier played devil's advocate to this choice, pointing out difficulties such as the single set and all-male cast, so that Forster and Britten might see 'whether the advantages they recognized in the story overweighed [the disadvantages], and they did. Britten was very excited about the project. And, so it came about that in 1949 – January – Forster and I for the first time travelled down to Aldeburgh to work on writing a libretto based on *Billy Budd*.'

Crozier knew very well what this work meant to Forster. Now seventy, his health caused persistent problems. He worried terribly whether incipient deafness might interfere with his enjoyment of music, and there was no escaping the irritant of scholars' and reviewers' persistent speculations about why he had written no more novels. 'He was enormously happy to be put into a creative situation, . . . Certainly he was working with eager people much younger than himself, who greatly respected him, but were determined to make him work hard. He loved it.'[137] After a long work session at

Aldeburgh in March 1949 Forster wrote in his diary that 'even if I achieve no more the scene is set. Were my life ordered and organised – as it was there – I might still go on creating. As it is, I see my furniture everywhere, my home nowhere.'[138] In June, after a visit to the United States, he was impatient for their next session to begin; he told Britten that during his American visit he had had enough of 'being famous . . . and should be glad to do a little work'.[139]

The work was also a source of some disquiet. Propelled forward once more by the excitement of creation, he could not seem to understand why Britten did not go steadily on with the score. Forster himself postponed some corrective surgery until after work on the score had begun.[140] But then Britten turned to other engagements, other compositions, and an American tour with Peter Pears. Although an American visit had taken Forster too away from the work, he was impatient for Britten to return to Aldeburgh, as if without Britten's example before him he dreaded a slackening in his own momentum. He did not really understand Britten's method of work, which was to concentrate intensely on a score once all was clear in his mind. The age difference became a handicap, and Britten hesitated to reprove a colleague so much older and so eminent. He was not pleased when Forster tactlessly expressed dissatisfaction with the music's setting for the cynical Claggert's monologue, which Forster had laboured to make a complete picture of a tragically warped personality. He wanted '*passion* – . . . not soggy depression or growling remorse'.[141] It was left to Crozier to patch things up. 'Oh dear! – when such a misunderstanding begins between two great men, one feverishly busy, the other not busy enough, it is most difficult to bring them to a frank exchange of views and to tolerance of each other's personal need for trust and loyalty.'[142] Still, by that time they all knew that *Billy Budd* would be a masterwork that overshone any frictions. Forster was moved to tears at one of the last rehearsals, and he was particularly gratified when Frederick Dalberg as Claggart thanked him for 'the superb words I had given him'.[143]

By 1951 life had settled into quieter channels. *Billy Budd*, although well received, did not create the immediate sensation of *Peter Grimes*. Librettists and composer were happier about their later version for BBC television in 1966, for which they condensed the original four acts as two.[144] Still, Forster was well satisfied with their work, and the impulses stirred by the Aldeburgh connection continued into the 1950s. He gathered the essays for *Two Cheers for Democracy*, first published in 1951. He collected the letters from India that he had asked his mother and aunt to save, and in 1953 they became *The Hill of Devi*. In 1956 he published *Marianne Thornton: A Domestic Biography*, which repaid his long-standing debt to his great-aunt and is a portrait of both the Thornton family and their moral landscape, so much of which became Forster's own. Between 1948 and 1960 he appeared six times on the Third Programme to speak about the Aldeburgh Festivals, which became the annual international event that they now are. Memories of *Billy Budd* carried him on into the 1960s. There was a Covent Garden performance in 1963, which Forster attended with Britten, Pears and Crozier. Forster told his American friend, the painter Paul Cadmus, that he was spending more time playing records, 'chiefly Janacek and Bach', and that this was 'part of the excitement that has seized me through the stage success of Billy Budd'. He had not expected much of this production, for another singer had replaced the American Theodor Uppman in the title role. 'Au contraire, wild enthusiasm.' An unexpected and very welcome 'sense of expansion and success . . . has given me a shove into 1964'.[145]

Since the mid-1950s, however, such moments of exhilaration had been increasingly rare. In 1955 he begged Leonard Woolf to tell him how to get on with his literary life. Reviewing was decent work but he no longer found it satisfying. His royalties were more than sufficient; in fact, he sometimes found the balance in his current account embarrassing and, true to Clapham's philosophy and example, he busied himself with putting it to work, to buy some uninterrupted working time for another writer, to help a friend faced with unexpected expenses, to help a museum or a worthy society in need of funds for specific causes. But this was all apart from being creative himself: 'I want another long piece of work which I might hope to live to finish', he told Woolf.[146] He turned instead to his short stories, rewrote and repolished them, but not really with a good heart, for he knew that those he cared most about could not be published because they dealt with homosexual themes. There seemed no prospect that Parliament would approve the Wolfenden Report, which advocated removing homosexuality from the category of criminal offences. 'What a world. . . . ' he wrote to Ackerley. 'There is nothing left for me that I want to do.'[147] One cannot say that he no longer cared about Culture, but his letters after the mid-1950s often seem more a retrospective than a call to action. He gave his approval to Santha Rama Rau's 1960 stage adaptation of *A Passage to India* but left script and production to her and to its director, Frank Hauser. The aspect of the production that particularly pleased him was the actor Zia Mohyeddin, who he thought perfect as Aziz. He did have very positive opinions about director and cast when the play moved to New York in 1961 after an excellent London run, but this was a defensive action out of his abiding distrust of high-powered American agents and publicity.[148]

His talks for the Third Programme came to an end in 1960, appropriately enough with a new reading of his 1941 talk on Crabbe, during the interval of a performance of *Peter Grimes*.[149] He participated in a number of radio interviews and discussions. The Third Programme retrospective with Britten and Crozier in 1960, on the making of *Billy Budd* and the process and problems of literary-musical composition, was the last of the discussions.[150] He was now one of 'the Masters', and was featured on a 1963 programme that included appreciations by friends and colleagues, with excerpts from some of his earlier broadcasts.[151]

During the 1960s the Third Programme, as conceived by Sir William Haley and George Barnes, was approaching its end. Its last transmission was on 4 April 1970. Its music offerings were then reassigned to a new Radio 3, which assumed, among four reorganised networks, the place of principal broadcaster of fine music. However, it retained only eight hours a week of the evening plays, features, poetry-readings and talks that had given the Third such distinction. Its other programmes of that kind went to Radio 4. The present became more intrusive, in the form of news and news commentary. The stated purpose of this new system was to 'clarify the character of each network and thus to make it easier for listeners to find the type of programming they are looking for, whether it be serious or light music, light entertainment, drama or pop'.[152] Whitehead sees the beginning of the end in a '"streamlining" of 1957 [that] had both cut the hours and undermined the method of the Third Programme, ending the sense of cultural "mission"'.[153] From King's College in January 1970 came a letter from twenty-eight signatories, Forster of course among them – almost his last declaration on behalf of Culture – to lament the prospect of Radio 3 as only a '"music-tap"' while speech, features and documentaries on Radio 4 were 'strait-jacketed into simple fixed categories to compete with the music and drama on Radio 3 to which they were once thought to be complementary.' The 'flexibility and surprise' that had distinguished the Third 'should be fostered, not stifled. Streaming, narrowing, segregating, stunting, such actions are short-sighted and show a callous disregard for the future.'[154] A Third Programme Defence Society sprang up, but it was only a rearguard action. The stronger forces of BBC politics and administration won the day, and despite all the efforts of its supporters the Third Programme was streamlined out of existence.

There is a sombre symmetry in the fact that the Third Programme's end came just two months before Forster's own death on 7 June 1970. Still, that other fact remains: he had helped to set an international standard, still available for ready reference by those who care, of excellence in broadcasting. 'I can think of few other people who had equal gifts in speech and writing', Jean Rowntree says, ' – and perhaps it was only in a very short period of history that this was possible. I am glad E.M.F. flourished in that period.'[155]

5

The Lonely Voice

Three posthumous volumes completed the list of Forster's new publications up to 1980: *Maurice* in 1971, *'The Life to Come' and other stories* in 1972, and *'Arctic Summer' and other fiction* in 1980.[1] This last is a collection of working fragments, fascinating and very valuable for the light that they shed on the composition of other completed works. *Maurice*, the 'homosexual novel' that most of his friends knew about and many had read in manuscript, appeared before the story collection, but it was his work on the stories that inspired Forster to make one last effort to put the manuscript of *Maurice* into the form in which he wished to leave it to his literary executors.

Although Forster defined himself as novelist, the short story is the literary form with which his writing career really began and to which he returned with great seriousness after he had given up work on any new novels. In 1902, when he wrote his first story, 'The Story of a Panic', he was one of the number of experimenters who were making the English short story modern. The Irish writer Frank O'Connor has called it 'The Lonely Voice': lonely because 'almost from its beginnings it abandoned the device of a public art in which the storyteller assumed the mass consent of an audience to his wildest improvisations.' The modern short story, O'Connor says, 'began, and continues to function, as a private art intended to satisfy the standard of the individual, solitary, critical reader'.[2] For both author and reader it is as personal as the lyric poem. Its crucial action is interior to a central character or characters or to a first-person narrator. It turns upon an epiphany of some kind, a revelation or sudden insight that works an irreversible change. It makes that point obliquely. Its plot is open-ended, and it leaves a question, to which the reader must find the answer, that bears upon an important personal issue and sometimes upon connections between the personal and the social, as in the stories of James Joyce's *Dubliners*. The more interior the action, the more closely the reader, if brave enough to follow the author's lead, must examine his own motives, actions, values.

Forster particularly valued the stories that came to him as a kind of literary epiphany: simply there, fully developed and waiting for him to take them in hand. 'The Story of a Panic' came to him in that way, and the revelation was the 'assurance that his gift, or as he called it, his "equipment" *mattered*'. He saw a way of substituting 'warmth' for the influential pessimism of Flaubert and Zola.[3] That was the point at which 'something had shifted in his soul, and energies he had only half-glimpsed in himself were now in his possession.'[4] That story, and the five with it in his first collection, *The Celestial Omnibus and Other Stories*, are fantasies of transformation, sometimes for better and sometimes for worse, in which the prosaic and the philistine fail to comprehend a supernatural or semi-supernatural phenomenon that offers enlightenment and liberation. Forster frequently embodied that phenomenon in the god Pan, an Edwardian conceit that he himself mocked gently when he gave the title 'Pan Pipes' to Rickie Elliott's stories in *The Longest Journey*, but the principal target of his mockery was the commercialism that the unimaginative Pembrokes try to impose upon them.

Despite his new-found feeling of power and competence, Forster realised that he depended a great deal on his friends' approval. When 'The Celestial Omnibus' and Other Stories was in preparation in 1910, he thought of Roger Fry to design end-papers but wanted to know whether Fry disliked the stories and therefore might find the work 'uncongenial' or even '"contemptuous"', but he told Trevelyan that he himself felt confident about them.[5] When the book appeared in 1911 a number of critics agreed with the *Athenaeum*'s reviewer, who thought that the stories 'all have a smack of the fantastically supernatural' that failed to convince.[6] Perhaps, when James Barrie added Peter to Pan he coarsened the idea of the classical Pan whom Forster made his *deus ex arboribus*. When his next collection, 'The Eternal Moment' and Other Stories, appeared in 1928, the critics' reaction was similar; this time it was the awful reality of the 1914 War that had intervened to make irrelevant the Edwardian fascination with fantasy and supernatural whimsy. Subsequent history made such fantasy seem even more remote, so that by 1964 Samuel Hynes could dismiss in one paragraph all of Forster's stories published up to that time as full of 'Pan-ridden goings on' and 'not distinguished enough to survive without the support of the novels'.[7] At least two of the stories revised in the 1950s and first published in 1972 must modify that judgement.

Knowing Mohammed el Adl in Egypt during the First World War

had liberated Forster to follow a new line in his stories during the 1920s and 1930s. He became sternly selective with respect to both the stories and the friends to whom he showed them, even though, since the public attitude toward homosexuality deprived him of both a public of thoughtful solitary readers and 'the mass consent of an audience', friends' opinions and encouragement were more necessary than ever. In a letter from Egypt he had told Siegfried Sassoon about a wartime story that he had begun, called '"Inferior" . . . But it was an inferior story.' He gave it up.[8] 'Copy' was still his problem. The war had uprooted him from Suburbia. India as a subject was at a standstill. His military environment in Egypt was uncongenial. By 1922, however, the work in hand was again *A Passage to India*, and in that year he burned most of the stories that he had classified as 'indecent'. He destroyed them not because he had become prudish about them but because they were a distraction from work on the novel. 'They were written not to express myself but to excite myself', and even when he had first begun to write them he had felt that they put his literary career in jeopardy because they were self-indulgent.[9] The best of those stories he preserved, and in 1923 he asked Sassoon to read 'The Life to Come', which was one of the survivors. Forster rather wished that he had given it a different ending although he suspected that even if he were to continue working at it, 'it would never have satisfied you'.[10] But after Sassoon called it a '"lovely story"' as it stood, Forster agreed. That was what he had thought all along.[11] He had simply needed a discriminating reader to say so. A little later he read it to Lytton Strachey, who also reassured him. 'I am very glad about this', Forster told Sassoon.[12]

'The Life to Come', dated 1922, is the earliest of eight of the surviving complete stories on the theme of homosexual love. The latest of those is 'The Other Boat', which was intended for a novel but was left as a fragment and not completed until 1957–8. These two, which are among his most powerful works of fiction, may be considered together as Forster's damning verdict not only on public prejudice toward homosexuals, but also on the colonisers who followed upon the heels of the merchants to consolidate British control of the Eastern Empire: the missionary and the soldier. In *Passage* he lets the missionaries off lightly by making them shadowy, ineffective figures who live among the outcaste leather-workers on the fringe of Chandrapore. But in 'The Life to Come' all his distrust of missionary motives and hatred for the consequences of their efforts are undiluted. In 'The Other Boat' the central figure is a young English officer in the Indian Army, an upstanding model of the type, certain to rise in his profession, destined for officialdom. But when the youthful charm has worn away he would certainly be found compressed into the narrow mould of a Captain McBryde.

'The Life to Come' began, as Forster told Sassoon, 'with a purely obscene fancy of a Missionary in difficulties'.[13] But as the story progressed, his own 'sorrow and passion' took its place. The story had passed through the refiner's fire and emerged as gold. In it, Paul Pinmay, the homosexual missionary, tries through strenuous evangelisation to atone for his one night with Vithobai, the young village chief who, in embracing both Pinmay and Christianity, fatally conflates religious with sexual love and Pinmay with Christ. Pinmay re-names him Barnabas. Like the biblical Barnabas, who vouched at Jerusalem for the good intentions of the converted Saul, the pagan Barnabas persuades his village to trust Paul Pinmay and follow his lead. But this Paul is not trustworthy and does not understand the obligations of either religious or sexual love. His missionary colleagues honour him for thoroughly Christianising the village, but in the process he destroys its culture and makes it a debased miniature of a Western industrial society. In the end, Vithobai-Barnabas, dying of tuberculosis, stabs Pinmay to death and kills himself so that they may be together in the Eternity that Pinmay has promised. Forster considered adding an extra chapter, a kind of Shavian 'Mr Pinmay in Hell', in which Pinmay and Vithobai would have been together in an Underworld that is Vithobai's heaven. There Pinmay, simply because he died first, is a slave, while Vithobai, who had the last word, 'reigns with his peers'.[14] However, Pinmay's sentence to a perverse Eternity is less the point of this parable than the truth that the distortion of love is a crime against the spirit, and Forster wisely resisted the extra chapter. Pinmay has distorted the meaning of love as cruelly as he has distorted the indigenous culture.

In 'The Other Boat' the distortion of love proceeds from caste-consciousness: not from Cocoa, who being half-caste has no caste at all, but from Lionel, the model young officer. They had met as children on an earlier passage from India when Lionel's mother fled with her children from the scandal that resulted after her husband, he too rising rapidly in the Indian Army, 'went native' and disappeared into Burma. Lionel now returns to India to redeem the family's reputation. Cocoa, now a fixer or hustler or possibly smuggler, has manoeuvred him onto the overcrowded boat and himself into Lionel's cabin. Lionel's double life on shipboard alternates between ecstatic interludes in the cabin with Cocoa, and the pukka Anglo-Indians above, with their bridge games and vocabulary of racist terms and jokes: wog, tar-brush, darkies, dagoes, black that comes off on the sheets. Lionel is like Ronny Heaslop, who feels competent and self-possessed when he can get away from Indians. When Lionel fears for his professional reputation if this new scandal were to become public, he begins 'to recover his poise and his sense of leadership' as soon as he joins the Anglo-Indians on the deck above. When sexual guilt overwhelms him, he hides among sanctimonious reflections about English womanhood and the girl he thinks he might marry. He blames Cocoa, who 'had woken up so much that might have slept'. But sex, which Lionel, properly brought up and correctly disciplined, had thought under control, had come 'charging back like a bull'. This story too ends in a murder and a suicide, with Cocoa strangled and Lionel drowned, victims of Lionel's guilty feelings about sex that is homosexual, interracial and contrary to caste – his own.[15] P. N. Furbank remembers how work on 'The Other Boat' revitalised Forster, and not only because he had taken an early fragment suggested by observations of shipboard passengers and had made it into a new and finished piece of fiction. He knew that he had produced something 'at his very best level, and in a way, of a new kind for him'. It also 'revived Forster's interest in his own career and reputation'.[16] He sorted the manuscripts of the stories, and he told Ackerley: 'I should like this side of me to have a chance of survival.'[17]

The revival of interest turned him once again to *Maurice*, which had had so long a literary life of stops and starts. One difficulty was probably the superfluity of opinions from friends who had read the manuscript. Forster wrote it in 1913–14 and by 1915 Edward Carpenter, who had been so important an influence for its beginning, had read and had liked it. Edward J. Dent and Roger Fry and Sydney Waterlow also had read it. Fry thought it 'beautiful', Forster's best work. Waterlow thought it truly moving and 'admirable as a sociological tract', but he thought that its virtues rather weighed down the characters.[18] Forster could not have been entirely happy to be told that it was sociological rather than artistic. He had confessed to Dent how much he needed the opinions of understanding critics, but he also felt confident that in this book he had taken an entirely new line, which he found satisfying because not even Whitman had been able to follow it to its logical conclusion. Lytton Strachey read it, liked the beginning, thought the ending flagged, and queried what seemed to be too much identification of Forster's views with Maurice's.[19]

In 1926 Forster thanked Ackerley for his criticisms but said that he could do no more with *Maurice*. Following Ackerley's suggestions would be a matter of virtually beginning again. He had put so much of himself into the novel that he could not repeat that effort. It was too late. 'So I shall destroy.'[20] Presumably he destroyed Ackerley's suggestions. Sassoon read the manuscript at some time before October 1929, and Forster told him how much trouble the dialogues, in particular, had caused him. The carnal element was the most troublesome, 'but it has to be got in I'm sure'. He offered to send Sassoon some stories, presumably those on homosexual themes. He had done his best, and he felt that he had achieved something really original, 'though possibly the real right thing, shaming our clumsy efforts, lies buried in a hundred drawers.'[21]

Certainly another of Forster's difficulties was the old one of being too close to his material. Again it is suburbanism and differences of class. Maurice is prosaically suburban, socially dutiful, rather slow of both body and imagination. Clive, whom he meets at Cambridge, is the heir to a run-down country estate. He is quick and literary, and he is homosexual when he and Maurice meet at Cambridge. His friendship begins the transformation of Maurice through realisation of his own homosexual temperament, but after Cambridge their relative stance is reversed. Clive decides that he is not, or no longer wishes to be, homosexual; he marries, becomes the complete squire and abandons Maurice, who cannot reverse his course with such apparent ease and deliberateness. Class consciousness, inseparable from the action-time of the story, which is 1912, enters in the person of Alec Scudder, Clive's gamekeeper, who sizes up the situation and assumes a place of his own in Maurice's life. Forster struggled long with this third part of the novel. He told Christopher Isherwood that in 1914 he had not known enough about the complexities of class to write that section to his own satisfaction. Class-consciousness was the very framework of Suburbia, but it was a cramped framework. What he then knew of class differences beyond those limits 'stimulated my imagination, that was all'.[22]

But his own hard-won emotional experience *was* the very heart of the novel. When both Society and the Law forbade candour on the subject of homosexuality the only solution in that dilemma was 'a priestlike secrecy and a faith in the Cause and the Subject'.[23] The point that he most wanted to make was not only socially unacceptable but certain to frighten off every publisher: that homosexual love need not end in violence or tragedy. This was the truth of the ending that he wanted his readers to take away with them. In this happy ending Maurice and Alec simply disappear together somewhere in a still-pristine English countryside. If it had ended with a hanging or a suicide some brave publisher might be persuaded to consider it as a moral tract. But Maurice and Alec are presumably happy in some unidentified greenwood and 'consequently recommend crime'.[24] Victorian literary morality still kept its grip on English fiction, and for Forster the 'nonsense and cruelty' that forced individuals like himself into 'priestlike secrecy' was simply 'the inversion of Victorian complacency'.[25]

In 1963 Forster informed Ackerley that he had classified all of his surviving short stories according to their degree of seriousness, and the most serious made the smallest pile. This last sorting was a valedictory to his literary career. Both the short stories and *Maurice* must now make their own way. *Maurice* belonged to the '"Love that dares not say its name" period which has now definitely ended'.[26] What Forster most wanted now was to be able to think about *Maurice* as neither a sociological tract nor a risk of criminal penalty, but as a literary production. In his 'Terminal Note' attached to the final revision, dated 1960, he observed that like Edward Carpenter he had hoped that knowledge about homosexuality would bring understanding, but 'what the public really loathes about homosexuality is not the thing itself but having to think about it'. If legalised in such a way that no one would notice, like the hundreds of measures that slipped through Parliament without causing a ripple in public opinion, all might be well. But England had got herself into a predicament for which Parliament must determine the issue, and Parliament was obliged to act publicly. When he made his final revision in 1960 Forster still despaired of a future for the recommendations in the Wolfenden Report. The twentieth century was more than half over, but he now understood the consequences of the whole Victorian class system, which still controlled his life and the lives of others like him, for he saw no hope of change. Maurice, born into the respectable middle class, 'may get off'.[27] England's Clives will continue to be magistrates, and the Alecs will go to prison. The manuscript bears Forster's query applicable to either literary or legal reactions to publication: 'Publishable – but worth it?' As a precaution, he sent Isherwood a copy with the exclusive rights for publication in the United States. Even with the American tendency to periodic fits of puritanical anxiety, publication seemed more likely there than in England. At the time he expected little more for either *Maurice* or the homosexual short stories. However, in l960 there was a new Obscene Publications Act, and once again Forster appeared as a witness for the defence of a novel. This was at the trial of *Lady Chatterley's Lover*, published by Penguin; the new Act had made defence possible even if the novel were judged obscene, on the rather antiseptic ground of being 'in the interests of science, literature, art, or learning'. The favourable verdict did not yet free *Maurice*, but it was a step in the right direction.

Forster's literary life drew toward its close with the general recognition that he was indeed one of 'the Masters'. On the 1969 New Year's Honours List he received the Order of Merit, England's highest award for artistic achievement. The symposium, *Aspects of E. M. Forster*, was published that year, its title a tribute both to Forster and to the influence of *Aspects of the Novel*, and the new book was presented to him at a ninetieth-birthday luncheon planned with special care by King's College.[28] However, none of this could have pleased him more than the fact that he had lived to see enactment at last of the Wolfenden recommendations, as the Sexual Offences Act of 1967, which decreed that Parliament cease to try to legislate public morality except in cases of offence to public decency. When *Maurice* appeared in 1971, one year after his death, reviewers agreed that it was not vintage Forster but that it was an important book. Several pointed out that it bore the disadvantages of a thesis novel: over-concentration on a single issue, transitions less leisurely and reflective than in his earlier fiction, and a certain grimness to Forster's usually lighter and more salutary sense of the absurd. The defects were the result of his being for too long the too-literally lonely voice. On the other hand, the novel contained much that was true Forster, of warmth and concern with the truth, and the holiness of the heart's affections as the first principle of life. He would have been the first to admit that the language and the class environments dated the novel and to agree with Walter Allen that it was a pre-Wolfenden 'plea for the public recognition of the homosexual and his right to express his love'.[29] In a way, that very datedness became its contribution to the present. The novel was true, C. P. Snow wrote, 'not of many people, but of a section of a small class, for a short period. They may have been unlucky in their temperaments and sexually diffident; but it did happen, and just for once, we can say that things are somewhat better now.'[30] George Steiner, from a younger generation of critics, made the really important critical judgement not only of *Maurice* but of all of Forster's work:

> But it is not the weaknesses in *Maurice* that bring a sense of sadness. It is the simple fact that there will never again be an autumn book list with a new novel by that late and most eminent Fellow of King's College, Cambridge.[31]

Abbreviations

By E. M. Forster:

AH	*Abinger Harvest* (1936)
CB	*Commonplace Book* (1985)
Diary	'Locked Diary' (King's College, Cambridge)
Forster	P. N. Furbank, *E. M. Forster: A Life* (1977–8)
HD	*The Hill of Devi* (Abinger Edition, 1983)
HE	*Howards End*
Letters	*Selected Letters of E. M. Forster* (1983, 1985)
LC	*The Life to Come and other stories* (Abinger Edition, 1972)
LJ	*The Longest Journey* (Abinger Edition, 1984)
MT	*Marianne Thornton: A Domestic Biography* (1956)
PI	*A Passage to India* (Abinger Edition, 1978)
RWV	*A Room with a View* (Abinger Edition, 1977)
TCD	*Two Cheers for Democracy* (Abinger Edition, 1972)
WAFT	*Where Angels Fear to Tread* (Abinger Edition, 1975)

Other:

CP	Crewe Papers (University Library, Cambridge University)
HP	Hardinge Papers (University Library, Cambridge University)
WMCJ	*Working Men's College Journal* (London)

Notes

PREFACE

1. *New Age*, 7 (12 May 1910), 26.
2. As used here, Anglo-Indian applies to a novel about India by an English writer, or to English living in India during the period of the Raj: not the present term for persons of English-Indian descent.
3. Quoted in P. N. Furbank, *E. M. Forster: A Life*, 2 vols. (London: Secker & Warburg; New York: Harcourt Brace Jovanovich, 1977–8), II, 64.

1. E. M. FORSTER: SELF AND NEIGHBOURS

1. Editor's note, 'The Challenge', *Listener*, 35 (1946), 264.
2. EMF, 'The Claims of Art', in series, 'The World We Want', ibid., 30 (1943), 742–3.
3. Arthur Koestler, 'The Challenge of Our Time', ibid., pp. 355–6. The other speakers were Sir E. L. Woodward (1890–1971), historian, 'Has All This Happened Before?' ibid., pp. 387–8; J. D. Bernal (1901–71), physicist, 'The Social Responsibility of Science', pp. 419–20; EMF, 'The Challenge of Our Time: The View of the Creative Artist', pp. 451–2; Benjamin Farrington (1891–1974), classicist, 'What Light from the Ancient World?' pp. 499–500; Michael Polanyi (1891–1976), physical chemist, 'Can Science Bring Peace?' pp. 531–2; J.B.S. Haldane (1892–1964), geneticist, 'The Challenge of Our Time: the View of the Biologist', p. 563; V. A. Demant (1893–1983), theologian, 'The Fairy Ring of Civilisation', pp. 599–600; C. H. Waddington (1905–75), geneticist, 'Science and the Humanities', pp. 631–2; A. D. Ritchie (1891–1967), philosopher, 'The Challenge of Our Time', pp. 667–8.
4. EMF, 'The Challenge of Our Time', reprinted, *Two Cheers for Democracy*, Abinger Edition, ed. Oliver Stallybrass (London: Edward Arnold, 1972), pp. 54–8. On Rooksnest, see Margaret Ashby, *Forster Country* (Stevenage, Herts.: Flounden Press, 1991).
5. EMF, 'The Ivory Tower', *London Mercury*, 39 (1938), 119–30.
6. Information from P. N. Furbank.
7. Eric Crozier, transcript of privately taped discussion, 'Talking about Morgan', 5 July 1971. Eric Crozier was Play Producer for BBC Television, 1936–9 and produced operas at Sadler's Wells, among them Britten's *Peter Grimes*. He was Britten's producer and librettist, 1945–51; co-founder of the English Opera Group, 1947, and of the Aldeburgh Festival, 1948. Robert Joseph Buckingham (1904–75) joined the Metropolitan Police in the mid-1920s. Forster met him in 1930. In 1932 Robert married May Hockey; their son, Robert Morgan, was Forster's godson.

8. EMF to Robert Buckingham, 3 August 1948. Edwin Keppel ('Francis') Bennett (1887–1958), after the study at the Working Men's College in London, went to Gonville and Caius College, Cambridge, on a scholarship from G. M. Trevelyan. He became a Tutor in 1926 and Senior Tutor, 1931–52. He was President of the College, 1948–56, and known for his work in German studies.
9. EMF, 'Notes on the English Character', *Abinger Harvest* (London: Edward Arnold, 1936), pp. 3–15.
10. F.M.L. Thompson, *The Rise of Respectable Society: A Social History of Victorian Britain 1830–1900* (Cambridge, Mass.: Harvard University Press, 1988), p. 197.

2. THE SUBURBAN NOVELS

1. EMF, 'Rooksnest', Appendix to *Howards End*, Abinger Edition, ed. Oliver Stallybrass (London: Edward Arnold, 1973), pp. 341–51.
2. EMF, *Marianne Thornton: A Domestic Biography* (London: Edward Arnold; New York: Harcourt Brace, 1956), p. 35. See *Forster* pp. 3–9. Edward Morgan Llewellyn Forster (1847–80) met Alice Clara ('Lily') Whichelo (1855–1945) when the Thorntons took an interest in her after her father died. Lily and Edward Forster married in 1877.
3. Noel Annan, 'The Intellectual Aristocracy', in *Studies in Social History: A Tribute to G. M. Trevelyan*, ed. J. H. Plumb (London: Longmans, Green, 1955), pp. 244–85. See p. 250: 'They valued independence and recognized it in others. Because they judged people by an exterior standard of moral and intellectual merit, they never became an exclusive clique and welcomed the penniless son of a dissenting minister as a son-in-law if they believed in his integrity and ability.'
4. *MT*, p. 59.
5. Ashby, *Forster Country*, p. 53.
6. Quoted in *Forster*, I, 15.
7. *MT*, p. 113.
8. On EMF and money, see his correspondence with Hilton Young, Lord Kennet, in EMF, *Selected Letters*, ed. Mary Lago and P. N. Furbank. 2 vols. (London: Collins; Cambridge, Mass.: Harvard University Press, 1983, 1985), II, 171–4; Mary Lago, 'E. M. Forster: Clapham's Child,' *Biography*, 17 (1991), 117–37.
9. *MT*, p. 113. The bank became Williams and Glyn's and kept the old address, 20 Birchin Lane, London EC3.
10. EMF, Notebook Journal, 3 August 1898.
11. EMF, 'Rooksnest', *HE*, p. 350. King's College keeps the mantelpiece.
12. EMF, 'Author's Introduction to *The Longest Journey*, Abinger Edition, ed. Elizabeth Heine (London, Edward Arnold, 1984), p. lxvi.
13. EMF, *Commonplace Book*, ed. Philip Gardner (Stanford, Calif.: Stanford University Press, 1985), p. 198. First published in facsimile edition by Scolar Press (London, 1978), with Introduction by P. N. Furbank, pp. ix–xiv. 'First book': *The Aeneid of Virgil*, trans. E. Fairfax Taylor.

Introduction and Notes by E. M. Forster, B.A. Temple Greek and
Latin Classics, Vol. 1 (London: J. M. Dent, 1906).
14. *Forster*, I, 49, 52.
15. Ibid., p. 50.
16. EMF to G. L. Dickinson, (postmark) 11 May 1902. Goldsworthy
     Lowes Dickinson (1862–1932) went to King's College, Cambridge, in
     1882. He intended a career in medicine but turned to modern history
     and became known as an advocate of the League of Nations.
17. Piers Brendon, *Thomas Cook: 150 Years of Popular Tourism* (London:
     Secker & Warburg, 1991), p. 85.
18. Quoted in ibid., p. 6. See Newman, 'Knowledge Viewed in Relation
     to Learning', *The Idea of a University*, Discourse VI, Part 5.
19. George Macaulay Trevelyan, *The Recreations of a Historian* (London:
     Thomas Nelson, 1919), pp. 139, 142, 146. Trevelyan's 'Muggleton' is
     not Lodowicke Muggleton (1609–98), the puritan heresiarch, who
     never left England. However, the fictional Muggleton shares
     Lodowicke Muggleton's determination to step aside from prescribed
     paths and find inspiration in his own way.
20. *MT*, p. 93.
21. EMF, Italian Diary, 6 October 1901.
22. Ibid., 10 October 1901.
23. Ibid., 11 October 1901.
24. Ibid., 10 October 1901.
25. Daniel Defoe, *A Tour through the Whole Island of Great Britain*, abridged
     and edited by P. N. Furbank, W. R. Owen, and A. J. Coulson (New
     Haven and London: Yale University Press, 1991), p. 53.
26. Quoted on title page, Richard Cobb, *Still Life: Sketches from a Tunbridge
     Wells Childhood* (London: Chatto & Windus/Hogarth Press, 1983).
27. EMF, Diary, 19 July 1912.
28. EMF, 'Notes on the English Character', *AH*, p. 3.
29. See David Cannadine, *The Decline and Fall of the British Aristocracy*
     (New Haven and London: Yale University Press, 1990), p. 55: 'One-
     quarter of the land of England and Wales was owned by 710 indi-
     viduals, and nearly three-quarters of the British Isles was in the
     hands of less than five thousand people [in 1861]. Even more remark-
     ably, it emerged that twelve men between them possessed more than
     four million acres, and that 421 owned nearly twenty-three million
     acres.'
30. *The Victoria History of the Counties of England: Surrey*, ed. H. E. Malden,
     4 vols. (London: Constable, 1902–11), III, 476.
31. *Letters*, I, 61, note 2.
32. *The Victoria History: . . . Surrey*, I, 486.
33. *Forster*, I, 133.
34. EMF to Alice Clara Forster, 8 February 1901.
35. J.F.C. Harrison, *A History of the Working Men's College 1854–1954*
     (London: Routledge & Kegan Paul, 1954), p. 20.
36. *The Life of Frederick Denison Maurice, chiefly told in his own letters*, ed.
     Frederick Maurice, 2 vols. (London: Macmillan, 1884; Farnborough:
     Gregg International, 1969), II, 176. On F. D. Maurice's educational

philosophy, see his *Learning and Working*, ed. W. E. Styles (London: Oxford University Press for Hull University Press, 1968).

37. 'Moral imagination': see Gertrude Himmelfarb, *Poverty and Compassion: The Moral Imagination of the Late Victorians* (New York: Knopf, 1991), pp. 4–5: 'In fact, the moral imagination of the late Victorians, in public affairs as in private, was neither sentimental nor utopian. It was every bit as stern as the old religion – perhaps because it was a displacement of the old. . . . Compassion had its reasons of mind as well as of the heart. A sharp, skeptical intelligence was required to ensure the proper exercise of that sentiment.'

38. *CB*, p. 302.

39. See Mary Moorman, *George Macaulay Trevelyan: A Memoir* (London: Hamish Hamilton, 1980), p. 72: Trevelyan 'also advised men who had recently left Oxford or Cambridge to join in concerts and debates there "before the doors of their profession close for ever between them and all chance of experience and change of idea."' Trevelyan (1876–1962) was educated at Harrow and Trinity College, Cambridge. He was Regius Professor of Modern History, 1927–40, and Master of Trinity, 1940–51.

40. Quoted in *Forster*, I, 93–4. For a photograph of Trevelyan 'as a prim and priggish young Fellow of Trinity in the early 1900s: not surprisingly, Lytton Strachey found him "very – I think too – earnest"', in David Cannadine, *G. M. Trevelyan: A Life in History* (London: HarperCollins, 1992), facing p. 128.

41. 'College Notes', *The Working Men's College Journal*, 8 (1903), 59. EMF made graceful acknowledgement of Trevelyan's influence with 'Dr Trevelyan's Love of Letters', first published in *Cambridge Review*, 1953; reprinted as Appendix B, in Cannadine, *G. M. Trevelyan*.

42. EMF, 'Pessimism in Literature', *WMCJ*, 10 (1907–8), 6–10, 26–33.

43. EMF, *Letters*, I, 60. Robert Calverley Trevelyan (1872–1951) chose poetry as a career, in which he was not very successful, but obscurity did not deter him.

44. Ibid., p. 84.

45. *WMCJ*, 10 (1907–8), 110.

46. EMF, Notebook Journal, 19 September 1907; 12 June 1907.

47. EMF, 'Dante', *WMCJ*, 10 (1907–8), 261–4, 281–6, 301–6.

48. EMF, Notebook Journal, 16 June 1908.

49. EMF, 'The Beauty of Life', *WMCJ*, 12 (1908), 153–7.

50. G. M. Trevelyan, 'An Autobiography', in *An Autobiography and Other Essays* (London: Longmans, Green, 1949), p. 23. See also his 'The College and the Older Universities', in *The Working Men's College 1854–1904. Records of Its History and Its Work for Fifty Years, by Members of the College*, ed. J. Llewelyn Davies (London: Macmillan, 1904), pp. 188–98.

51. Quoted in *Browning's Trumpeter: The Correspondence of Robert Browning and Frederick J. Furnivall*, ed. William S. Peterson (Washington DC: Decatur House Press, 1979), p. xxiv.

52. *Forster*, I, 97, and see pp. 75–9. See also below, note 83.

53. EMF, 'Old Lucy', *The Lucy Novels: Early Sketches for* A Room with a

View, Abinger Edition, ed. Oliver Stallybrass (London: Edward Arnold, 1977), pp. 21–2.

54. *Forster*, I, 160–6.
55. EMF, *A Room with a View*, Abinger Edition, ed. Oliver Stallybrass (London: Edward Arnold; New York, Knopf, 1977), p. 97.
56. Ibid., p. 126.
57. Ibid., p. 103.
58. Ibid., p. 126.
59. Ibid., pp. 108–9.
60. EMF, Notebook Journal, 15 December 1903.
61. EMF, *Where Angels Fear to Tread*, Abinger Edition, ed. Oliver Stallybrass (London: Edward Arnold, 1975), p. 1.
62. *RWV*, pp. 116–20.
63. *WAFT*, p. 6.
64. Ibid., p. 7.
65. Ibid., p. 56.
66. Ibid., pp. 62–3.
67. Ibid., p. 73.
68. Ibid., p. 76.
69. Ibid., p. 78.
70. Ibid., p. 81.
71. Ibid., p. 91.
72. *RWV*, p. 173.
73. Unsigned review, *Spectator*, in *E. M. Forster: the Critical Heritage*, ed. Philip Gardner (London and Boston: Routledge & Kegan Paul, 1973), p. 119.
74. *Letters*, I, 83–4.
75. Ibid., p. 139.
76. EMF, 'Pessimism in Literature,' *WMCJ*, 10 (1907–8), 6–10, 26–33.
77. Unsigned review, *Tribune*, in *CH*, p. 65.
78. Unsigned notice, *Evening Standard & St. James's Gazette*, in *CH* p. 72.
79. Unsigned review, *Tribune*, in *CH*, p. 66.
80. Unsigned review, *Nation*, in *CH*, p. 69.
81. Unsigned review, *Spectator*, in *CH*, p. 94.
82. Unsigned review, *Times Literary Supplement*, in *CH*, p. 68.
83. EMF, Notebook Journal, 21 March 1904. See Michael Holroyd, *Lytton Strachey: A Critical Biography*, 2 vols. (New York: Holt, Rinehart & Winston, 1967–7), I, 129–30; EMF, Notebook Journal, 21 March 1904.
84. EMF to Koestler, 13 November 1941.
85. EMF, Author's Introduction, *The Longest Journey*, Abinger Edition, ed. Oliver Stallybrass (London: Edward Arnold, 1984), p. lxvi.
86. Unsigned review, *The Spectator*, in *CH*, p. 93.
87. Ibid., p. 92.
88. EMF to G. L. Dickinson, 12 June 1907.
89. *Forster*, I, 149.
90. Unsigned review, *Times Literary Supplement*, in *CH*, p. 67.
91. EMF. *LJ*, p. lxviii.
92. Ibid., pp. 62–3; but compare p. lxviii.
93. EMF, 'Notes on the English Character', in *AH*, pp. 4–5.

94. *LJ*, p. 278.
95. Ibid., pp. 7–8.
96. Ibid., pp. 10–11.
97. Ibid., p. 15.
98. Ibid., p. 31.
99. Ibid., p. 32.
100. Ibid., p. 33.
101. Ibid., p. 37.
102. Ibid., p. 38.
103. Ibid., pp. 159, 172.
104. EMF, 'Notes on the English Character', *AH*, p. 14.
105. EMF to Florence Barger, 17 December 1917. Florence Emily Barger (1879–1960) studied educational theory at Liverpool University and worked as a school inspector. In 1904 she married her cousin, George Barger, EMF's King's College friend. For many years she was EMF's confidante and closest woman friend.
106. EMF to Florence Barger, 9 January 1918.
107. EMF to Lorna Wood, 12 December 1917. Miss Wood (1891–1944) was Matron at the Alexandria hospital where EMF worked for the Red Cross during the First World War.
108. EMF, 'Notes on the English Character', *AH*, pp. 5, 8.
109. *LJ*, p. 160.
110. Ibid. p. lxviii.
111. Ibid. pp. 29–31, 137–8.
112. Ibid., p. 263.
113. *Letters*, I, 51. See EMF, 'Nottingham Lace', *'Arctic Summer' and Other Fiction*, ed. Elizabeth Heine, Abinger Edition (London: Edward Arnold, 1980), pp. 1–66.
114. *Forster*, I, 92.
115. *LJ*, p. lxvii.
116. *HE*, p. 164. Margaret Ashby (*Forster Country*, pp. 109–10) traces the source of this passage to EMF's 'short prose meditation' in the visitors' book at a guest house near Pulborough, Sussex, dated 2 November 1915. *Forster Country*, pp. 109–10.
117. Ibid., p. 173.
118. Ibid., p. 70.
119. Ibid., p. 192.
120. Ibid., p. 181.
121. Ibid., p. 97.
122. Ibid., pp. 229–30.
123. Ibid., pp.242, 243.
124. A. N. Monkhouse, initialled review, in *CH*, pp. 123–4.
125. Noel Annan, 'Oh, What a Lovely War', *New York Review*, 14 May 1992, p. 4.
126. *HE*, p. 144.
127. Ibid., p. 97.
128. Ibid., 194.
129. Ibid., pp. 132, 133.
130. Ibid., p. 257.

131. Ibid., p. 178.
132. EMF, Notebook Journal, 29 January 1909.
133. Ibid., p. 197.
134. Ibid., pp. 303–5.
135. The *Daily Telegraph* reviewer thought that 'Leonard's seduction of Helen Schlegel is an unlikely incident. At any rate, it strikes a false note'. R. A. Scott-James, in the *Daily News*, thought that 'poor squalid Mr. Bast . . . is an exquisite piece of diabolical character-drawing'. See *CH*, pp. 131, 138.
136. *HE*, pp. 331–2.
137. Ibid., p. 50.
138. EMF, Notebook Journal, entries for 18 April, 1 May 1908.
139. *HE*, p. 29.
140. Trilling, *E. M. Forster* (Norfolk, Conn.: New Directions, 1943), p. 118.
141. EMF, 'Pessimism in Literature', *WMCJ*, 10 (1907–8), 26–7.
142. *HE*, pp. 200–1, 262–3.
143. EMF to Robert Buckingham, 18 April 1950.
144. Elizabeth Poston to EMF, 3 October 1960. Miss Poston (1905–87), composer, writer and pianist, was noted for clarity of compositional style and as an editor of folksong.
145. EMF to Henry Brooke, 8 October 1908. Brooke (1903–84), later Lord Brooke of Cumnor, was Minister of Housing and Local Government and Welsh Affairs, 1957–61; and Conservative Home Secretary, 1962–4.
146. *HE*, p. 172.
147. Ibid., p. 184.
148. Ibid., p. 184. 'Telegrams and anger': pp. 25, 101. 'Panic and emptiness': pp. 23, 61, 169.
149. Ibid., pp. 183–4.
150. Ibid., p. 337.
151. Ibid., p. 25.

3. THE INDIAN NOVEL

1. See reviews collected in *CH*: R. A. Scott-James (*Daily News*), pp. 135–9; A [rchibald] M[arshall] (*Daily Mail*), pp. 143–5; unsigned review (*Daily Graphic*), pp. 130–1; unsigned review (*Times Literary Supplement*), pp. 125–6; unsigned notice (*Standard*), pp. 128–9.
2. EMF, Notebook Journal, 12 June 1907; *Letters*, II, 131.
3. *Forster*, I, 191, 192; EMF, Notebook Journal, 14 May 1911, 27 March 1904.
4. *Forster*, I, 191.
5. EMF, Diary, 14 May 1911.
6. David Lelyveld, *Aligarh's First Generation: Muslim Solidarity in British India* (Princeton, NJ: Princeton University Press, 1978), p. 105. The 'influential English book': Sir William Muir, *The Life of Mahomet and History of Islam, to the Era of the Hegira*, 4 vols. (London: Smith, Elder,

1858–61). It had fifteen editions by 1895. Sayyid Ahmad Khan (1817–98), son of an honorary official in the Moghul Court at Delhi, was a judge in the subordinate judicial administration of the North West Provinces where Muir (1819–1905) became Lieutenant-Governor in 1868.

7. Lelyveld, *Aligarh's First Generation*, p. 109.

8. See ibid., pp. 124–5.

9. Ibid., p. 213.

10. Obituary, 'Sir Theodore Morison: Moslem Renaissance in India', *The Times*, 15 February 1936, p. 14. Morison (1856–1936) was on Lord Curzon's Council, 1903–4, and presided over the important All India Educational Conference in 1904. He was on the Council of India 1906–16. Besides education, his great concern in later years was the 'drain theory': how could India find capital for modern industry, to supplement her own inadequate resources? See his *The Economic Transition in India* (London: John Murray, 1911).

11. EMF, Notebook Journal, 9 July 1908. Compare *A Passage to India*, Abinger Edition, ed. Oliver Stallybrass (London: Edward Arnold, 1978), pp. 64, 135. Syed Ross Masood (1899–1937) was born in Aligarh. At Oxford he studied at New College, then was called to the Bar. After a few years' practice in Bankipore, in 1910 he became Director of Public Instruction in Hyderabad State, and after retirement there was Aligarh Vice-Chancellor. In 1934 he resigned in protest after an administrative setback. He was knighted in 1933.

12. Crewe to Hardinge, 28 June 1912. HP, Vol. 74. Crewe refers to the Lords' India debate, in which he stated that he saw 'no future for India' in the 'experiment . . . of attempting to confer a measure of self-government, with practical freedom from Parliamentary control, upon a race which is not our own race, even though that race enjoyed and appreciated the advantages of getting the best service of men belonging to our race – I do not believe that experiment is one which could be tried'. *Parliamentary Debates*, Lords, 24 June 1912, Vol. 12, col. 155. He reiterated his position of 1911, that the Government of India had no plan to offer any formal system of federation nor even any policy 'leading in the direction of something like a federal system in India. I wish to dispel altogether the idea that anything of the kind is intended'. See ibid., col. 243.

13. Hardinge remained convinced that his statement was only mistimed. He did *not* intend to imply self-government under colonial status, which would 'practically mean independence, which would be quite incompatible with the permanency of Br. rule in India . . . '. (Hardinge to Lord Carmichael, Governor of Bengal, 2 July 1912. HP, Vol. 84/2.) Indians did not know how colonial government operated: 'Since there are not the ties of blood, race, and religion to bind India to us as our Colonies are bound, this form of government is impossible for India.' Hardinge to Sir William Clarke, Governor of Bombay, 2 July 1912. HP, Vol. 84/2.

14. Montagu, Memorandum, 'Indian Public Services Commission', 24 August 1911. CP, Box I/8 (1). For a very detailed but discursive and

sometimes unreliable biography of Edwin Samuel Montagu (1879–1924) see Naomi B. Levine, *Politics, Religion and Love: The Story of H. H. Asquith, Venetia Stanley and Edwin Montagu, Based on the Life and Letters of Edwin Samuel Montagu* (New York and London: New York University Press, 1991).

15. Hardinge to Crewe, 10 November 1911; and Note dated 19 September 1911, on the Montagu Memorandum. CP, Box I/8 (1).

16. Butler, Note [n.d.] on Montagu's Memorandum, ibid. See also Butler to Du Boulay, Private Secretary to Hardinge, 28 November 1911. HP, Vol. 51. Sir (Spencer) Harcourt Butler (1869–1938) was one of Hardinge's more forward-looking advisers, inclined to liberalise measures when possible within the Raj framework. He was Lieutenant-Governor of Burma, 1915–17; then of the United Provinces, 1918, and Governor, 1921–3; and Governor of Burma, 1923–7.

17. Crewe to Hardinge, 4 July 1912, ibid.

18. Crewe to Islington, 15 August 1912. CP, Box I/8 (1).

19. Fisher to Crewe, 19 July 1912, ibid. H.A.L. Fisher (1865–1940) began his career as a classicist, then turned to European history. In 1914 he became Vice-Chancellor of Sheffield University, where he promoted cooperation between science and industry. He was Minister for Education in Lloyd George's Cabinet, 1916–22; and Warden of New College from 1925. On Oxford's influence, see Richard Symonds, *Oxford and Empire: The Last Lost Cause?* (London: Macmillan, 1986).

20. Francis Knollys, 1st Viscount Knollys, Private Secretary to King George, to Crewe, 23 July 1912. CP, Box I/8 (1).

21. Abdur Rahim, Note on the Medical Services, in *Reports and Commissions*, IV (1916); Vol. 7 of *Blue Books*, 1916, Vol. 1, pp. 464–84.

22. Lelyveld, *Aligarh's First Generation*, pp. 337–8.

23. A 'helping of Africa': see *HE*, p. 193. Paul Wilcox cannot marry unless and until he finds a woman who can 'stand the climate' of Nigeria 'and is in other ways – ' suitable: that is, one who will conform to the imperial code of behaviour (p. 18). When he returns ill to England Margaret Schlegel is beguiled sufficiently to revise her earlier estimate of him as 'a ninny' and to admire him when he returns to Nigeria, 'out to his duty' (p. 109). The Empire provides the Wilcoxes' wealth, but they are ignorant about its far reaches 'and would at times dismiss the whole British Empire with a puzzled, if reverent, sigh' (pp. 25–6). The visiting memsahibs enjoy Evie Wilcox's grand Shropshire wedding as a miniature durbar, a setting in which to feel pampered and appropriate (pp. 208, 213, 220). Finally, Charles Wilcox, as he speeds his motor car past the plodding Leonard Bast, is 'another type whom Nature favours – the Imperial. Healthy, ever in motion, it hopes to inherit the earth. . . . But the Imperialist is not what he thinks or seems. He is a destroyer. He prepares the way for cosmopolitanism, and though his ambitions may be fulfilled, the earth that he inherits will be gray' (p. 320).

24. G. E. Moore, *Principia Ethica* (Cambridge: The University Press, 1903), pp. 203, 204.

25. Quoted in *Forster*, I, 145.

26. EMF, Notebook Journal, 29 December 1907. 'Heddy': Cecil Headlam, *Oxford and Its Story* (London: J. M. Dent, 1904): Oxford romanticised, with emphasis on the Gothic revival, so that Masood's mother might think it excessively sectarian.

27. EMF, Notebook Journal, 8 December 1908; Diary, 2 March 1911. Compare *PI*, p. 60: Aziz is 'sensitive rather than responsive'.

28. Ibid., 25 April 1911.

29. Ibid., 17 July 1911.

30. EMF to Masood, 8 May 1907.

31. EMF, Diary, 10 January 1911.

32. EMF to Masood, 21 November 1910.

33. Masood to EMF, quoted in *Forster*, I, 194; EMF, 'Syed Ross Masood', *Two Cheers for Democracy* (New York: Harcourt, Brace, 1951), p. 292.

34. Crewe to Hardinge, 25 November 1911. HP, Vol. 73. On Bengali politics as background to Partition, see J. H. Broomfield, *Elite Conflict in a Plural Society: Twentieth-Century Bengal* (Berkeley and Los Angeles: University of California Press, 1968).

35. See *The Times*, 13 December 1911: 'Imperial and Foreign Intelligence: The Changes in India: Official Correspondence', p. 5; 'Imperial Delhi: The Future Capital of India', and 'First Impressions: A Mixed Reception', p. 8; leading article, 'A Great Imperial Announcement', p. 9.

36. See EMF, *'The Hill of Devi' and other Indian writings*, ed. Elizabeth Heine. Abinger Edition (London: Edward Arnold, 1983), pp. xxii–xxiv.

37. EMF's 1957 Preface, Appendix A in *PI*, pp. 313–14.

38. See ibid., p. 311.

39. Montagu to Crewe, 12 November 1912. CP, Box I/8 (9).

40. Crewe to Montagu, 15 November 1912. CP, Box I/5 (10).

41. Montagu, 1910 Budget Speech, in *Parl. Deb.*, Commons, Vol. 4, 26 July 1910, cols. 1950–2063.

42. Crewe to Hardinge, 12 April 1912. HP, Vol. 74.

43. EMF, 'Indian Journal', in *HD*, pp. 128–9.

44. Montagu to Crewe, 8 December 1912. CP, Box I/5 (11).

45. Montagu to Crewe, in ibid. The change of name was not finally allowed until 1921.

46. See John W. Cell, *Hailey: A Study in British Imperialism, 1872–1969* (Cambridge: The University Press, 1992), p. 129.

47. Hardinge, quoting Crewe, to Butler, 21 July 1912. HP, Vol. 84 (2).

48. Crewe to Hardinge, 5 September 1912. HP, Vol. 74.

49. Hardinge to Butler, 30 July 1912. HP, Vol. 84 (2).

50. EMF, *Letters*, I, 144.

51. Crewe to Carmichael, 15 January 1912. CP, Box C/6.

52. Crewe told Hardinge (18 September 1913. HP, Vol. 75): 'You may be sure that no sort of encouragement will be given to Mohammedan firebrands, such as Mohammed Ali, when they come to England.'

53. Dr Mukhtar Ahmed Ansari worked to reconcile Hindus and Muslims politically and was President of the Indian National Congress, 1927. The Government of India came to regard him as one of those moderates who might help to integrate control with progress. See

Muslims and the Congress: Select Correspondence of Dr. M. A. Ansari 1912–1935, ed. Mushirul Hasan (New Delhi: Manohar, 1979). Two letters of 1912 (pp. 1–2) comment on his activities while EMF was in India. EMF found him charming and delightfully hospitable; see *Letters*, I, 141, 149.

54. Sir Malcolm Lyall Darling (1880–1969) had been Tutor and Guardian to the Maharaja of Dewas Senior, 1907–8, and thus a link between EMF and the Maharaja, to whom he was Private Secretary in 1921. Although Morison was the direct link to Masood, EMF felt closer to Darling. When *Passage* appeared, EMF wrote to him (31 May 1924): 'I am sending you a copy – to you, not to Josie [Jessica, Mrs Darling], after long deliberation, tell her: it is you who originally linked me to India.' After retirement in 1940 from agricultural work in the Punjab, he was Indian Editor for the BBC, until 1944. See his *The Punjab Peasant in Prosperity and Debt* (London and New York: H. Milford for Oxford University Press, 1925).

55. See *Men and Memories: Recollections 1872–1938 of William Rothenstein*, abr. and ed. Mary Lago (London: Chatto & Windus; Columbia: University of Missouri Press, 1978), p. 162; *Imperfect Encounter: Letters of William Rothenstein and Rabindranath Tagore 1911–1941*, ed. Mary Lago (Cambridge, Mass.: Harvard University Press, 1972), pp. 13–17, 27–8. Official concern about Rothenstein would have been due in part to his intention to visit Abanindranath Tagore, an artist nephew of the Bengali poet Rabindranath Tagore (1861–1941), then under surveillance as a former leader of Bengal Partition protests during which huge crowds marched through Calcutta streets singing his nationalist songs.

56. EMF, 'Indian Journal 1912–13', for 5 January 1913, in *HD*, p. 173.
57. *PI*, p. 2.
58. *Letters*, I, 180.
59. Sir John Hewett to Sir James Du Boulay, Private Secretary to Hardinge, 18 and 19 March 1912. HP, Vol. 49.
60. P. N. Furbank to ML, 28 September 1992.
61. *PI*, pp. 55, 58–9.
62. Ibid., p. 162.
63. Hardinge to Carmichael, 13 July 1912. HP, Vol. 84/2.
64. *PI*, pp. 22, 27–8.
65. Ibid., p. 74.
66. Ibid., p. 30.
67. Santha Rama Rau, *A Passage to India* (stage script, author's collection). Produced at the Oxford Playhouse and Comedy Theatre, London, 1960; Ambassador Theatre, New York, 1962.
68. *PI*, p. 245.
69. *PI*, pp. 205, 210.
70. Ibid., p. 172.
71. Ibid., p. 174.
72. Ibid., p. 23.
73. Ibid., p. 154.
74. Ibid., pp. 155–6.

75. Ibid., p. 161.
76. Hardinge's feelings about the coming of a Royal Commission to investigate the Civil Service struck the same tone as Turton's apologia. Each was genuinely hurt by unfavourable reflections upon his administration. 'It has been a great disappointment to me and has caused me much depression. I do not think that I have done a single unkind thing to anybody since I have been in India, and it seems hard that I should be treated in this way. However, there is no accounting for people, and after all one must continue to do one's best.' Hardinge to Montagu, 7 January 1913. HP, Vol. 85/2.
77. *PI*, p. 136. Aziz says to Adela: 'Nothing embraces the whole of India, nothing, nothing, and that was Akbar's mistake.'
78. Ibid., p. 27.
79. Ibid., p. 79.
80. Ibid., p. 67. Tagore renounced his 1915 knighthood in 1919, a solitary and courageous protest against the Amritsar Massacre, an act construed in many quarters as arrant disloyalty. For the letter of resignation, see Edward J. Thompson, *Rabindranath Tagore: Poet and Dramatist* (London: Oxford University Press, 1926), pp. 273–4.
81. *PI*, p. 178.
82. Ibid., pp. 44–5.
83. Jane Harrison to Gilbert Murray, 7 August 1913.
84. Montagu, quoted in Levine, *Politics . . . Edwin Montagu*, p. 186. See EMF on his impression of official attitudes (*Letters*, II, 156): '[The missionary George Turner at Lahore] is the only Englishman I have met who seems to care for the people. The Officials &^{ct} may understand them, but it is always against the grain in their case.'
85. *PI*, p. 160.
86. Ibid., p. 73.
87. Ibid., p. 246.
88. Charles Edward Trevelyan, *On the Education of the People of India* (London: Orme, Brown, Green, & Longmans, 1838), pp. 165–6. For Macaulay's 1835 Minute on Education, see *Sources of Indian Tradition*, comp. Wm. Theodore de Bary et al. (New York: Columbia University press, 1958), pp. 596–601.
89. EMF, 'Indian Journal', in *HD*, p. 216.
90. *PI*, p. 28.
91. Ibid., p. 36.
92. Ibid., p. 69.
93. Ibid., p. 48.
94. Ibid., p. 56.
95. Fisher to Du Boulay, 17 February 1914. HP, Vol. 60.
96. *PI*, p. 102.
97. Ibid., p. 56.
98. Ibid., p. 19.
99. On Annie Besant, see Anne Taylor, *Annie Besant: A Biography* (Oxford and New York: Oxford University Press, 1992). On Sister Nivedita (Margaret Noble) and other Englishwomen in India, see Barbara N. Ranusack, 'Cultural Missionaries, Material Imperialists, Feminist

Allies: British Women Activists in India 1865–1945', in *Western Women and Imperialism: Complicity and Resistance*, ed. Nupur Chaudhuri and Margaret Strobel (Bloomington: Indiana University Press, 1992), pp. 119–26.

100. *PI*, p. 62.
101. Ibid., p. 70.
102. Ibid., p. 87.
103. Ibid., p. 119.
104. Ibid., pp. 121–2.
105. Ibid., p. 127.
106. Ibid., p. 136.
107. Ibid., p. 144.
108. Railways Board to Du Boulay, 23 May 1913. HP, Vol. 57.
109. EMF, *Letters*, II, 125.
110. *PI*, p. 184.
111. Ibid., pp. 185, 188.
112. Ibid., p. 240.
113. Ibid., pp. 241–2.
114. EMF, *Letters*, II, 267.
115. *PI*, pp. 68–9.
116. Ibid., p. 72.
117. EMF, *Letters*, I, 228.
118. Ibid., p. 284.
119. For a brief exposition of Vaishnava faith and examples of the lyrics, see *In Praise of Krishna: Songs from the Bengali*, trans. Edward C. Dimock, Jr. and Denise Levertov, with Introduction by Edward C. Dimock, Jr. (Garden City, NY: Doubleday Anchor Books, 1967). See also, *Krishna: Myths, Rites and Attitudes*, ed. Milton Singer (Honolulu: East–West Center Press, 1966).
120. William G. Archer, *The Loves of Krishna*. Ethical and Religious Classics of East and West, No. 18 (New York: Macmillan [1957]), p. 65.
121. EMF, *Letters*, I, 165. Compare *PI*, p. 277. See also *Letters*, I, 171; and *PI*, pp. 274–6. See also *HD*, p. 203, note 95, on a Mr Gokhale who sang for EMF – but the Yaman Kalyana raga, not a Vaishnava lyric; also pp. 73, 81–3, 153–4, 157–8, 159. Adwaita P. Ganguly, *India: Mystic, Complex and Real* (Delhi: Motilal Banarsidass, 1990), Ch. 10, 'Adela's "Illusion" and Godbole's Philosophy of "Good and Evil" and "Suffering"', pp. 208–40.
122. *PI*, p. 7.
123. Ibid., pp. 47, 48.
124. Ibid., p. 52; see also pp. 175–6: the subaltern makes an interesting slip when he calls the Barabar Hills 'Barabas Hill', and EMF describes the general attitude toward Ronny as that toward 'a martyr . . . he was bearing the sahib's cross' (p. 176). In fact, Major Callendar 'had got hold of the subaltern, and set him on to bait the schoolmaster' (p. 177).
125. Ibid., p. 53.
126. Ibid., p. 90.
127. Ibid., p. 96.

128. See M.A.K. Ghalib, *Dastanbuy: A Diary of the Indian Revolt of 1857*, trans. Khwaja Ahmad Paruqu (New York: Asia Publishing House [1970].) For samples of Ghalib's poems, see *Ghazals of Ghalib: Versions from the Urdu by Aijaz Ahmad et al.*, ed, Aijaz Ahmad (New York: Columbia University Press, 1971).

129. G. K. Das, *E. M. Forster's India* (London: Macmillan, 1977), pp. 60–1.

130. *PI*, pp. 50, 97. G. K. Das emphasises the enduring connections from Ghalib's poems, however anachronistic, to twentieth-century politics: 'By the time *A Passage to India* was published the Khilafat movement had of course ended, but the revolutionary consequences of the movement remained permanently, and they have crystallised into some significant themes and conflicts in Forster's story.' Aziz claims disinterest in politics but wants his Afghan ancestors to rule India once again, and '"whatever Ghalib had felt, he had anyhow lived in India, and this consolidated it . . . "'. See Das, *E. M. Forster's India*, p. 60; *PI*, pp. 96–7.

131. Morison, *Imperial Rule in India: Being an Examination of the Principles Proper to the Government of Dependencies* (London: Archibald Constable, 1899), p. 4.

132. *HD*, p. 38.

133. *PI*, pp. 64.

134. Ibid., p. 97.

135. Ibid., p. 284.

136. Ibid., pp. 296–7.

137. Ibid., p. 307.

138. Ibid., p. 311.

139. Ibid., pp. 311, 312.

140. EMF, 'Indian Journal', *HD*, p. 227.

141. *PI*, p. 270.

142. EMF, 'Three Countries', quoted in ibid., p. xxv.

143. Quoted in ibid., p. xi.

144. EMF, *'Arctic Summer' and other fiction*, ed. Elizabeth Heine. Abinger Edition (London: Edward Arnold, 1980): 'Nottingham Lace', pp. 1–66; 'Arctic Summer', pp. 118–215.

145. Quoted in *Forster*, I, 257.

146. *Letters*, I, 274.

147. On the interaction between the Rowlatt Acts and Amritsar, see Broomfield, *Elite Conflict*, pp. 140–2.

148. *Parl. Deb.*, Commons, Vol. 131, 8 July 1920, cols. 1706–7.

149. See Woolf, *Growing: An Autobiography of the Years 1904–1911* (London: Hogarth Press, 1967): his account of his career as an administrator in Ceylon. He concludes by saying (pp. 247–8) that 'I was born in an age of imperialism, and I disapproved of imperialism and felt sure that its days were already numbered.'

150, *PI*, p. xv.

151. *Letters*, II, 47.

152. Ibid., p. 63. Here EMF, as was his habit, crosses out words but leaves them legible so that the process of his thought is traceable. For 'where the two might be combined' he substituted 'are combined'. For 'the Cambridge view' he substituted 'King's view'.

4. THE BBC BROADCASTS

1. See reviews collected in *CH*: L. P. Hartley (*Spectator*), p. 225; S. K. Ratcliffe (letter, *New Statesman*), pp. 24–5; 'D.L.M.' (*Boston Evening Transcript*), p. 261; Arnold Bennett (*Journals*), p. 288; Leonard Woolf (*Nation & Athenaeum*), p. 205.
2. In *CH*: R. Ellis Roberts (*Bookman* [London]), p. 232; Rose Macaulay (*Daily News*), p. 198.
3. In *CH*: unsigned review (*Times Literary Supplement*), p. 200; I. P. Fassett (*Criterion*), p. 273.
4. In *CH*: unsigned review (*Observer*), p. 211; Edwin Muir (*Nation* [New York], p. 280; E. A. Horne (letter, *New Statesman*), p. 248.
5. In *CH*: H. C. Harwood (*Outlook*), p. 203.
6. In *CH*: H. R. Massingham (*New Leader*), p. 209.
7. In *CH*: E. A. Horne (letter, *New Statesman*), p. 248.
8. In *CH*: Sylvia Lynd (*Time and Tide*), p. 216; Bhupal Singh (*A Survey of Anglo-Indian Fiction* [1934]), p. 294.
9. In *CH*: unsigned notice (*Times of India*), p. 239.
10. In *CH*: Laurence Stallings (*World* [New York]), p. 241.
11. In *CH*: J. B. Priestley (*London Mercury*), p. 229.
12. In *CH*: 'A.S.B.' (*Nation & Athenaeum*), p. 289.
13. For a later comment, see Francis King, *E. M. Forster and His World* (New York: Scribner, 1978). However, EMF 'could have sworn I had heard the phrase used (with a touch of archness perhaps) to and of a collector by other English people. Was of course wrong.' (To Darling, 16 September 1924.) Perhaps not: Chandrapore's Anglo-Indians, would have known whether the Collector enjoyed that old form of address.
14. EMF to Darling, 4 September 1925.
15. Quoted in *Forster*, II, 106. See also EMF to D. H. Lawrence, in ibid., p. 124.
16. See *PI*, p. 312.
17. EMF to Reid, 9 January 1925. Forrest Reid (1875–1947), novelist, was born in Belfast, went to Cambridge and after graduation settled in Ulster. His novels deal principally with boyhood feelings and experiences, and although Forster felt that the later work was not up to his earlier standard he took pains to keep Reid in touch with London literary life.
18. EMF to Florence Barger, 19 September 1924.
19. EMF to Florence Barger, 2 October 1924.
20. EMF to Ackerley, 19 January 1925.
21. *Letters*, II, 67.
22. EMF to Ackerley, 6 May 1925. Joe Randolph Ackerley (1896–1967) attended Cambridge University after the First World War, then spent some years trying to write, while financed by an allowance from his father, a partner in the fruit importers Elder and Fyffes. In 1928 he became a BBC Talks Producer and was Literary Editor, *The Listener*, 1935–59; EMF became one of his regular reviewers. They met in 1922 after EMF wrote Ackerley an appreciative letter about his poem

'Ghosts', which coincided with EMF's mourning the death of Mohammed el Adl.
23. EMF to Darling, 12 June 1926.
24. EMF to Darling, 15 November 1928. See EMF, 'My Wood, or the Effects of Property upon Character', *New Leader*, 13 (15 October 1926), p. 3; reprinted as 'My Wood', *AH*, pp. 22–6.
25. EMF, 'Fallen Elms', *CB*, pp. 56–7.
26. EMF to Florence Barger, 1 November 1925.
27. *Letters*, II, 97.
28. Briggs, *The Birth of Broadcasting*, Vol. 1 of *The History of Broadcasting in the United Kingdom*, 4 vols. (London: Oxford University Press, 1961–79), I, 4.
29. Jean Rowntree to ML, 13 October 1988. Also, Mary Lago, 'E. M. Forster and the BBC', *The Yearbook of English Studies*, 20 (1990), 132–51.
30. EMF to Darling, 18 July 1928. 'Of Railway Bridges', reprinted in *HD*, p. 174. For a complete list of EMF's broadcasts, see B. J. Kirkpatrick, *A Bibliography of E. M. Forster*, 2nd edition (Oxford: Clarendon Press, 1985), pp. 263–71.
31. EMF to Darling, 18 July 1928.
32. *CB*, p. 38.
33. Reith, quoted in Briggs, *The Golden Age of Wireless*, Vol. 2 of *The History of Broadcasting in the United Kingdom*, p. 185. John Charles Walsham Reith (1889–1971), later Lord Reith, was the son of a Moderator of the Church of Scotland. He attended the Royal Technical College, Glasgow, and was an apprentice in a locomotive works. In 1922 he answered an advertisement for General Manager of the new British Broadcasting Company, then became Director General of the Corporation. In 1938, at the Government's suggestion he left to become Chairman of Imperial Airways, then served in several wartime administrative capacities, but never returned to the BBC. See Reith, *Broadcast over Britain* (London: Hodder & Stoughton, 1024); *The Reith Diaries*, ed. Charles Stuart (London: Collins, 1975).
34. Corporation Licence, quoted in ibid., p. 128.
35. Reith, quoted in ibid., pp. 128–9.
36. Briggs, *Golden Age of Wireless*, pp. 124, 125.
37. Hilda Matheson, *Broadcasting*. Home University Library of Modern Knowledge (London: Thornton Butterworth, 1933), pp. 74, 76.
38. EMF to Orwell, 2 June 1943, in *Orwell: The War Broadcasts*, ed. W. J. West (London: Duckworth/BBC, 1985), p. 256.
39. Orwell to John Arlott, quoted in King, *E. M. Forster*, p. 97.
40. EMF to Ackerley, 9 August 1928.
41. Lionel Fielden, *The Natural Bent* (London: Andre Deutsch, 1960), p. 105. Fielden (1896–1974) joined the BBC in 1927. In 1935 he went to India as Director of Broadcasting to the Government of India, a title much grander than the facilities as he then found them.
42. Matheson, *Broadcasting*, p. 176.
43. Ibid., pp. 193.
44. Ibid., p. 206.

45. *CB*, p. 27.
46. Fielden, *Natural Bent*, p. 114.
47. Ibid., p. 116.
48. Briggs, *Golden Age of Broadcasting*, p. 143.
49. EMF, Locked Diary, 30 January 1932.
50. EMF to Florence Barger, 27 November 1917.
51. EMF, Diary, 12 November 19.
52. Fielden, *Natural Bent*, p. 115.
53. Interview with Jean Rowntree, 29 March 1992.
54. EMF, *Aspects of the Novel* (London: Edward Arnold, 1927); 'The Art of Fiction', 24 November 1944, BBC Eastern Service.
55. Barnes, Private Notes [1946].
56. *Forster*, II, 155; see also *Letters*, II, 85–7.
57. *Letters*, II, 155.
58. EMF, 'Notes on the Way', *Time and Tide*, 15 (1934), 695–6: quoted in *Letters*, II, 122, note 3.
59. EMF to Kilham Roberts, 20 May 1939. Denys Kilham Roberts (1903–76), barrister, as Secretary of the Society of Authors helped to create the League of Dramatists, Composers Guild, Screenwriters Association, and Radiowriters Association.
60. EMF, Introductory Talk for Sixth-Form Students, 24 September 1937. Forster, Broadcast Scripts, I, 1930–43. Series I.
61. BBC to Fielden, quoted in *Natural Bent*, p. 206. Copious italics, although not identified as such, as presumably Fielden's.
62. EMF to Elizabeth Trevelyan, 3 October 1939. In 1900 Trevelyan married Elizabeth des Amorie van der Hoeven. Their house at Holmbury St Mary was not far from West Hackhurst.
63. Priestley to Barnes, 5 April 1943.
64. Kilham Roberts to EMF, 14 February 1940.
65. EMF to Kilham Roberts, 15 February 1940.
66. EMF to Kilham Roberts, 19 March 1940.
67. EMF to Barnes, 23 May 1940.
68. EMF to Barnes, 5 February 1942.
69. Quoted in Lago, 'E. M. Forster and the BBC', *Yearbook of English Studies*, 20 (1990), pp. 138–9.
70. W. J. West, ed., *Orwell: The War Broadcasts* (London: Duckworth/BBC, 1985), p. 14.
71. See 'British Aims in India: A Common Basis. Assurance by "Friends in the Commons"', *The Times*, 24 December 1940, p. 2.
72. See, for example, 'Proceedings', *Journal of the Royal Society of Arts*, 58 (1909–10), 287.
73. See Partha Mitter, *Much-Maligned Monsters: History of European Reactions to Indian Art* (New Haven: Yale University Press, 1981), on indirect effects of such attitudes on Indian administration.
74. EMF, 'Indian Photographic Exhibition', 22 November 1940. Reprinted as 'The Individual and His God', *HD*, pp. 237–40. Cf. 'The World Mountain', *Listener*, 52 (2 December 1954), 977–8.
75. Briggs, *The War of Words*, Vol. 3 of *The History of Broadcasting in the United Kingdom*, p. 506.

76. *New Statesman*, 5 July 1941, quoted ibid.
77. Fielden, *Natural Bent*, p. 214.
78. Briggs, *War of Words*, pp. 505–6.
79. *Letters*, II, 195, note 1; EMF to Darling, 24 November 1940.
80. *Letters*, II, 194–5; and p. 195, note 1.
81. EMF, 'Three Anti-Nazi Broadcasts', *TCD*, pp. 31–42.
82. EMF, Diary, 31 May 1940.
83. EMF to Elizabeth Trevelyan, 1 May 1940.
84. EMF, Diary, 23 May 1940.
85. EMF, Diary, 13 May 1940.
86. EMF, Diary, 25 July 1940.
87. EMF, Diary, 4 September 1940.
88. EMF to Koestler, 7 March 1943.
89. EMF to Elizabeth Trevelyan, 10 October 1940.
90. Quoted in *Forster*, II, 240.
91. Quoted in *Letters*, II, 191, note 2.
92. EMF to Darling, 20 March 1941.
93. *Letters*, II, 191, note 3.
94. Ibid., 193.
95. *CB*, pp. 150–1.
96. EMF, 'India Again', *TCD*, pp. 315–23. Reprint of first of two talks, 'Has India Changed?' 27 January and 3 February 1946; first published as 'India after Twenty-five Years', *Listener*, 35 (31 January and 7 February 1946), 133–4, 171–2.
97. Kate Whitehead, *The Third Programme: A Literary History* (Oxford: Clarendon Press, 1989), p. 1.
98. BBC Central Control Board Minutes, quoted in Briggs, *Golden Age of Broadcasting*, p. 27.
99. Harold Nicolson to Barnes, 11 July 1943.
100. Quoted in Whitehead, *Third Programme*, p. 19. Sir William Haley (1901–87) worked on Manchester newspapers, then was Director of the Press Association and Director of Reuters, 1939–43; BBC Editor-in-Chief, 1943–4 and Director-General, 1944–5; then Editor of *The Times*, 1952–66 and Chairman, Times Newspapers, 1967.
101. Interview with Jean Rowntree, 29 March 1992.
102. Rowntree, Personal Memoir, p. 18.
103. Barnes, American Travel Notes, 1945.
104. Barnes, Notes for the Third Programme [1945].
105. Barnes to Taylor, 25 April 1946.
106. See Briggs, *Sound and Vision*, Vol. 4 of *The History of Broadcasting in the United Kingdom*, p. 72.
107. See 'A Third Choice', *Listener*, 36 (26 September 1946), 400; Sir William Haley, 'Breaking New Ground in Radio', Supp. p. i; George Barnes, 'The Aims of the "Programme"', pp. i–ii.
108. EMF, 'Does Culture Matter?', *TCD*, pp. 95–104; reprinted from *Time and Tide*, 16 (16 November 1935), 1657–8.
109. 'A Third Choice', *Listener*, 36 (26 September 1946), 400.
110. For a complete list of EMF's BBC broadcasts and of his manuscripts in the BBC Written Archives, see B. J. Kirkpatrick, *A Bibliography of*

E. M. Forster. Soho Bibliographies, 2nd edition (Oxford: Clarendon Press, 1985), pp. 233–53.

111. EMF, 'The Fifth Anniversary of the Third Programme', 29 September 1951; *Listener*, 46 (4 October 1951), 539–41.

112. Grisewood, *One Thing at a Time: An Autobiography* (London: Hutchinson, 1968), p. 61.

113. Ibid., pp. 161–2.

114. Ibid., pp. 162, 163.

115. Ibid., pp. 166, 167.

116. Ibid., p. 170.

117. Ibid., p. 172.

118. Morris to Sprott, 17 December 1952. John Morris (1895–1980) had studied anthropology while at King's College, Cambridge, then had military service in India and taught English in two Japanese universities. He was Head of the BBC Far Eastern Service, 1943–52, and Controller of the Third Programme, 1952–8. Walter John Herbert Sprott (1897–1971) was at Clare College, Cambridge, then went to University College, Nottingham, where he was Professor of Philosophy, 1948–64. EMF had become acquainted with him as an undergraduate.

119. *Letters*, II, 247–8.

120. Morris to EMF, 14 January 1953.

121. *Letters*, II, 148, note 2.

122. Quoted in Barnes, Typescript Report, 'The First Ten Years of the Third Programme', April 1956, p. 15.

123. Rowntree, Memoir, p. 16.

124. EMF to Barnes, 14 October 1946; to Plomer, 12 June 1941.

125. Interview with Nancy Evans Crozier, 12 April 1992.

126. EMF to Plomer, 17 July 1948. His letter is Mrs Stainforth's immortality: 'Now that I have written to you about Mrs Stainforth so "amusingly", she will doubtless live for a little. But on what a thread she hung!'

127. EMF, 'Chormopuloda' (review, *The Ascent of F6*.), *Listener*, 16 (14 October 1936), Supp., p. vii; reprinted in *TCD*, pp. 257–9.

128. See above, note 92.

129. Interview with Eric and Nancy Crozier at University of Missouri, Columbia, 1986.

130. Benjamin Britten (1913–76), later Lord Britten of Aldeburgh, began his study of music with the English composer and teacher Frank Bridge. Britten was in the United States, 1939–42. Charles Montagu Slater (1902–56) was an editor of the *Left Review* in the 1930s. See Donald Mitchell, 'Montagu Slater (1902–56): who was he?', 1981 interview with Enid Slater and others, including Peter Pears and Eric Crozier, in Philip Brett, *Benjamin Britten: Peter Grimes* (Cambridge: University Press, 1983), pp. 22–46. Peter Pears (1910–86) was educated at the Royal College of Music and was with the BBC Singers, 1934–7, and the Sadler's Wells Opera, 1943–6. Britten composed many songs for him, and he created leading roles in all of Britten's principal operatic works.

131. Interview with Eric Crozier, 1986.
132. Ibid.
133. Philip Brett, *Benjamin Britten: Peter Grimes*, p. 189. For the libretto, see *The Operas of Benjamin Britten*, ed. David Herbert (London: Hamish Hamilton, 1979), pp. 181–205.
134. EMF, 'The Aldeburgh Festival of Music and the Arts', 20 June 1948, Third Programme; published as 'Looking Back on the Aldeburgh Festival', *Listener*, 39 (8 July 1948), 1011, 1013.
135. *Letters*, II, 234.
136. EMF, 'Some Books', 12 February 1947, BBC Talks. At that time *Billy Budd* was by no means the familiar work that it is now. The Melville revival did not begin in the United States until the 1920s, and 'until 1967 there were essentially only two (and both textually deficient) editions of *Billy Budd*: Raymond Weaver prepared one for the Constable Edition of Melville's works in 1924, and then, in 1928, came out with another somewhat improved edition in his *Shorter Novels of Herman Melville*' (New York: Liverwright). A 1948 edition by F. Barron Freeman, *Baby Budd, Sailor*, is eminently unreliable. A definitive text, by Harrison Hayford and Merton Sealt, did not appear until 1967 (University of Chicago Press). Forster and Crozier used William Plomer's *Billy Budd, Foretopman* (London: John Lehmann, 1946), 'derived from Weaver', probably from his 1928 version. For the concise summary quoted here I am indebted to Professor Thomas Quirk.
137. Interview with Eric Crozier, 1986.
138. EMF, Diary, 12 April 1949.
139. EMF to Britten, 19 June 1949.
140. EMF, Diary, 20 October 1949.
141. *Letters*, II, 242.
142. Crozier to Nancy Evans, quoted in *Letters*, II, 242, note 3.
143. Ibid., p. 245.
144. Libretto, *Billy Budd: An opera in four acts*, in *The Operas of Benjamin Britten*, pp. 181–205.
145. EMF to Cadmus, [?]1 January 1964. Paul Cadmus, painter and etcher, noted as an artist in tempera, is widely represented in major galleries. Theodor Uppman, American baritone, created the role of Billy, and Peter Pears was Captain Vere. Uppman received his musical training at the Curtis Institute, Philadelphia, and made his Metropolitan Opera debut in 1952, two years after *Billy Budd*.
146. EMF to Woolf, 7 December 1955.
147. EMF to Ackerley, 6 October 1957.
148. See *Letters*, II, 276–8. Santha Rama Rau, essayist and novelist, dramatised *Passage* as her response to a dinner-party challenge and an observation that Broadway had never seen a play about India by an Indian. This *Passage* was not literally a play by an Indian, but she chose adaptation because she regards the novel as the greatest about India by a Western writer. Frank Hauser, who had reopened the Oxford Playhouse in 1956, produced the play there in 1960. It quickly moved to the Comedy Theatre, London, and subsequently to the Ambassador Theatre, New York. Hauser had met the Pakistani actor

Zia Mohyeddin during a tour of India and Pakistan, and *Passage* was his first London appearance.

149. EMF, 'George Crabbe and Aldeburgh', 20 January 1960. Third in series, 'The Poetry of Place', BBC General Overseas Service; repeated on Third Programme as 'The Poetry of Place', 24 January 1960.

150. EMF, Britten and Crozier, discussion of *Billy Budd* and 'how they made an opera from Melville's story', 12 November 1960, Third Programme.

151. 'The Masters: E. M. Forster', 27 March 1963, BBC General Overseas Service; repeated on Home Service, 16 July 1963.

152. Gerard Mansell, 'The New Plans for Radio', *Listener*, 83 (15 January 1970), 82–4.

153. Whitehead, *Third Programme*, p. 227.

154. 'Dissatisfied' (letter), *Listener*, 83 (29 January 1970), 150.

155. Jean Rowntree to ML, 18 November 1988.

5. THE LONELY VOICE

1. EMF, *Maurice* (London: Edward Arnold, 1971); *'The Life to Come' and other stories*, ed. Oliver Stallybrass. Abinger Edition (London: Edward Arnold, 1972); *'Arctic Summer' and other fiction*, ed. Elizabeth Heine (London: Edward Arnold, 1980).

2. Frank O'Connor, *The Lonely Voice: A Study of the Short Story* (Cleveland and New York: World Publishing/Meridian, 1965), p. 15.

3. Furbank, in *Letters*, I, viii. For 'The Story of a Panic', see EMF, *The New Collected Short Stories* (London: Sidgwick & Jackson, 1985), pp. 18–39.

4. *Forster*, I, 92.

5. *Letters*, I, 62. E. J. Dent (1876–1957), musicologist known for his work on Scarlatti manuscripts and Mozart libretti, became a King's College Fellow in 1901 and Professor of Music in 1926. Roger Fry (1866–1934), painter and art critic and historian, was a member of the Bloomsbury set and leading English advocate of Post-Impressionism. Sydney Philip Waterlow (1878–1944), Foreign Office official and aspiring writer, was Forster's friend in a somewhat marginal manner; but it was through him that Forster went to Germany as tutor to children of Elizabeth von Arnim, Waterlow's aunt.

6. Unsigned notice, *Athenaeum*, in *CH*, p. 177.

7. Samuel Hynes, 'The Old Man at King's: Forster at 85', *Edwardian Occasions: Essays on English Writing in the Early Twentieth Century* (New York: Oxford University Press, 1972), p. 155.

8. EMF to Sassoon, 2 May 1918. Forster's friendship with Siegfried Sassoon (1886–1967) began during World War One. His war poems in stark contrast to the romanticised recruiting of the time made him one of the influential young war poets. He retired to his country estate to write memoirs, travel books, and occasional novels.

9. Quoted in *LC*, p. xiii.

10.   EMF to Sassoon, 21 July 1923.
11.   EMF to Sassoon, 1 August 1923.
12.   EMF to Sassoon, 20 December 1923.
13.   EMF to Sassoon, 1 August 1923; again, one of Forster's revealing deletions: he substituted 'fancy' for 'vision'. Complete text of 'The Life to Come', *LC*, pp. 65–82.
14.   EMF to Sassoon, 27 July 1923.
15.   EMF, 'The Other Boat', *LC*, p. 193; complete text, pp. 166–97.
16.   *Forster*, I, 222.
17.   EMF to Ackerley, 12 September 1959.
18.   *Letters*, I, 222.
19.   See Strachey to EMF, 12 March 1915, in *CH* , pp. 429–32.
20.   EMF to Ackerley, 20 June 1926.
21.   EMF to Sassoon, 11 October 1929.
22.   *Letters*, II, 158.
23.   EMF to Plomer, 4 December 1936.
24.   See EMF, 'Terminal Note', *Maurice*, pp. 235–41.
25.   EMF to Isherwood, 28 March 1938. Christopher Isherwood (1904–86), English poet, novelist and travel writer, was at Cambridge, 1924–5; then in medical school at the University of London, 1927–8; after which he taught English in Berlin, 1928–33. After four years of travel in Europe and China he settled in California in 1939, where he taught and wrote film scenarios. He became an American citizen in 1946.
26.   EMF to Ackerley, 13 January 1963.
27.   See EMF, 'Terminal Note' to *Maurice*.
28.   *Aspects of E. M. Forster*, ed. Oliver Stallybrass (London: Edward Arnold, 1969).
29.   Walter Allen, 'The least of Forster', *Daily Telegraph,* in *CH*, pp. 437–8.
30.   C. P. Snow, 'Open Windows', *Financial Times,* in *CH*, pp. 433–6.
31.   George Steiner, 'Under the Greenwood Tree', *New Yorker,* in *CH*, pp. 475–82.

Index

163